Iconicity - A Fundamental Problem in Semiotics

Troels Degn Johansson, Martin Skov, and Berit Brogaard (Eds.)

ICONICITY

A Fundamental Problem in Semiotics

NSU Press

Production editors: Troels Degn Johansson, Martin Skov, and Berit Brogaard
Layout: NORDIC SUMMER UNIVERSITY
The book is typeset in Garamond
Printing: Centertryk, Aalborg, Denmark
Printed in Denmark 1999

ISBN 87-87564-80-7 Danmark, Nordisk Sommeruniversitet
1st Edition, 1st Printing

NSU Press
NORDIC SUMMER UNIVERSITY
Katrinebjergvej 89 G
DK-8200 Århus N
Denmark
Tel. +45 8942 4496
Fax. +45 8616 6086
E-mail: nsu@cfk.hum.aau.dk
URL: http://www.au.dk/nsu

NSU Press publishes research papers from the NORDIC SUMMER UNIVERSITY. Publications from the **NSU Press** are available in book-shops and on application to the NORDIC SUMMER UNIVERSITY.

The NORDIC SUMMER UNIVERSITY was founded in 1950. The basic aim of the NORDIC SUMMER UNIVERSITY is to contribute to research by the development of ideas and interdisciplinary research networks within fields that are yet to be approached systematically in research.

The NORDIC SUMMER UNIVERSITY is sponsored by the Nordic Council of Ministers.

Contents

Cognitive Semiotics

Foreword

The articles collected in this volume were for the most part first presented as papers in the Copenhagen Semiotics Circle, a seminar that formed part of the Nordic Summer Unversity's aesthetics studies circle "Modernity and Visual Aesthetics" (1996-98). This informal Copenhagen group of dedicated semioticians was however formed already in 1994 in the spirit of earlier circles such as the Moscow and St. Petersburg groups, or the linguistic circles in Prague and, indeed, Copenhagen. Soon after, a group of scholars and artists from the five Nordic countries came together under the auspices of the Nordic Summer University. Their aim was to study visuality and aesthetics in the context of modernity. Although the connection between the two was not obvious for all parties immediately, a bond was soon created, and in 1996 both groups fomed part of the aesthetics studies circle.

Visual aesthetics should not be seen as just an arbitrary branch of contemporary studies in the humanities. With its implication of seeing something more or less directly "as it is", it becomes tied up with not only the scopic regimes of modern urban culture but also with some fundamental questions of Truth and Knowledge, reverberating down through the history of philosophy. We soon realized that this goes for semiotics as well: Far from being just a local problem in semiotic theory, the "visual", or "iconic" in fact represents a fundamental problem for semiotician the context of philosophy.

As the editors of this book and coordinators of the Copenhagen Semiotics Circle we wish to express our gratitude to all participants, not only of the Copenhagen group but also those of the aesthetics studies circle who, although not being represented in this book, made contributions of pivotal importance nevertheless. A special thanks goes to the non-Copenhagen residents who took the time to visit the Copenhagen circle's seminars: Peer Bundgård, Göran Sonesson, and Svend Østergaard.

Last but not least we wish to express our gratitude to Stacey Marie Cozart who has gone beyond the call of duty in proof-reading and correcting the English of these papers. Should the reader find this book intelligible at all, she is not the least responsible.

December 1999

Troels Degn Johansson
Martin Skov
Berit Brogaard

Introduction: Iconicity and Semiotics

Martin Skov & Troels Degn Johansson

In this book we present a number of articles on *iconicity* — one of the concepts dear to semiotic theory, yet a concept that is treated very differently by semiotic theory depending on the theoretical position taken.

A reader with no prior knowledge of semiotics may wonder what the term "iconicity" stands for. The answer is that it designates the field of semiotic investigation dealing with the similarity between a *sign* and the *object* it stands for, or denotes. While some signs appear to signify by means of pure convention (that is, according to a rule, or habit as for instance when the acoustic sound-wave /*hun*'/ signifies the concept "dog" in Danish), others seem to signify by means of the fact that sign and object share some quality, or property (a photo of Bill Clinton *looks like* a certain human being that is the current president of the United States). The first type of relation between sign and object is usually refered to as "symbolic" (following the terminology of the american philosopher Charles Peirce), the second type as "iconic". The substantive "icon" is most often used specifically to designate a certain type of sign-relation (within the framework of Peirce a wery well defined relation, as it is!), whereas iconicity can be taken to embrace more broadly the various topics associated with the notion of "signification by similarity". The problem of semiotic iconicity can in this sense be seen to include the ontology of iconic signs (i.e.,hypo-icons in Peirce), the relation of inference to (visual) perception, or — as we shall see — epistemology.

It contrast to symbols, it may seem easy to deal with icons; they simply look like the objects they signify. However, the semiotician soon realizes that this is not the case. Defining icons and understanding their nature is highly difficult. What exactly is similarity? Under what circumstances can a sign be said to look "like" an object? Is a mathematical proposition iconic in its relation to its referent (Peirce thought so)? On the other hand, if the icon is a sign that stands for some object, it cannot be *exactly* identical to this object; otherwise it would not be a sign but a mere replica of the object (it would be "the same"). Thus iconic sign-relations must contain some properties or quality not "like" the object. How does such containment work? Furthermore, it is not immediately obvious if icons only allow perceptual likeness or also abstract likeness, or even both at the same time. Iconicity is a messy business!

Depending on your conception of the notion, iconicity can in fact be confused with "symbolicity". The symbol could, for instance, be seen in a "romantic" vein as linking a material signifier to a transcendental signified by virtue of some extraordinary law of analogy. As Hanne Roer remarks in her contribution to this book, the so-called symbolic mind of the Middle Ages, largely seeing the earth as a book written by the finger of God (*quasi quidam liber scriptus digito Dei* — a phrase immotalized by Hugh of St. Victor in the 12th century), may be more fruitfully understood as a case of Peircean iconicity. On the other hand, as another contributor, Göran Sonesson, is careful to point out in his paper, the term icon is not really used within semiotics 'in its most common religious and art historical sense, to refer to a pictorial representation of persons or events derived from the sacred history of Christianity', at least if it is taken in the Peircean sense. The religious icon is a highly styliziced and conventional depiction of a non-existent entity or event, whereas the icon in Peirce designates the relation of representation and object by way of pure quality or firstness. The religious icon actually has more in common with the Peircean symbol, relating representamen and object via some type of a conventional rule. However, things are not that clear cut. The medieval mind did not see the rule relating the icon to the transcendental realm of God as merely "conventional", but as truly *manifestating* this realm. The design of the work was thought to correspond to the actual proportions of the Great Design located in God's mind. At least in medieval semiotics a conception of signs, we would happily call "symbolic", is hence admittet, where "conventional" rules can be thought to display very iconic properties. Such confusion is not unfamiliar to semiotic theory, not even today.

The stakes are hightened if we take the study of iconicity to include epistemology. From Plato to Husserl, and beyond, a widespread theory of knowledge has existed to the effect that the world is thought to *appear* before our senses (and their artificial extensions) in a way which has to be analyzed and explained in order to yield its true meaning. Consequently, it is one of man's great challenges to develop methods of investigations which secures that our sense experiences and explanations are correct. If semiotics, with its sign-mediation of mind and object, is seen as embodying this epistemological problem, then it immediately presents itself as a pivotal question if iconic sign-relations can be taken as the foundation of such methods? Now, it could be argued that the technical matter of defining "icon" has nothing to do with epistemology — a theory of sign-types could possibly be carved out without any commitment to a specific epistemological stance. (As the opposite is also true: a theory of true knowledge could very well be formulated without dwelling upon the correct definition of the iconic sign.) However, most semioticians would probably acknowledge that the two problems are co-dependent: how you view epistemology presupposes some idea of iconicity, and how your technical theory of iconic signs is crafted begettets a lot to your underlying epistemological position. At least, this is a fact historically: The question of semiotic iconicity and epistemology has been tigthly interwoven throughout the history of thought. Scepticism and realism leads to two very different kinds of semiotic theory, and call for different types of scientific strategies of investigation. In fact, a substantial part of the history of modern semiotic theory could be told by tracing the treatment of iconicity in various theoretical contributions, from Saussure and onwards, or in the reception of Peirce and his realist phaenoroscopy. This is a story that directly connects itself to earlier philosophical attempts to understand how humans conceptualize the surrounding universe, and inherits the same traditional conflicts: Should meaning be seen as *constructed* is some way or another (by man, language, culture, or otherwise; this is the scepticist position)? Or should it be seen as *determined,* or constrained at least, by real structures in the world (be they natural or transcendental; this is the realist position)? Semiotics has been influenced by both positions, and the jury is still out on this one.

To summarize: Semiotic iconicity involves a range of hard problems. Above all the concepts of *similarity* and *difference* which structure in a very basic way the notions of the "icon" and the "symbol": At the basis of semiotic theory we find the idea that the functives of a sign-function can be either similar to, or different from each other. Understanding what this means, what similarity and difference really is, belongs to something like what the Greeks called "first" philosophy; they are both prerequisites for further philosophical reasoning and should thus be determined in a purely *formal* way. Yet, to some degree they must remain co-dependent, since it would make no sense to say that something is similar to some other thing if such a comparison does not include an amount of distinction. Several of the papers collected here examine very closely these fundamental questions.

Secondly, we face the problem of how signs can model (or however you want to put it) any phenomenon correctly, making use of the concepts

11

of similarity and difference. This problem is composed of several different sub-questions. First of all it consists of both an *ontological* aspect and an *epistemological* aspect. To be able to compare sign and object we really need to know what the object at hand is "in itself" — its essence as Aristotle would have it. That is, we seek a theory of what the nature of the object really amounts to. But we also need some theory of how we can know with certainty that a given sign-function really match sign and object. Again, the two problems seem co-dependent and can be difficult to separate. It should be noted, however, that the epistemological question of truth is not exactly same as the ontological question of what some thing is in itself.

Thirdly, the epistemological question of truth should be distinguished from the *psychological* question of how human beings cognitively come to judge certain signs in a certain way. As shown convincingly by Husserl in his *Logische Untersuchungen,* our on-going *hinc et nunc* psychological acts of perceiving, feeling, judging, etc. (the act-quality of our experience), must not be conflated with the ideal meaning of such acts (the act-material of our experience), even though the two are dependent upon each other, since truth belong to another realm than psychology. Psychology underpins logical reasoning and confronts us with problems of its own, such as how perception is created, how perception relates to cognition, and how both are tuned in to the features of the surrounding world.

Finally, any semiotic theory proper, surely, will have to address the nature of the sign itself — how it is composed and how it functions. At least two important questions pose themselves *vis à vis* the problem of iconicity. The first has to do with how the sign motivates inference. Traditionally semiotics has dealt with two major types of motivation, either motivation by virtue of the object, or motivation by virtue of the rule governing the sign-function (that is: *arbitrarity*). Considering how important this notion of motivation is, and how often it is envoked, it is strange how seldom the concept itself is examined.

These types of problems are schematized in the following figure:

Metaphysics	*Similarity - Difference*
Ontology	*Essence - Non-Essence*
Epistemology	*Truth - Error*
Psychology	*Perception and Cognition*
Sign-Motivation	*Object/Rule*

Fig. 1.

Ideally, a theory of semiotics should deal with all five levels of iconicity, and it should be able to explain how they relate to each other. In practise, it is usually the case that individual levels are singled out, or that several levels are run together in reductive strategies.

With these short remarks on the notions of "icon", "hypo-icons", and "iconicity" we now turn to the individual papers. This book consists of three parts. In the first, *Apologies,* Frederik Stjernfelt, Göran Sonesson, and Erling Davidsen & Helle Munkholm Davidsen identify the basic arguments that should be taken to support the necessity of a concept of iconicity in semiotics and in its application in pictorial semiotics. In the second part, Per Aage Brandt, Hanne Roer, and Troels Degn Johansson present three particular and distinct *contexts,* each of which may prove helpful for a further understanding of iconicity beyond the focus of general semiotics: The question of the origin of iconicity in human evolution (Brandt), notions of similarity, or perhaps even iconicity in Middle Age philosophy and literature (Roer), and finally iconicity in specific pictorial mediations (Johansson). The third and final part of the book is dedicated specifically to *iconicity and cognitive semiotics.* Here Svend Østergaard, Michael May, Berit Brogaard, and Torben Fledelius Knap establish the relevance of iconicity for the understanding of cognition and perception, and in Fledelius Knap more specifically for the understanding of music.

The first part of the book moves on from a general to a rather specific approach. In Frederik Stjernfelt's paper 'How to Lean More: An Apology for a Strong Concept of Iconicity' we are introduced to the concept of iconicity in the context of the philosophical problem of similarity. Here Stjernfelt

13

defends Peirce's concept as a special and indeed necessary way of substantiating for signification facts which are obviously grounded on similarity in some sense. In the course of his argumentation, Stjernfelt systematically works through first Nelson Goodman and then Umberto Eco in order to demonstrate that in both critics the concept of iconicity was perhaps too hastily rejected. Stjernfelt then proceeds by discussing some much broader and perhaps overlooked perspectives of Peirce's concept of iconicity; first and foremost that icons are the only signs through which it is possible for us to "learn more", as Peirce has it. More specifically, iconicity should according to Stjernfelt be taken to constitute not only algebraic and diagrammatical reasoning but also, more generally, fiction and imagination.

In 'Iconicity in the Ecology of Semiotics', Göran Sonesson too works through Goodman and Eco but with reference specifically to the problem of iconicity in pictorial semiotics. Sonesson argues here that iconicity is indispensable as a concept of ground in Peirce, and that iconicity as a general pictorial ground in turn leads to what Sonesson takes to be the ecological foundation of semiosis. Setting off from James Gibson's notion of perceptual ecology and Edmund Husserl's life-world concept, Sonesson suggests that we should conceive of pictures fundamentally as mediations of a life-world of iconicity that is itself to be disclosed as a strictly hierarchical order of assymmetry and similarity; an order which Sonesson identifies with George Lakoff and Mark Turner's conception of a "Great Chain of Being" and which in Sonesson's recent work serves as a ground for a general semiotics of culture.

Erling Davidsen & Helle Munkholm Davidsen proceed in an even more specific manner to maintain a more sceptical, yet apologetic approach to the concept of iconicity, although their scepticism is primarily directed towards Sonesson. In 'Iconicity and Evidence' Davidsen & Munkholm Davidsen argue that although a hierarchical life-world order of prominence in Sonesson might be seen as that ground that makes iconic representations secondary to what they represent, such argumentation does in their view nevertheless lead to relativism, i.e. the view that in some respect "anything ultimatively may be an icon of anything." The notion of "iconic sign" there becomes irrelevant. Davidsen & Munkholm Davidsen then return to what they see as the fundamental problem of iconic signs, namely that the level of expression and content in iconic signs have "collapsed". This Hjelmslevian observation in turn leads Davidsen & Munkholm Davidsen to perform an analysis of the phenomenal status of the icon.

The second part's presentation of various contexts of iconicity as a concept, or a problem consists of three, very different pieces. In 'Grounding Iconicity', Per Aage Brandt ventures to formulate and answer the question: 'Where do icons come from?' This leads him to outline a scenario of the very origin of iconicity in the evulution of Man. In Brandt's evolutionary scenario, icons stem originally from body and facial painting which for Brandt is both the most primitive and original mode of symbolization. Facial painting are later taken over by painting on masks and shields, and subsequently on cave walls, argues Brandt, but this primitive mode of symbolization remains an iconic presentation of mental life; a symbolization that is based on a facially grounded empathy. Brandt develops his scenario further by suggesting that today's communication via computer media "inter-faces" has brought about a renaissance for such "facial iconicity". This examplifies what he sees as a rather evident fact about communication, which earlier technologies and evolutionary stages seem to have hidden, or neglected.

In 'The Barrel Hoop and the Trinity. Some Ideas of Iconicity in the Middle Ages,' Hanne Roer also outlines a historical perspective although Roer deals specifically with notions of iconicity, or similarity in Middle Age philosophy (Augustine, Bacon), modistic grammar (Martinus and Boethius de Dacia), and literature (Dante Alighieri). According to Roer, 'there is in the Middle Ages a general fascination with the power and reality of icons, images, and pictures.' As already mentioned, Peirce's concept of iconicty, therefore, constitutes a fruitful starting point for a more systematic analysis of what this fascination amounts to. In her paper, this inquiry is performed as a careful study of those canonical examples which have often been addressed in Middle Age philosophy and literature.

The last paper in the context section is Troels Degn Johansson's 'Towards a Meta-Rhetorics of Pictorial Media. Specificity, Pictorality, and Compound Signs.' Johansson's paper addresses a well-know problem in pictorial semiotics, namely whether the specificity of pictorial media should be considered relevant when one is to account for the orgainization of signification in given texts. According to Johansson, this issue addresses the problem of iconicity inasmuch as he, along with Sonesson, takes images to be pictorial mediations of a common ground of iconicity. Johansson sets off from Sonesson's recent work, that is, his influence by Belgian research team Groupe μ's visual rhetorics and his parallel ecological life-world order cosmology of semiosis. However, unlike Sonesson, Johansson attributes rather great importance to the specificity of pictorial media; a factor which for Johansson too problematizes Sonesson's key concepts of pictorality and compound sign.

Svend Østergaard opens the third part of the book, *Iconicity and Cognitive Semiotics,* with a paper entitled 'Schemas and Symbols'. Here Østergaard explores the relation between the cognitive schemas, which seems to be determining our conceptual understanding of the world, and the symbolic representation of language. Østergaard approches this relation as a problem of motivation: Some types of schemas are obviously motivated by external topological and dynamic properties; still the expression, or communication of any schematic content requires a procedure of symbolic representation. Interestingly, iconicity may operate in two very different ways here, that is, either in terms of external motivation, or of cognitive symbolization.

Michael May's paper 'Diagrammatic Reasoning and Levels of Schematization' deals with verbal categories (e.g. "seeing as", "seeing in") for our perception of pictorial representation, that is especially of diagrams. Following certain analyses, May sets off from the hypothetical conviction that logically and/or intuitively we must be able to maintain a "three-fold attention" to images, i.e. that our attention could be characterized by three distinctively different categories if we are to understand pictorial representation the way we do. This problem of pictorial attention leads May to discuss whether a logical, or cognitive approach is the most relevant for our understanding of diagrams. However, for May what seems evident in this respect is to recognize the necessity of a common ground which is both logical and semantical. Gilles Fauconnier's concept of mapping between mental spaces becomes important here for an understanding of how different semantic domains may interconnect, and thus how we are to account for a perhaps three-fold pictorial attention that both amounts to a logical and cognitive semantics.

Berit Brogaard continues in some respect May's train of though by re-addressing the basic question of cognitive semantics, i.e. "how we can think something with respect to what we see". Having recourse to Peirce's basic sign-object trichotomy (icon, index, and symbol), she outlines the "mental theater" of fuzzy set theory in order to throw light on the relation between sense qualities (i.e. icons), given, or bounded frames (i.e. symbols), and fuzzy frames (i.e. indices).

In the fourth and final paper of this section, Torben Fledelius Knap has recourse to cognitive semiotics to understand music as a mode of expression. As Fledelius Knap states initially, music is not a 'reliable medium in a standard information theoretical way', and music has, therefore, always constituted an incessant challenge to semiotics. For Fledelius Knap, however, iconicity — when understood either in terms of the purely qualitiative, or kinaesthaetic aspects of music — may be taken for a fertile ground if we are to understand how music builds up "spaces of meaning" in a cognitive sense. Also Fledelius Knap refers here to the mental space theory of Gilles Fauconnier. To examplify his point, the author refers to an experiment performed by playing Saint-Saëns's *Carnival of Animals* before a class of students. The author here points to what he sees as a remarkably high rate of recognition of the 13 Animals represented in Saint-Saëns's piece (i.e. lions, hens and roosters, fast animals, turtles, etc.), although the individual fragments were played in a random order.

To sum up, we can already conclude that the following articles will bring forth further problems on all those five levels of iconicity that are outlined above. Both "realist" and "sceptical" approaches to semiotics try their hand at the puzzle of iconicity. We hope that the reader will find this collection of papers stimulating, and that he/she, upon reading the last entry, will set out to contribute to the science of semiotics himself/herself.

Apologies

How to Learn More

An Apology for a Strong Concept of Iconicity

Frederik Stjernfelt

Iconicity is generally conceived of as the sign-relation making one phenomenon signify another by similarity in some respects. Iconicity is hence built on similarity, but it is not simply defined by it, for a very simple reason. Similarity is generally symmetrical: if *a* is similar to *b,* then *b* is also similar to *a,* while sign-relations are generally asymmetrical: if *a* signifies *b,* it does not follow that *b* signifies *a.* Iconicity adds to similarity an intention aimed at *b,* using *a* as a means to this end.[1] This difference is acknowledged by most schools, for instance Peirce, who states that

> An Icon is a sign which refers to the Object that it denotes merely by virtue of characters of its own, and which it possesses, just the same, whether any such Object actually exists or not. It is true that unless there really is such an object, the Icon does not act as a sign; but this has nothing to do with its character as a sign. Anything whatever, be it quality, existent, individual, or law, is an Icon of anything, in so far it is like that thing and used as a sign of it. [Peirce, *CP*: 2.247].

Here, similarity as well as being used as a sign are necessary prerequisites for the Icon, but only taken together, they become sufficient prerequisites. In the other great phenomenologist Husserl, we find a similar distinction in the sixth *Logische Untersuchung:*

---

[1] One could add that the opposite seems to be the case regarding transitivity. Similarity is not transitive: if A is similar to B and B is similar to C, then A is similar to C, is generally not the case, not even if we restrict similarity to deal with one single type of quality. One shade of red may be similar to another which in turn is similar to a third shade — without it being the case that the first and the third are similar. Take, on the other hand, transitivity in signification: if A signifies B, and B signifies C, then A signifies C. This is, if not generally realized in discourse, then in general a possible, that is, valid construction in the system in question, at least given certain contexts. Peirce seems to admit this principle under the notion 'nota notae': "The logical principle Nota notae est nota rei ipsius, that is, the predicate of the predicate is the predicate of the subject, which is laid down in several places by Aristotle as the general principle of syllogism" (Peirce, *CP*: 3.590).

Das Zeichen hat mit dem Bezeichneten inhaltlich zumeist nichts gemein, es kann ihm Heterogenes ebesowohl bezeichnen, als ihm Homogenes. Das Bild hingegen bezieht sich auf die Sache d u r c h Ä h n l i c h k e i t, und fehlt sie, so ist auch von einem Bilde nicht mehr die Rede…. Es wäre eine deskriptiv unrichtige Auffassung der Sachlage, wenn man denken würde, der ganze Unterschied bestehe darin, dass dieselbe Intention, die einmal an die Erscheinung eines dem gemeinten Objekt ä h n l i c h e n Objektes geknüpft ist, ein andermal an die Erscheinung eines ihm u n ä h n l i c h - e n objekts geknüpft sei. Denn auch das Zeichen kann dem Bezeichneten ähnlich sein, ja vollkom- men ähnlich. Die Zeichenvorstellung wird dadurch aber nicht zur Bildvorstellung. Die Photographie des Zeichens A fassen wir ohne weiteres als Bild dieses Zeichens auf. Gebrauchen wir aber das Zeichen A als Zeichen für das Zeichen A, wie wenn wir schreiben: A *ist ein römisches Schriftzeichen,* so fassen wir A trotz bildmässiger Ähnlichkeit nicht das Bild, sondern eben als Zeichen.

Also die objektive Tatsache der Ähnlichkeit zwischen Erscheinendem und Gemeintem bestimmt keinen Unterschied. Gleichwohl ist sie für den Fall der Bildvorstellung nicht belanglos. Dies zeigt sich in der möglichen Erfüllung; und es ist ja nur die Erinnerung an diese Möglichkeit, welche uns die "objektive" Ähnlichkeit hier heranziehen ließ. Die Bildvorstellung hat offenbar die Eigentümlichkeit, daß, wo immer ihr Erfüllung zuteil wird, ihr als "Bild" erscheinender Gegenstand sich mit dem in erfüllenden Akte g e g e b e n e n Gegenstand durch Ähnlichkeit identifiziert. Indem wir dies als Eigentümlichkeit der Bildvorstellung bezeichnet haben, ist schon gesagt, daß hier die E r f ü l - l u n g d e s Ä h n l i c h e n d u r c h Ä h n l i c h e s d e n C h a r a k t e r d e r E r f ü l - l u n g s s y n t h e s i s a l s e i n e r i m a g i n a t i v e n i n n e r l i c h b e s t i m m t [Husserl, 1980a: 54-55]

Similarity is not sufficient to define an icon — a Husserlian "Bild" — for mere signs (*Zeichen*, which in Husserl do not possess any iconic content) may share similarity with their object. In order to function as a *Bild*, similarity needs to be invoked by a certain type of conscious act, imagination, which is defined by addressing its object "durch ähnliches". Thus, Peirce as well as Husserl agree in the need for a further determination of the Icon than mere similarity. In Peirce it is the functioning of a phenomenon as a sign for a similar object; in Husserl it is the notoriously asym- metrical concept of intentionality incarnated in a certain subtype named *Bildbewusst- sein* which introduces the asymmetry. Thus, there is a seminal difference between exactly which kind of support similarity needs in order to become an icon. In Peir- ce, the sign character is carefully defined without any reference to consciousness; in the still pre-egological Husserl of the *Untersuchungen*, similarity is defined objecti- vely, but not so imagination, which is seen as an intentional act with a certain kind of "Erfüllungssynthesis", that is, defined by phenomenological consciousness (a not yet transcendental consciousness, it must be admitted). The Peircian solution intro- duces the assymmetry not by means of an intentionality-like concept, but through the pragmatic concept of "use as a sign", elsewhere "function as a sign". Implicitly, then, Peirce makes the concepts of "use" and "function" more broad than (human) consciousness, true to his naturalized semiotics. For instance, the well-known biological phenomena of mimicry would by his definition (but not so by Husserl's) be unproblematic instances of iconicity.[2] To us, the Peircian solution is the one to be preferred in order to avoid any dualism between man and nature or the like, and it seems quite likely that Husserl's idea may be reinterpreted in a Peircian frame (so as to make intentionality a concept depending on the more general concept of a (teleological) system). On the other hand, Husserl's rendering of the special character of the *Bild* makes apparent an important feature which is in Peirce (at best) more implicitly present: similarity between two phenomena and the use of one as a sign of the other are not sufficient if just added as two independent features. To make up a *Bild* — or an icon, we could say — a sign must signify *through* its similarity to its object. We shall return to this elsewhere to concentrate on that other defining feature of iconicity, in addition to its intentionality/use/function part: its *similarity*, whose objectivity both authors invariably stress.

It is probably not to say too much to state that similarity has been given a bad press during the last century or so. Many currents in recent philosophy, psychology, linguistics, etc. have seen the objectivity of similarity as highly questionable and have consequently sought to eliminate the concept as a piece of common-sense ideology. The attack has come from two principal sides. One is what could be called the Nietzschean side in general, claiming that similarity is only a construct by a weak mind in order to control an overwhelmingly non-self-similar ontological Being. In Nietzsche himself, we find the prototype of this idea in his ontological concept of the world as *werdende*, as a current of constant change, in which it is of course impossible to isolate stabilities other than by means of artificially stiffening and controlling what cannot be controlled. This idea has been prominent in various existentialisms, nihilisms, Lebensphilosophien, and the like throughout our century and one of its latest incarnations is of course the famed "philosophies of difference", which teach that difference is always presupposed by any identity or similarity. In this kind of thought, similarity is most often identified with identity as being part of the despised "Identitätsphilosophie"; by this operation all the non-trivial difficulties in the concept of similarity are concealed by reducing it to the trivial idea that A = A.

Another line of attack on the notion of similarity has come from almost the

---

[2] The insect known as a "walking stick" evidently functions as a sign fooling hungry birds, but there's no conscious, let alone human intention behind this function.

opposite side of philosophy, analytical philosophy. The idea of a purely symbolic calculus as the ultimate aim of science and philosophy has been thriving at least since Leibniz, but during the last century this idea has enjoyed greater prominence than ever before. The history of this idea is long and cannot be mapped in detail here, but some crucial points can be sketched out. A source for it is of course the influential success of Newtonian mechanics, which gave rise to a lot of philosophical attempts at explaining the reasons for this success. One of the ideas was the "algebraisation" of Newton's laws. Taken together with Descartes' analytical geometry, which made transformations between geometrical figurae and algebraic expressions possible, this indicated that algebraic calculi were the ultimate aim of a science that be successful. This — in itself, sound — idea was sharpened through a series of developments in the 19th century. First, the problem of formalizing imaginary and complex numbers gave rise to the construction of autonomous algebra in the first half of the century: the insight that algebraic structures may be investigated with no reference to what the algebraic symbols might be used to symbolize, yielding the famous results of group theory and the like. Second, the development of non-Euclidean geometries by variations on the famous parallel-axiom in Euclid's system. Originally, these geometries sprang from the attempts at showing that the axiom might be proved as a theorem by using the simpler Euclidean axioms; one way to show this would be to assume the contrary and derive a contradiction. This procedure did not, in fact, result in contradictions, but merely in new, consistent, formal systems which could now be interpreted to yield Lobat-chevskijan and Riemannian geometries, respectively. Now, the crucial point was that in these new geometries, the symbols of the old Euclidean systems were to be given new interpretations. What was in Euclid a straight line, for instance, became in Riemann a great circle. Thus, the interpretation of algebraically expressed propositions tended to be marginalized, a tendency which came in full power in the formal logic of Frege, Peirce, Schröder, Russell, etc. around the turn of the century — and which rose to metamatemathical fame in Hilbert's famous idea of the possibility of making mathematical proofs by a mere "formale Redeweise" in which the symbols involved were treated as mere letters equipped with certain rules of transformations, placing their interpretation between brackets. It is necessary to understand that this whole development is extraordinarily fertile and by no means contrary to the idea of similarity *in itself.* The vast research in the autonomous regularities of algebra, symbol systems, and formal logic is one of the richest developments in science during the last centuries. But somehow two perversions of this ingenious idea emerged. One was that formalization was purely logical in a very restricted use of the word, as meaning consisting in a purely conventional, symbolical calculus.

Another was that formalization is not only crucial to science, but formalization *is* science, so that the very interpretation of formal systems tended to be conceived of as a source of error to be avoided. In fact, we almost ought to coin a new word in order to characterize this exaggerated belief in formalism — "formalisticism", or the like. In Hilbert, it was still the case that the "formale Redeweise" was only to be maintained within proof theory — in the previous meta-mathematical determination of definitions, of axioms, rules for the manipulation of symbols, etc., the interpretation of the terms was ineradicable, as well in the subsequent understanding of the conclusion proved.[3] But in many heirs to his formalist program, this crucial distinction was forgotten, and the ideology spread that by establishing a formal calculus the very aim was to *exterminate* intuition, not merely to control it. In the humanities, this idea spread through logical variants on structuralism, cf. for instance Hjelmslev's formal — or should we say formalisticist — rendering of Saussure, in which the mere algebraic dependencies between terms was all linguistics might hope to map. All in all, it is no wonder this overall tendency to privilege symbolic and algebraic calculi at the expense of interpretation and intuitive presentation became hostile to iconicity and its basis in similarity. Thus, we find in two of the major figures in analytical philosophy, Quine and Goodman, attempts at reducing the notion of similarity completely — just like we in psychological or logical structuralism, for instance Greimas or early Eco, find analogous ideas.

In recent years, a new "morphological turn" or even "iconic turn" as a part of the vast domain of cognitive science has changed the picture. Here, continuous models not reducible to algebra are introduced alongside feature-preserving mappings of such models between (mental) domains not thoroughly defined by these mappings. The aim of this paper is to isolate the notion of similarity implicit in these procedures — by contrasting them with the fallacious attempts at getting rid of similarity altogether.

Let us examine the famous arguments of Goodman (1972) which have often been conceived of as the definitive burial of similarity in the American context, the "Seven Strictures of Similarity" — "Similarity, ever ready to solve philosophical problems and overcome obstacles, is a pretender, an impostor, a quack." (p. 437)

The first of the seven arguments runs as follows: 'Similarity does not make the

---

[3] Thus, it could be argued, Hilbert, the father of formalism, was no formalist (Hempel, in Benacerraf and Putnam (1982) makes this point). He insisted not on formalism but on finitism, that is, the formal means of proof should be finite, even if the metamathematical content of the theorems proved might be infinite, and thus it was his attempt at solving the same infinity problem as the intuitionists, not to make formalisms the only goal of science.

difference between representations and descriptions, distinguish any symbols as peculiarly "iconic", or account for the grading of pictures as more or less realistic or naturalistic.' Here, Goodman's idea is that the conviction of resemblance as 'the necessary and sufficient condition for representation is so deeply engrained that the evident and conclusive arguments to the contrary are seldom considered' (*ibid.*). Now, this conviction is at least not shared by any of the two great phenomenologists Peirce and Husserl, as we have already seen: each of them make similarity a necessary but not sufficient condition for representation — and only for certain kinds of representations: namely, the iconic ones. Accordingly, Goodman's argument precisely presents examples of resemblance lacking the asymmetry of the sign function: "Yet obviously one dime is not a picture of another" etc. He realizes that this only proves that resemblance is not sufficient to define representation, and then turns to the idea that resemblance *and* reference should be sufficient. His example here is of precisely the same character as Husserl's with the *A* above — it involves the *suppositio materialis*:

> Consider a page of print that begins with "the final seven words on this page" and ends with the same seven words repeated. The first of these seven-word inscriptions surely refers to the second, and is as much like it as can be, yet is no more a picture of it than is any printing of a word a picture of another printing [*ibid.*]

But Goodman draws completely different conclusions from the example than does Husserl. He hastily concludes while continuing to the next issue:

> Still, once pictures are somehow distinguisthed from other denotative symbols — and this must be by some other means than similarity — does not comparative naturalism or realism among pictures depend upon their degree of resemblance to what they represent? Not even this can be maintained [p. 438].

It is strange that an heir to the Frege-tradition like Goodman does not see that it is the oblique reference ("When I say 'A' I am referring to A ...", etc.) so crucial to the Fregean distinction between *Sinn und Bedeutung* which is invoked here — and which of course is a type/token relationship, not an iconic relation. His argument may be summed up as follows: neither similarity nor the sum of similarity and reference is sufficient to define a picture. In this, he is perfectly right. But his conclusion that icons do not involve similarity at all does not follow from this. In both Peirce and Husserl, the defining feature is similarity in a signifying and referring function, which is not the same as the mere aggregate of similarity and reference. The reference of the picture is *dependent* on similarity; in Husserl's vocabulary the reference of a picture is an "unselbständige Inhalt" because it depends on the similarity. Of course this is not the case in all kinds of signs, for instance in the *suppositio materialis* which both authors use as an example and where the icon is merely mentioned (or, object of an act of *Nennen*). In these cases, the reference takes place as a result of deictic — or, in Peirce's wording, indexical — sign use. Thus, the failure of Goodman is here to recognize that there are several different ways of referring (iconically, indexically, symbolically, at least). This fault is then in Goodman's hasty style mixed up with another in the argument already quoted. Similarity should be independent of the degree of realism of a representation for reasons of cultural relativism: realism is a function of culturally specific systems and hence similarity is an effect of these and not the opposite way around. This crude argument oversees that the fact that similarity is "culture-dependent" does not make it a mere effect of cultural norms. Cultural norms *require* similarity in their description; one could say that one culture differs from another because it emphasizes other similarities. In that respect, the similarities perceived are of course "culture-dependent", but this is merely because the very notion of culture is defined by systems of similarities. So to say that "similarity is relative, variable, culture-dependent" merely amounts to saying that any *particular* judgment of similarity is dependent on the classes of similarities envisaged, which is a mere truism, more apt, in fact, to dissolve the concept of culture than the concept of similarity.

Now, the "second stricture": 'Similarity does not pick out inscriptions that are "tokens of a common type" or replicas of each other.' The token-type problem of course involves the problem of nominalism versus realism, and the very terminology of token and type is a (probably unconscious) Peircian heritage. Here, Goodman invoked various variants on written types, such as for instance a B, a B where the middle horisontal line is not attached to the vertical bar, and an O — and, again hastily, concludes that the second B is topologically more like the O than the proper B, because the first two both possess one interior part only, the second two. Goodman simply fails here to see that more than one topology exists; for instance a topology distinguishing singularities would not hesitate to identify the to Bs as having similar (but not identical) systems of singularities, different from the O. In fact, Goodman's example does nothing but say that a green circle and a red circle are not similar, because one is green and the other is red. But both are still round. The problem is, of course, to focus upon the right level of comparison, and this is not always as easily done as in this deludingly simple example. In fact, typefaces constitute a very complicated case of similarity as argued by Douglas Hofstadter (1985) and myself (1992) — but complexity is not an argument against similarity

27

either.[4] Goodman's topological deliberation permits him to conclude that

> I suspect that the best we can do is to say that all inscriptions that are d's must be alike in being d's. That has the solid ring of assured truth, but is hardly electrifying. Moreover, notice that to say that all d's are alike in being d's amounts simply to saying that all d's are d's. The words 'alike in being' add nothing: similarity becomes entirely superfluous. [p. 439].

This conclusion displays an overall strategy found in similar versions in various anti-similitarists: "similarity" can be reduced to identity. But this short-circuit overlooks the non-trivial fact that many propositions of the form "All A's are A's" conceal complex cognitive skills used to detect objective similarities. "All A's are A's" is not trivial, because in this proposition, the first 'A' refers to tokens, the second 'A' to the type; and the question at stake is: which bundle of (different, to be sure) similarity-preserving transformations connects the various subtypes of A's with each other? Or to put it differently: how do we recognize a given token A as a type A when we have no access whatsoever to an extensional definition of A-ness, that is, to the "set of all A's," the unproblematic existence of which and access to which Goodman is much too quick to presuppose.

The "third stricture" says: 'Similarity does not provide *the* grounds for accounting for two occurrences performances of the same work, or repetitions of the same behavior or experiment.' The structure of the argument is the same as in the first stricture, as supposed by our italicization of "*the* grounds". Of course similarity is not sufficient, it takes a supplementary indexical indication of which aspects of similarity are relevant. 'Repetitions of the same behavior, such as hitting a tennis ball against a barn door, may involve widely varying sequences of motion.' (p. 439). Actually, in this stricture Goodman does not draw any distinction between two issues involved: kind of similarity and indexical reference. When he sums up 'In each of these cases, the grouping of occurrences under a work or an experiment or an activity depends not upon a high degree of similarity but upon the possession of certain characteristics. In the case of performances of a Beethoven symphony, the score determines what those requisite characteristics are ...' The score in this example actually performs two tasks: it determines "requisite characteristics" which we must still suppose can be instantiated in a host of variants which consequently will

---

[4] Actually, this similarity problem involves Gödel's well-known incompleteness theorem and entails that the set of possible A's may not be delimited beforehand because it is not computable. Of course, insights of this complexity do not interest the crusader of difference.

be similar with respect to a subset of those characteristics — and it codifies this set of characteristics by making them explicit and indexically attaching a stabilizing name ("Beethoven's Xth") to them. Thus, all in all, this "third stricture" is no argument against similarity at all; the fact that '... the principle of classification varies with our purposes and interests' does not imply that there is not similarity at stake in each one of the cases mentioned, and the similarity is then relevant to a standard selected by the *purpose or interest* in question (notice these categories and their relatedness to Peirce's *sign function* or Husserl's *Bildbewusstsein*).

The fourth stricture is more controversial: "Similarity does not explain metaphor or metaphorical truth" (p. 440). Here, we find Goodman's most famous denial of similarity: "Anything is in some way like anything else". This leads him to conclude, like in the second stricture, that similarity is the result of a process, be it similarity between tokens or the parts of a metaphor, rather than its prerequisite: 'In both cases a reversal in order of explanation might be appropriate: the fact that a term applies, literally or metaphorically, to certain objects may itself constitute rather than arise from a particular similarity among those objects' (p. 440). There is an interesting tension here between the two parts of Goodman's argument. The first is actually a statement of a stunning extension: "Anything is in some way like anything else". Of course, Goodman intends by this statement to reduce similarity to insignificance because of its omnipresence, but if we take his words at face value, it is a statement of enormous a priori breadth. It is of course impossible empirically to undertake the task of actually comparing all known phenomena two and two; how then is it possible to state this amazing theorem? The idea is probably that if the *tertium comparationis* chosen is sufficiently general, some property will show up shared by both. Yet, we cannot presuppose that this property will in all cases be an empirical property (given one phenomenon, we can simply define another phenomenon by giving it another empirical property for each property of the first one — a property chosen beyond the limits of any chosen similarity function). Consequently, the property shared must in this extreme case be of an a priori character, having no opposite. For instance: both are phenomena. Both have a certain form (the formless being also a form). Etc. Given this deliberation, we can surely subscribe to Goodman's a priori law: anything is in some way like anything else. But then this is in flagrant contradiction with his consequent: that metaphorical use constitutes similarities rather than being constituted by them. If similarities between any things always already exist, then metaphor must be constituted by the selection of certain of these similarities at the expense of others. This discussion is still relevant today when for instance Lakoff's cognitive semantics is based on the idea that similarities are not preexisting but are created by metaphorical mappings from one domain onto another. But if Goodman's a priori law is really correct, this cannot be the case: the similarity chosen must in some sense of the word exist beforehand, as a potentiality. This would of course be Peirce's solution and it seems evident that it is pertinent for most everyday judgments of similarity. The fact that it has never been asserted before that this orange on the table before me is similar in shape to the moon (given a certain granularity of similarity classes) might cause sensible souls to see me as a genius for creating metaphors, but modestly, it seems strange that this similarity should be something created by me. I merely discover (no great effort) this similarity by applying a certain *tertium comparationis* (a circle, give or take a certain rate of deformation). In rare cases, of course, it may take great pains to establish a new complicated *tertium comparationis* to see a similarity (Newton discovering the similarity between the movement of the apple and of the heavenly bodies, Eliot discovering the similarity between cruelty and the growth of April flowers) but this hardly implies that the similarity was not there before. Of course, artists will rage against this conclusion, for does it not imply that the work of art is not their creation; was it already in some sense a possibility before their effort? This is probably — if we for a moment allow ourselves the Nietzschean pleasure of getting personal — one of the reasons why it is so hard for many to give up the idea of similarities as something constructed: by doing so, one also gives up the self-flattering romantic-nihilist idea of the subject as artist, as genius, as *Übermensch*.

The fifth stricture deals with similarity in science: 'Similarity does not account for our predictive, or more generally, our inductive practice' (p. 441). Goodman sets out by stating that the fact that the future will be like the past is often regarded as highly dubious — but contradicts this idea: '... while I am sure the future will be like the past, I am not sure in just what way it will be like the past. No matter what happens, the future will be in some way like the past. This idea Goodman illustrates by drawing a curve plotting the relationship between two sets of variables. Now, there will exist a curve covering any possible extrapolation of the sets of data already given, he argues.' The idea seems to be that the drawing of curves is our means for retroactively assuming a similarity which we were not able to see during the process, and of course it is mathematically correct that any amount of points in the plane can be connected with one line with an increasing x-variable. But this argument proceeds as if science had never, in a large number of cases, established any *laws* delimiting this infinite set of possible curves to a small class of related curves. 'Along which, among countless lines of similarity, do our predictions run?', Goodman rhetorically asks, and of course this question can only be answered in each specific case. When letting go of a stone, I of course suppose it will behave similarly to the stone I let go of yesterday, that is, according to the same law of gravity, — Peirce's favourite example.

The sixth argument: 'Similarity between particulars does not suffice to define qualities'. This is not the fact, Goodman argues, because it does not follow from the fact that each two of several particulars are alike, that they are all alike. Objects may pairwise have a color in common without all of them having any color in common. Hence, 'Dyadic likeness between particulars will not serve to define those classes of particulars that have a common quality throughout.' This is correct: similarity is not transitive. Similarity cannot define quality, it is rather defined by it. Goodman's argument here assumes that it should be possible to judge two objects alike without stating in what the similarity consists — which is of course not the case. Even in the cases in which it might be difficult to point out the precise similar feature, as between parent and child, it is possible to reason about it and close in on it: "it is something about the form of the eyes", etc. Even if there thus might be cases in which the tertium is not obvious, it must exist as a not-yet-fully-articulated prerequisite to the similarity judgment.

The seventh and last stricture: 'Similarity cannot be equated with, or measured in terms of, possession of common characteristics.' Even if it was precisely what Goodman was about to do with the Beethoven œuvre in the 3rd stricture, this is proposed as the more general argument, underlying some of the earlier ones. The common-sense idea of similarity between two things — that they have at least one property in common — is once again contrasted with the idea than any two things have a property in common and that consequently this is insignificant. An attempt to rescue similarity by saying that two things having more properties in common are more alike than two things having less properties in common (p. 443) is counterargued by the idea that 'any two things have exactly as many properties in common as any other two'. Goodman gets this idea from the extensional definition of property by class membership, and each element in a given universe is a member of exactly the same amount of subsets as any other. This set theoretic triviality is then supposed to be the definitive argument, for

> I have, indeed, been counting only first-order extensional properties. ... The inevitable suggestion that we must consider intensional properties seems to me especially fruitless here, for identifying and distinguishing intensional properties is a notoriously slippery matter, and the idea of measuring similarity or anything else in terms of number of intensional properties need hardly be taken seriously [p. 444].

Now, it is not necessary to maintain that the idea of similarity needs quantification to be sustained, but it is comical that Goodman at this late point refuses to concern himself with intensional similarity because of its slippery nature — of course this is where the whole problem lies insofar as extensionally defined properties, as he rightly claims, make the concept trivial, just like it makes the whole idea of properties trivial (because the property "red" should then be defined by the set of all red objects, and this, again, is a set like all other sets and nothing in particular distinguishes it from the other. Then, how do you zoom in on this set, knowing nothing at all about redness before you know the set with all its elements ...). Of course, he adds, one could restrict oneself to counting the *important* properites — a solution he discards rightaway because importance is a "volatile matter". But of course similarity is relative to what in a given case is considered "important", and this of course lies in the Peircian and Husserlian framing of similarity in icons by "function" and "intention" respectively.

In a concluding remark, Goodman sums up his alleged results:

> similarity is much like motion: "Clear enough when confined by context and circumstance in ordinary discourse, but hopelessly ambiguous when turned loose". Talking about motion is pointless if no frame of reference is established. ... We have to say what a thing is to the left of, what it moves in relation to, and in what respects two things are similar. [p. 444].

In this we could not agree more. Yet, this is not sufficient for Goodman, because unlike motion, similarity cannot be saved by recognizing its relativity: adding a specification of the property in common, similarity is simply rendered superfluous.

To this, Goodman once more adds the superfluous argument that circumstances alter similarities (of course they do), and concludes

> Relativity, even volatility, is not a fatal fault. Physics does not stop talking of motion merely because motion is not absolute. But similarity, as we have seen, is a much more slippery matter. As it occurs in philosophy, similarity tends under analysis either to vanish entirely or to require for its explanation just what it purports to explain. [p. 445].

Now, one could argue that physics does not stop talking of matter either, even if it is slippery. And Goodman has not, in fact, proved that similarity evaporates under analysis. The idea is that the concept of common property makes it vanish. But a central point is that common property is not enough to define similarity: this property should be measured in relation to a certain granularity on the property scale in question. I might say that two objects are similar because they are both red (for instance two traffic lights), even if it is not precisely the same shade of red. But the property in common thus depends on a certain topology on the quality scale in question, in this case the color continuum. In some cases, this topology may divide the continuum in two areas only, for instance dark and light, in others, it may require thousands of nuances, in some cases the property classes overlap, in others they do not. This still makes it correct to assume that similarity is a mere shorthand for something else — but it is not a shorthand for something equally simple (for instance common property), because a given judgment of similarity implies a certain set of possible topologies on the property space (many different granularities may make the two red colors "similar"). Thus "similar" means "invariant under certain transformations in quality space with a certain topology and granularity". But this is not trivial. And this is why similarity is not eradicable: it is the phenomenological mode for such invariances to appear. In many cases the topology and transformations in the property space in question are evident, and in these cases the concept of similarity of course is trivial but in other cases similarity is a sign to be interpreted; the precise character of the property space in question and its topology and transformations is a question to be investigated. Thus, similarity calls for explanation.[5] In the easy cases, the explanation is of course, as are any trivial questions, trivial.

In the history of semiotics in our century, the preference for a purely symbolic calculus at the expense of iconicity had the wind behind it since the spread of formalism in the interwar period. In the American context, the logical semantics taking its point of departure in Carnap saw truth-conditions of expressions in purely formal systems as the decisive feature of scientific endeavors in semantics, later to terminate in Chomskianism. In the European context, the formalism of Hjelmslev,[6]

---

[5] The reason why Goodman does not think this is the case is probably because he sees the idea of a "common property" as something which may easily be formalized in a discrete symbolic algebra. If phenomenon 1 has the property a and phenomenon 2 has the property a, then it takes no great amount of insight to state that $a = a$. But in cases where quality spaces are continuous, this proposition is a mere surface of continuous transformations which need not be simple.

[6] It is illuminating to compare Husserl's doctrine of dependencies in the 3rd and 4th *Logische Untersuchungen* with Hjelmslev's formally analogous algebra in *Prolegomena* from 1943. In Husserl's formal ontology in the 3rd *Untersuchung*, two types of parts of a whole are distinguished; *selbständige und unselbständige Teile*, respectively, or *Stücke und Momente*. In the formal grammar built on this foundation in the 4th *Untersuchung* as the synthetic a priori basis for any possible specific grammar, these two mereological categories give rise to two corresponding categories of *Bedeutungen*, independent and dependent, respectively, and this in turn makes two overall categories of grammar possible, heirs to the categorematics and syncategorematics. These basic grammatical categories now may display three possible relations: the relation between two independent unities, the relation

with its claim that all language description should proceed in a simple algebra, was a forerunner of what was to come in structuralism, both in linguistics and in the structurally inspired humanities more broadly. This tendency had its heyday in the sixties with French structuralism, generative grammar, and symbolic Artificial Intelligence, supported by its biological counterpart in DNA-based neo-Darwinism, when all the world seemed be but one symbolic calculus — but the general tendency seems to be that it has been slowly receding since then, allowing for a comeback of an interest in iconicity. But still, the tendency is strong, and in semiotics it is necessary to respond to the arguments of the "formalisticists" in order not to fall prey to too naïve a concept of iconicity. Probably the most extreme anti-similitary movement in general semiotics is Greimas' theory, the so-called Paris School. Even if the overall architecture of the theory includes a Merleau-Pontian "sémiotique naturelle", allegedly phenomenologically functioning prior to the intervention of language, still the concept of iconicity is relegated to a very superficial level of discourse, as a secondary adornment of established meaning in order to render it similar to a given (and always ideological) conception of reality, that is, as promoting

---

between an independent unit and one dependent upon it, and finallly one between two units, each of them dependent on the other. Now, these are precise formal analogues to the three basic relations on which Hjelmslevian algebra was to be built: independence, dependence, and interdependence, respectively. But while Husserl envisaged his system as a formal prerequisite to any grammar whatever, which would in turn add its own regularities to be described, Hjelmslev made the demand that the three types of relation should be the only descriptive tool allowed in his algebra for the empirical description of languages, thereby making these systems of interrelations the only object of linguistics. The whole material thus organized — be it phonic or graphemic matter on the side of expression or semantic substance on the side of content — was to be left out of the scope of linguistics. This comparison clairifies the fact that the word formalism in fact covers two different ways of using the same formal systems: in one, formalisms do not exhaust the empirical field they describe; Husserlian formal ontology is of course valid for any empirical field whatsoever, and even if further formalisms may of course be needed to cover the material ontologies, then these formalisms can never cover a whole empirical field entirely, the demand being that formalization shall proceed according to *die Sachen selbst*, cf. Husserl's interpretation of the famous demand of *adequatio rei ac intellectus*. Another more radical version of formalism (which, as proposed above, might be nicknamed formalisticism), here exemplified in Hjelmslev, sees a definition formalism as exhausting the empirical field in question, no matter, as it were, is left out for further research because matter is conceived of as nothing but what is organized through formalization, and consequently the (iconical) interpretation of the content of the formalism in use becomes irrelevant. In the first version, formalization is indispensable to control a certain content; in the second it simply and reductionisticallly substitutes any content.

Barthesian "effects of reality".[7] In this view, icons are simply seen as a secondary and necessarily illusionary addition to basic conceptual ("semio-narrative") meaning already well-established, and all of it supposedly describable in a Hjelmslevian meta-language in which the denominations remain algebraic throughout and hence arbitrary. In contrast to this consequent and untenable position, Umberto Eco's famous attack on iconicity in the 60s and 70s is at the same time much more multi-faceted and much more unclear.[8] It almost seems as if Eco is steadfastedly determined to "get rid of" iconic signs, as he does not hesitate to say, because he brings forth a whole series of widely varying arguments, often not even mutually consistent. His "Critique of iconism" forms a part of his "Theory of Sign Production" framed in a comical semi-Marxist language of production and labor, and even if it does not figure explicitly as an argument, this overall ontology is probably crucial in his critique of iconism: iconicity, or natural, motivated, analogical signs of any kind seems to come into being "without work" so to speak. But in Marxism, there must be no free lunch, and consequently these apparently spontaneous signs must have their basis in the human production of codes and conventions revealed: they are bourgeois signs whose apparent freedom is built upon the suppression of more hardworking signs. It might seem like kicking a more than dead horse to counterargue claims like these nowadays, but it still has relevance because of the underlying idea that human subjectivity is responsible for all semiotic activity. This idea is not a privilege for Marxism, and one finds it in various disguises in existentialisms, deconstructionisms and other heirs to the subjectivist strand in German Idealism on the one hand, as well as in formalisticists like Hjelmslev on the other[9] — and this

---

[7] Thus, there must be an internal contraction in the theory; the idea of a "sémiotique naturelle" being impossible without the possibility to identify similar phenomena as similar. I hasten to say that this theory has in other respects, in particular concerning narrative questions, proved extremely fertile.

[8] Of course, Eco has left this anti-iconic position long ago, and his most recent book is in fact a threatise on iconicity. Still, his old position is worth dismantling; first, for the reason that it is a prototypical version of modern semiotic anti-iconism; second, because it has been, and in many currents still is, very influential.

[9] One can even find cooperations between the Nietzschean version and the formalisticist version of anti-iconism, as for instance in the actual Italian Hjelmslevo-Nietzscheanism of Alessandro Zinna, a direct heir to the Ecoists' Hjelmslevo-Marxism of the seventies. When first you get the strange idea it is easy to see how this coupling works: Hjelmslev's concept of sign-function destabilizes the sign in so far as it is no longer a part of the language system, and his definition of form of expression and form of content respectively as the giving form to amorphous substance yields a place for Nietzschean active nihilists to undertake these creative acts of producing not only signs, but also expression and

is probably a very widespread reason for skepticism towards iconicity that the acknowledgment of it invariably forms part of a Copernican revolution depriving the human subject of some of its privileges.

Within this overall frame, Eco's arguments are, as mentioned, various, to say the least. One argument goes against similarity as "shared properties" by attacking Morris' simplified version of Peirce, including the fairly reasonable statement that icons resemble their objects "in some respects" so that 'Iconicity is thus a matter of degree' (Morris, quote from Eco: 192) Instead of understanding the strength of this claim, Eco sees it as a weakness because when stretched to onomatopoeia it includes "completely conventional" expressions. Here Eco, in a Hjelmslevian craze, compares various linguistic expressions for a cock's crowing; English /cock-a-doodle-doo/, French /cocquerico/, and Italian /chicchiricchi/; the iconic relationship of these to the cock's crowing is 'very weak' (p. 192). In fact, this positive statement is not very plausible; the onomatopoeia mentioned are all close to a possible phonetic transcription of the actual sound, and they even display a large amount of similarity among them: all of them are four-syllable words with the same prosodic structure with a long and stressed last syllable; in all of them the two first syllables begin with /k/ and finally the first and last syllable contain the same vowel (all this goes as well for Danish /kykeliky/, by the way). Eco undertakes this — very weak — analysis in order to counterargue "shared properties", and his other example is not much more convincing. In this he compares the photo of a glass of beer in an advertisement with an actual glass of beer. The fact that the photo contains neither glass nor beer nor vapour nor coldness is not a very convincing argument against shared properties when the icon in question is actually a visual rendering of the object. Eco does, at least, admit the existence of "visual stimuli", but his explanation of their role in the sign process minimizes their effort to the extreme:

> I feel certain visual stimuli, colors, spacial relationships, incidences of light and I coordinate them into a given perceptual structure. The same thing [sic!] happens when I look at an actual glass of beer; I connect together some stimuli coming from an as yet unstructured field and I produce a *perceptum* based on a previously acquired experience. [p. 193].

He later questions even the notion of "the 'same' perceptual effect" and asks if it is not better to assume that "previous learning" is responsible for my viewing two different perceptual results as the same. Even if it is the "same" thing that happens

---

content forms — as against those who just take language for what it is.

in the two cases, the sameness is relegated from the sign and made the product of the I which in turn is made a product of previous learning, that is, culture. That is, an empirically easily verified similarity in form, color, texture, etc. is replaced with a completely unverifiable "previous learning" not further accounted for. Furthermore, this pseudo-explanation does not account for why "the same thing" does not happen when I am faced with other stimuli; if Eco's idea were correct I would see beer glasses all around me. Maybe he did. This analysis shows how formalisticism and its idea of the forming of a "yet unstructured field" (cf. the structuralist arch-idea of language's partition of an amorphous substance, standard in Saussure as well as Hjelmslev) can be coupled unproblematically with subjectivism and, in turn, culturalism. His further examples are similarly unconvincing: the iconic rendering of a horse by means of its contour is explained by a "graphic convention" instead of a geometrical transformation of objective properties of form coupled with knowledge of the animal as being one concluded object; and the "sweetness" of saccharine and sugar is allegedly "not a property of the two compounds, but the result of their interaction with our taste buds". Still, recent research in the physiology of gustation shows that it is a molecular property which is responsible for this similarity in function, namely the presence on the periphery of both macromolecules of morphologically similar "active sites", and even if this were not the case, the two tastes would still be phenomenologically similar, i.e. lie close to each other in taste space. The fact that various cultures prefer various tastes — which he adds as a culturalist argument — does not change these biochemical and phenomenological facts. All in all, his rejection of the shared property idea builds on a construction unluckily uniting subjectivism, culturalism and formalisticism.

A geometrical case is now made against the notion of similarity (which he surprisingly finds a more scientific notion than shared properties — presumably because similitude has a use in geometry defined by invariance in certain transformations).[10] Here, Eco's argument is even more coarse, to put it bluntly. A Lockean tabula rasa is invoked in the shape of a "naive interlocutor" or "non-trained informant" who is not able to perform the transformations required (and so compare the Cheops pyramid with a small model, for instance). That transformations such as these should be completely conventional is now argued with the presentation of some simple graphic theoretical figurae which are similar in so far as they connect the same set of points with the same set of lines (but where the points do not inhabit

---

[10] Even if Eco does not know the Erlanger program and thinks that geometrical similitude is only invariance to scalar transformations (and not, for instance, projections, rotations, mirrorings, topological "stretchings", etc.).

the same places in the plane and the lines do not have the same form). These graphs are of course not similar in the sense that they are invariant in scalar transformation — and this is for Eco an argument that they are not 'spatially (and therefore geometrically) "similar"' (p. 196) even if they are, of course, topologically similar. Eco probably feels the danger of trying to drive out one kind of similarity with another, for he instantaneously adds: 'This kind of *isomorphism* may be called a form of similarity but it would be very difficult to assert that it is a geometric similitude. To call such a relationship "iconic" is a mere metaphor.' (p. 197). Now "mere" metaphor may in many cases contain genuine insight, and such is the case, of course, here. Isomorphism is iconic; the question is why Eco refuses to admit it. A positive answer could be that he fears a concept of iconicity which is spontaneous and substantial, maintaining a similarity without a *tertium comparationis* — this would explain the strange fact that he considers it an argument against iconicity to reveal the *tertium*, the underlying principle of similarity in each case. Of course, Eco's later work has shown a rationalist and well-placed fight precisely against unfounded similarity claims in various occult practices where no *tertium comparationis* and no correlative invariants under transformation are to be isolated.[11] But the fear of such "similarities" should be no argument against well-founded similiarities, and it seems that Eco in general mistakes the transformations guaranteeing the single types of similarities for being mere cultural conventions. Thus, in addition to the earlier arguments which pointed to large competencies on the part of the ego, this Lockean construction makes of the I a mere tabula rasa.

But more arguments follow. Eco confronts himself with a version of Peirce's concept of iconicity and criticizes Peirce for not abandoning his reference to objects in his definition of it, because it makes iconism an 'umbrella-term that covers many different phenomena such as a mental image, a graph, a painting.' (p. 199) This argument is very strange; it is precisely the reference to similarity with the object which gives the unity of Peirce's definition and which allows it to include the various phenomena mentioned. There are two points in this: one is what we have already touched on and what Eco emphasizes over and over again: that a transformation between sign and object '... does not suggest the idea of natural correspondence; it is rather the consequence of rules and artifice' and hence is "mere" convention. But rules can never be the *causes* of similarity, for they presuppose it in so far as their general formulation is of the type "Do *the same* as what is prescribed here

---

[11] Already Peirce, by the way, raged against the mysticist claims that the Gizeh pyramids document ancient Egyptian knowledge of the expansion of π, of e, the precise position of the North Star etc. - claims so well parodied in *Foucault's Pendulum*.

...". The same goes for his emphatic conclusion "Similitude is *produced* and must be *learned*" — it would be impossible to teach anybody anything if one were not allowed to say "Now, do *like I do* ..." and thereby presuppose similarity.[12] This argument of course is also valid against Goodman's similar claims. Another point is not stated explicitly, but it might seem as if Eco's implicit contrast to Peirce's alleged "umbrella" term is a rather narrow idea of iconicity restricted to the domain of vision only. This of course brings him in conflict with the culturalism stated so far, because vision and the possession of eyes can hardly be interpreted as cultural conventions which must be learned. This comes to the fore in his next argument, which is aimed against the symmetry of certain similarity phenomena which must consequently be excluded from the concept of iconicity: mirror images, doubles tokens of the same type,[13] and expressive signs. This argument is of course perfectly valid, cf. the central phenomenological distinction between symmetrical similarity and asymmetrical iconicity; yet it is no argument against the latter that it depends on the former, from which it must be distinguished. But in this almost sound argument totally new criteria sneak in all of a sudden:

> Secondly the presumed 'iconism' that should govern the correspondence of a token to its type is not a *theorem* that semiotics could demonstrate; it is one of its *postulates* .... The rules of this recognition are deeply rooted in the mechanisms of human perception and must be assumed as already given in any semiotic enquiry. [p. 203].

Here, semiotics is suddenly presented as a deductive science with postulates, proofs, theorems, etc., and token-type relations are wholesale reduced to biology. But why should it not be important to guarantee the soundness of the postulates of one's science's — which in this case are even empirical matter for other sciences

---

[12] The argument here is structurally analogous to Kant's argument for the inevitability of an *Urteilskraft*, an ability to judge. How can a rule be applied to a particular case? You may not propose another rule to take care of the application, for then you run into an infinite regress: how can this second rule be applied, then, and so on. The same goes for the attempt to get rid of similarity by means of conventions: how do you apply the conventions to similar cases — by means of yet other conventions ...?

[13] We shall not go into Eco's arguments here except to notice that his treatment of the token-type problem is at best superficial. He obviously thinks that expression types are "ruled by a *ratio facilis*", that is, they are easy to produce and reproduce, even if he admits that tokens of content types may be more difficult to handle. But even expression tokens constitute a very complicated problem, and the complexity of the bundle of transformations securing the various kinds of similarities between various subtypes of a type has been investigated by Douglas Hofstadter (1985) and myself (1992).

(cognitive psychology)? This sudden naturalist tendency culminates in the refusal of iconicity in the so-called "expressive" signs — Kandinskian lines signifying emotions, and the like: 'We may consider all these cases of empathy as mere *stimulations* that should be studied by the physiology of the nervous system.' (p. 203) — as if they were not semiotic phenomena at all. A strange theory: seeing a picture of a beer as a beer is a complicated cultural phenomenon, while seeing a line as a complicated psychological emotion is something perfectly natural. Just like some icons are thus "mere" conventions for a completely blank Locke-like culturalized subject, other icons are "mere" neurological phenomena in a naturalized physiological subject brimming with semiotic competence. It is a wonder that these two subjects may thrive in one and the same head. The problem of cutting the cake and dividing the iconic signs amongst these two "mere" categories is of course the numerous cases in which both are active and hard to distinguish. Eco elaborates on the conventionality at length, making clear that this is the semiotically interesting field (the natural "signs" not being signs but something even simpler than Pavlovian conditioned reflexes), but embarks finally on still another type of argument stating that measured on very general (we would call them formal ontological) terms, similarity becomes ubiquitous: '... on the level of very elementary formal phenomena such as high-low, right-left, or long-wide ‾ everything resembles everything else' (p. 212). Perfectly correct as this is, Eco takes it strangely enough as yet another argument for "arbitrary underlying codifications" and is close to concluding with a complete conventionalism. Crude as it is, he finally offers a totally different classification between grammar-oriented and text-oriented procedures, in which iconicity must fall on the text-oriented side because of its lack of distinct elements and their compositionality. Here, he suddenly — and in obvious contrast to his contour claim (p. 194) — admits that 'the drawing of a horse can be understood even by those who are not acquainted with visual conventions ...' (p. 214) because it is "*not further analyzable* either into signs or into *figurae*" (p. 215). And the equivalent of an iconic sign is not a word or a phrase but a text (why not a phrase in many cases, actually, cf. traffic signs?) whose units 'are established — if at all — by the context' (p. 216). It is difficult to see how this analysis at one and the same time can save iconic signs and reject their iconicity; the idea is probably that the context here does the work which codes, conventions or physiology cannot do. But how should one be able to recognize similar contexts if not by means of similarity (remember we are beyond conventionality now, so we must not posit codes for recognizing contexts ...).

Eco's conclusion - under the final solution heading of 'Getting rid of the "iconic signs"', — repeats the umbrella idea and adds a final stroke: it is not only the very idea of iconicity, but also the idea of a *sign* which must be discarded at the expense of the sign-function, an in itself sound Hjelmslevian term here diversified in various quasi-Marxist modes of sign production. This idea should finally dissolve the "iconic signs" because they are arguably produced by different procedures, interchangeably with other signs.

This final fallacy — to believe the product can be explained by the production — is as absurd as to claim that cars are not cars because some of them are produced by Germans, others by Japanese, but it permits us to conclude Eco's critique. His umbrella term thesis rests on this mode-of-production theory — and then the wildly differing critiques of iconicity might be understandable (to himself) as pertaining to different modes of production (even if they were not presented in this lingo). Conventionality, culture, and subjectivity is one source for apparent "iconicity", the physiology of the nervous system is another, formal ontology is a third, and the context of signs constitutes a fourth. Even if a wedding of some of these positions into a culturally formed subject strangely and completely independent of its own natural, physiological bases can be constructed and is indeed typical for the period, then no construction can involve all of them: where should the formal ontological constraints intrude: in the subject? — this would attack culturalism; in the nervous system? ‾ this would attack the independence of nature and culture. Where would "context" come in? — not in culture which is conventional through and through, not in the physiology of perception since no semiotics is possible here ... Eco's iconic cleansing project is doomed to fail, not only because he attempts to dissolve a category phenomenologically well-defined, but also because his umbrella argument ends up umbrellaing his own ontology such that it becomes a complete quagmire of a crude nature-culture dualism equipped with self-contradictory annexes. What can more generally be learnt from Eco's failures is that mode-of-production explanations in semiotics, be it of a quasi-Marxist brand as is the case here, be it of a Nietzschean brand as in various types of *Lebensphilosophie* and deconstructionism, or be it of a neurophysiological or any other brand, can never stand alone but must be based on a prior phenomenological descriptive rendering of the field, making coherent the objects, distinctions, and in general the phenomena involved.

This repudiation of various anti-iconisms takes us back to the Peircian definition of the icon. Nowadays, everybody seems to know and love the Peircian tripartition of signs into Icons, Indices, and Symbols, referring to their objects by means of similarity, contiguity, and habit, respectively. Yet, there is more to the Peircian notion of Iconicity than meets the eye in this deceptively simple definition. Let us run through some of the central descriptions of Iconicity in Peirce. As mentioned above, it must be borne in mind that Peirce, being a realist, does not proceed by *defining* his notions. Icons are to Peirce real existent phenomena, and they may be phenomenologically *described* in a series of different ways; no simple definition will exhaust them. In fact, as it will be clear, this feature of his realism is closely connected to the very notion of iconicity itself.

Let us present a range of his different descriptions of icons and discuss the crucial implications involved therein.

Similarity and Quality

First of all, as is well-known, iconicity is dependent upon similarity: icons are 'signs whose significant virtue is due simply to its Quality' (Peirce, *CP*: 2.92). Now, in a pure icon, this quality has a strange property: it is not general; still the icon can be used as an icon of a continuity of objects which has the same quality: "... neither icon nor index possesses generality" (*CP*: 1.372). The reason for this, of course, is that the objects of the single icon may differ in all other respects than the precise quality in question. The character of the quality mentioned is crucial; Peirce often invokes as examples sense qualities like colors or smells, but much more complex structures may also count as qualities, cf. the passage quoted at the outset of this paper:

> An Icon is a sign which refers to the object that it denotes merely by virtue of characters of its own, and which is possesses, just the same, whether any such Objects actually exists or not. It is true that unless there really is such an object, the Icon does not act as a sign; but this has nothing to do with its character as a sign. Anything whatever, be it quality, existent individual, or law, is an Icon of anything, in so far as it is like that thing and used as a sign of it. [*CP*: 2.247].

Here, similarity is simply equal to shared qualities. As already mentioned, a complete Icon would stand in a relation of identity to its object, except for its existence, which in Peirce's Kantian tradition is of course no predicate, no quality. Hence, Peirce does not subscribe to Leibniz' principle of the Identity of Indiscernabilities: two objects may be perfectly alike except for their existence in time and space, which is not counted as a quality but as a haecceity. An icon which shares only some qualities with its object has so to speak a general side in so far as it is blank with respect to the aspects not partaking in the Icon; these are prescinded in the Icon. Even if the very Icon in itself is not, as mentioned, general, one could say that any Hypoicon (Peirce's notion for any sign which primarily functions by means of iconicity) involves a germ of generality. This becomes the possibility of various more or less strict stylizations of Icons, rendering certain qualities important, others not so, which implies that the Icon acquires a certain degree of typicality, being able to subsume tokens under it. Thus, an Icon may be a type, a Legisign, without any intervention of Symbols; in fact this is the very basis of Peirce's realism.

I Predicates

In so far as Icons are the means of representing qualities, they generally constitute the predicative side of more complicated signs:

> The only way of directly communicating an idea is by means of an icon; and every indirect method of communicating an idea must depend for its establishment upon the use of an icon. Hence, every assertion must contain an icon or set of icons, or else must contain signs whose meaning is only explicable by icons. The idea which the set of icons (or the equivalent of a set of icons) contained in an assertion signifies may be termed the predicate of the assertion. [*CP*: 2.278].

Thus, the predicate in logic as well as ordinary language is essentially iconic. It is important to remember here Peirce's generalization of the predicate from the traditional subject-copula-predicate structure. Predicates exist with more than one subject slot; this is the basis for Peirce's logic of relatives and permits at the same time enlarging the scope of logic enormously and approaching it to ordinary language where several-slot-predicatives prevail, for instance in all verbs with a valency larger than one. In his definition of these predicates by means of valency, that is, number of empty slots in which subjects or more generally indices may be inserted, Peirce is actually the founder of valency grammar in the tradition of Tesnière. So, for instance, the structure "_ gives _ to _" where the underlinings refer to slots, is a trivalent predicate. Thus, the word classes associated with predicates are not only adjectives, but verbs, common nouns, circumstants; in short all descriptive features in language are predicates.

This in turn implies that the qualities invoked in an icon may be of widely varying generality (just like Eco noticed in the passing):

> But instead of a single icon, or sign by resemblance of a familiar image or "dream", evocable at will, there may be a complexus of such icons, forming a composite image of which the whole is not familiar. But though the whole is not familiar, yet not only are the parts familiar images, but there will also be a familiar image in its mode of composition.... The sort of idea which an icon embodies, if it be such that it can convey any positive information, being applicable to some things but not to others, is called a *first intention*. The idea embodied by an icon, which cannot of itself convey any

information, being applicable to everything or nothing, but which may, nevertheless, be useful in modifying other icons, is called a *second intention*. [*CP*: 3.433].

What Peirce distinguishes in these scholastic standard notions borrowed from Aquinas via Scotus, is, in fact, the difference between Husserlian formal and material ontology. Formal qualities like genus, species, dependencies, quantities, spatial and temporal extension (in short: logico-mathematical qualities) and so on are of course attributable to any phenomenon and does not as such, in themselves, convey any information in so far as they are always instantiated in and thus dependent upon First Intentions in a Husserlian manner, but they are nevertheless indispensable in the composition of descriptions of first intentions. The fact that a certain phenomenon is composed of parts, has a form, belongs to a species, has an extension, has been mentioned in a sentence, etc. does not convey the slightest information of it until it by means of first intentional icons is specified which parts in which composition, which species, which form, etc. Thus, here Peirce makes a hierarchy of icons which we could call material and formal, respectively, in which the latter are dependent on the former. One may note in the passing that the distinctions in Peirce's semiotics are themselves built upon such Second Intentions; thus it is no wonder that every sign must possess some Iconic element. Furthermore, the very anatomy of the proposition becomes just like in Husserlian rational grammar (of the 4th *Untersuchung*) a question of formal, synthetic a priori regularities.

II   Icons in Abduction and in Reasoning in General

Amongst Peirce's forms of inference, similarity plays a certain role within abduction, his notion for a "qualified guess" in which a particular fact gives rise to the formation of a hypothesis which would entail the fact in question as a consequence. Many such hypotheses are of course possible, and this inference is not necessary. Precisely for this reason, similarity plays a seminal role here: an

> ... originary Argument, or Abduction, is an argument which presents facts in its Premiss which *presents a similarity* to the fact stated in the conclusion but which could perfectly be true without the latter being so. [*CP*: 2.96, o.i.].

The hypothesis posed is abducted by some sort of iconic relation to the fact to be explained. Thus, similarity is the very source of new ideas — which must consequently be controlled inductively and deductively, to be sure. But iconicity does not only play this role in the contents of abductive inference, it plays an even more important role in the very form of logical inference in general:

> Given a conventional or other general sign of an object, to deduce any other truth than that which it explicitly signifies, it is necessary, in all cases, to replace that sign by an icon. This capacity of revealing unexpected truth is precisely that wherein the utility of algebraic formulae consists, so that the iconic character is the prevailing one. [*CP*: 2.279].

The very form of inferences depends on it being an icon; thus for Peirce the syllogistic schema inherent in reasoning has an iconic character: 'Whenever one thing suggests another, both are together in the mind for an instant.... *every* proposition *like* the premiss, that is having an icon like it, *would* involve ... a proposition related to it as the conclusion ...' (*CP*: 2.444). Thus, first and foremost deduction is an icon: 'I suppose it would be the general opinion of logicians, as it certainly was long mine, that the Syllogism is a Symbol, because of its Generality' (Eisele IV, p. 317) — but instead it is an icon, because it is the only type of sign that possesses the ability of *showing*, of evidence.

> The truth, however, appears to be that all deductive reasoning, even simple syllogism, involves an element of observation; namely deduction consists in constructing an icon or diagram the relation of whose parts shall present a complete analogy with those of the parts of the objects of reasoning, of experimenting upon this image in the imagination, and of observing the result so as to discover unnoticed and hidden relations among the parts. [*CP*: 3.363].

In this light, it is no wonder that synthetic a priori truths exist — even if Peirce prefers notions like 'observable, universal truths'; the result of a deduction may contain more than what is immediately present in the premises, due to the iconic quality of the inference.

III To Learn More

This leads us to what is probably the most decisive feature in icons: the fact that they are the only sign through the contemplation of which it is possible to learn more: 'For a great distinguishing property of the icon is that by the direct observation of it other truths concerning its object can be discovered than those which suffice to determine its construction' (*CP*: 2.279). But this epistemologically crucial property is nothing but an elaboration on the concept of similarity. The icon is not only the only type of sign involving a direct presentation of qualities of its object, it is also a sign through the contemplation of which one can learn more than lies in the directions for its construction. If one imagines a pure, icon-less index, then it would have a quality-deprived character of being-now, of mere insistence, about which we would never be able to learn anything except if it became possible to form some kind of icon of it. And if one imagines a purely symbolic sign, say for instance the variable x, we cannot learn anything about it except when it is placed in some iconical, that is, predicative, context or other. This implies the crucial fact that, in Peirce, iconicity also covers what we for formalistic reasons have been used to seeing as "purely symbolic formalisms", algebras and symbolic calculi of various sorts. But they are not deprived of iconicity; the very fact that we can learn some more from them is proof of their iconicity. Thus, the "learn some more" clause prevents Peirce's definition of similarity from being circular like most usual definitions are; similarity always involves the possibility of learning more than what is at present obvious. In this respect, icons play the central role in Peirce's evolutionary epistemology and his idea of science as a transpersonal endeavor of the infinite community of researchers: it is a steady growth in complicated predicates, in iconicity which characterizes science and guarantees its asymptotic movement towards ultimate truth, provided the pragmatistic maxims are followed.

IV   Icons, Algebra, and Syntax

As just mentioned, this vision of iconicity implies that it includes all kinds of algebraical systems (that is, those it is possible to manipulate in order to learn some more): 'As for algebra, the very idea of the art is that it presents formulae which can be manipulated, and that by observing the effects of such manipulations we find properties not to be otherwise discerned.' For this reason, algebra is even *'icons par excellence* ... no application should be made of such an abstract statement without translating it into a sensible image.' The sensible image in question here is that we are able to synthesize an abstract statement into for instance an equation which we can thereafter manipulate according to certain rules which are adequate to *die Sachen selbst* in question. The manipulation of an equation or of an algebraic statement is in this respect perfectly equal to the manipulation of a picture or a text or any other icon in order to make it reveal some more similarities than immediately observable. This might be an offensive idea for many — that symbolic calculi shall now count as prototypes for iconicity — but the argument is strong, and what is more, it even gives us a critical tool for distinguishing between good — that is, iconic — and less good formalization. A formalization in this optics is namely sterile in so far it does not permit any fertile possibilities of manipulation. Mere formalization without motivated syntactical, generative possibilities is in this view a blind alley. Of course, it can not always be told beforehand if a certain formalization is fertile, and the relevant experimentation might be very mediate: to write down a fifth grade equation might seem hopeless in so far as we now know it has no canonical solution, but the very fact that it is formulated in the same language as solvable polynomia of lesser grade ultimately did permit the proof that it in fact has no solution — which is an even more impressive manipulation of it. But the mere substitution of some objects by letters or the like makes no manipulable icon, and this is why so many algebraic attempts in the humanities have proved sterile: they have merely exchanged some concepts with letters and have not furnished a motivated, formal set of rules for their manipulation. An *iconic syntax* is invariably needed, and this is found already in *language*: 'That icons of the algebraic kind, though usually very simple ones, exist in all ordinary grammatical propositions is one of the philosophical truths Boolean logic brings to light' (*CP*, p. 2.280). We have already met icons in predicates, but the very syntax of language is in itself an iconic kind of algebra, because it is built in accordance with the crucial second intention distinctions in the object described: the distinctions between various kinds of predicates, various kinds of subjects, various kinds of copulas. In this respect, Peirce's iconic grammar can meet Husserl's *reine Grammatik* of the 4th *Untersuchung*, both are formal, general calculi in accordance with the mereological structure of the object described. Thus, 'Every assertion is an assertion that two different signs have the same object' (*CP*: 2.437) — namely an iconic sign pertaining to a certain quality and an indexical sign pointing out the object in question in some frame of reference. These two in themselves, taken separately, assert nothing; it is only their being placed alongside in iconic syntax which makes an assertion: 'Icons and indices *assert nothing*. If an icon could be interpreted as a sentence, that sentence must be in a "potential mood", that is, it would merely say "Suppose a figure has three sides .." etc.' (2.291). Here Peirce in fact discovers a logical category found around the same time by the Austrian logician Meinong, who coined it *Annahme* — an assertion deprived of its assertive character and hence consisting of nothing but icons and indices (or of symbols of them, to be precise) in Peirce's terminology, a kind of weaker copula.[14] In fact,

---

[14] Peirce does not identify the copula with the verb to be, rather it is the very assertion of the predicate+subject structure. Here, he anticipates speech act theory by admitting questions, imperatives and the like as propositions on a par with assertions. Of course, one must distinguish here two different dimensions, that of the relation to the adressee (the

his deliberation makes it possible to distinguish two kinds of Annahmen, the merely iconic and the both iconic and indexical. "Imagine three sides .." would be an example of the first, while "Suppose Socrates has three sides ..." would be the other. A purely indexical Annahme is probably impossible except as a limit case ‾ or is at least empty: "Suppose something is the case right now ..." In the Brentanian tradition, to which Meinong also belongs, Husserl's *Bildbewusstsein* would be an example of the as if-character of the Annahme. This idea of an iconic grammar permits Peirce to develop yet another iconic parallel to these Austrian thinkers, namely Stumpf's famous coinage of *Sachverhalt* as a notion for the signification (not the reference) of a proposition. In Peirce, we find a direct expression of this idea when he states that 'What we call a "fact" is something having the structure of a proposition, but supposed to be an element of the very universe itself' (*NEM* IV, p. 239). Of course, this definition explicitly deals with what is supposed to be the case, that is, supposed reference and not signification, but it is entirely consistent with Peirce's intensional semantics to operate with "possible facts", phenomena supposed to be able to be the case, which would then be entirely coextensive with *Sachverhalte*. Thus, in general it is the iconicity between grammar and facts that permits sentences to be understood:

> The arrangement of words in sentences, for instance, must serve as *Icons*, in order that the sentence may be understood. The chief need for the icon is in order to show the Forms of the synthesis of the elements of thought. For in precision of speech, Icons can represent nothing but Forms and Feelings. [*CP*: 4.544].

As a consequence, Peirce may of course reproach the logicians which claim they do not use icons but merely symbols, that they invariably must introduce icons as the basis of their syntax of manipulation. The character of whole propositions in contrast to mere icons is that a proposition, or, in Peirce's coinage, a 'Dicisign ... *conveys* information, in contradistinction to a sign [such as an icon] from which information may be derived' (2.309). We have already learnt that a mere icon does not assert anything; still it is possible to derive information from it by experimentation, which so to speak makes it speak, in using it as material for a proposition. In contradistinction to this, a proposition already asserts something. Looking back on what is usually conceived as pure icons, they now differ on a scale between mere icons and dicisigns. A proposition, Peirce says elsewhere, is a sign making explicit

---

enunciation, in Benveniste's terms: is the proposition performed convincingly?) and that of the logical status of the proposition (is it an assertion, an *Annahme*, a question...?).

the object to which it refer. A mere icon does nothing of the kind: a painting of a man is an icon of many possible men, but as soon as an index is added, for instance "Portrait of Mr. P.", the painting now becomes a proposition saying something like "Mr. P. looks like this". Of course the index need not be in the title, but may lie in the information conveyed by the painting itself.

All in all, the idea that algebraic, formal, and linguistic syntactic systems must be iconic in order to be able to convey information is a very remarkable consequence of the concept of iconicity.

V Mathematics and Diagrams

As an implication of this fact, icons now acquire a very special relationship to mathematics:

> The reasoning of mathematicians will be found to turn chiefly upon the use of likeness, which are the very hinges of the gates of their science. The utility of likenesses to mathematicians consists in their suggesting in a very precise way, new aspects of supposed states of things [*CP*: 2.281].

Mathematics is merely hypothetical, all its statements are of the form if-then; given such-and-such axioms, such-and-such symbols, such-and-such rules of transformations, this and that will be a consequence. This makes it a science of icons, in so far as all this if-thening deals with iconic structures. Icons, unlike symbols, cannot deceive, in so far as they always portray something logically possible (you cannot make an icon of the round square, etc.). Hence,

> It will be observed that the icon is very perfect in respect to signification, bringing its interpreter face to face with the very character signified. For this reason, it is the mathematical sign *par excellence*. But in denotation it is wanting. It gives no assurance that any such object as it represents really exists. [*NEM* IV: 242-3].

But given this character, mathematics rests entirely objective, it is so to speak a mapping of the field of possibilities, and in so far as Peirce conceives of the field of qualities to be — at least potentially — one vast continuum, mathematics in fact ought to be able to detect the hypothetical relations of all qualities, including even, in principle, sense qualities. Mathematics does not assert anything about the world; it is more like a vast repertoire of possible complicated qualities to be used in descriptions; for this reason every science depends on mathematics as a large stock of second intention language — even if it does not derive its actual truths from there. It contains only perfect truths, which Peirce in a play of words coin as imperfect — not actual:

> A proposition is not a statement of perfectly pure mathematics until it is devoid of all definite meaning, and comes to this — that at property of a certain icon is pointed out and is declared to belong to anything like it, of which instances are given. The perfect truth cannot be stated, except in a sense that it confesses its imperfection. The pure mathematician deals exclusively with hypothesis [*CP*: 5.567].

The special kind of instrument used for deriving mathematical and other hypothetical truths is to Peirce the subset of icons named "diagrams". I shall not go into the special problems of them here,[15] but let me run through the central features: 'Remember it is by icons only that we really reason, and abstract statements are valueless in reasoning except so far they aid us to construct diagrams.' (*CP*: 4.126) Diagrams are explicitly Peirce's heirs to Kant's schemata; they make possible the inferencing of synthetic a priori propositions, or, in Peirce's terms, they make it possible to infer iconically about general matters. A diagram is an icon governed by a symbol such that it stands generally as a type for a whole set of token instantiations like it ⁻ just like the premises of a general syllogistic inference. This guarantees that the manipulation of the diagram holds for all these token cases involved. Certain rules for manipulation are implied by the structure of the icon itself, others are imposed by the symbol regulating it, and the outcome of this is that it is not possible to predict beforehand what the results of the transformations of it will be. This in turn becomes Peirce's explanation of the surprising fact that mathematics (as well as the special sciences using mathematics) is still able to discover new regularities: all truths are not given in and by the definition of a branch of mathematics, new truths may yet be discovered by observation. Thus, this opens the way for his version of a "Geschichte der reinen Vernunft": it is in fact possible to obtain a unforeseeable growth in synthetic a priori knowledge, and at the same time it introduces in a certain sense experiment and observation on the a priori level: the mapping of this field is due to the experiments of imagination in the "reiner Anschauung", Kantianly spoken, or in the Husserlian *Bildbewusstsein* including *kategoriale Anschauung*. It is rarely surprising in a continuistic theory like Peirce's to find traces of diagrammatic features in most icons. Still it must be possible ⁻ in a further

---

[15] I refer to my "Symbol og skema i neo-kantiansk semiotik" and May and Stjernfelt, "Measurement, Diagram, Art", as well as my "The Diagrammatic Interpretation Process".

synthetic a priori research — to erect a typology of possible diagrams. Peirce himself gives us the idea of such an endeavor when in a description of diagrammatic reasoning he notes in passing that

> Modern exact logic shows that every operation of deductive reasoning consists of four steps as follows:
>
>> 1st, a diagram, or visual image, whether composed of lines, like a geometrical figure, or an array of signs, like an algebraical formula, or of a mixed picture, like a graph, is constructed, so as to embody in iconic form, the state of things asserted in the premise (there will be but one premise, after all that is known and is pertinent is collected into one copulative proposition). [*NEM* IV: 275].

The following three steps consist in scrutinizing the diagram and trying an experiment; in observing the results of this and trying to find a new relation between the parts of it 'not mentioned in the precept by which it was constructed ...' (*CP*: 276); finally, in repeating the experiment and inferring inductively that every diagram constructed the same way would yield the same result. But the crucial point in this context is the three subtypes of diagrams mentioned; Michael May and I have preliminarily proposed to call them maps, graphs, and algebra, respectively.

VI The Imaginary Moment

Now, at a certain moment in the diagrammatical procedure just mentioned, a certain phase is reached in which the icon performs its full impact, a moment of imagination, one could call it. It lies already in the very description of its character of pure quality: 'The role of an icon consists in its exhibiting the features of a state of things as if it were purely imaginary' (*CP*: 4.449); here we find *in nuce* how Peirce's icon entails the idea of purely fictitious *Sachverhalte*. Peirce describes it in more detail as follows:

> Icons are so completely substitutions for their objects as hardly to be distinguished from them. Such are the diagrams of geometry. A diagram, indeed, so far as it has a general signification, is not a mere icon; but in the middle part of our reasonings we forget that abstractness in great measure and the diagram is for us the very thing. So in contemplating a painting, there is a moment when we lose the consciousness that it is not the thing, the distinction between the real and the copy disappears, and it is for the moment a pure dream — not any particular existence, and yet not general. At that moment we are contemplating an *icon*. [*CP*: 3.362].

This moment of fiction is crucial to the possibility of thought, of imagination, or of the contemplation of pictures to approaching the object intended. In many cases, of course, this imaginary moment may be unrestricted as the free play of imagination; in others it is constrained by various, more or less severe regulations pertaining to the object, for practical, æsthetical, scientific, or other purposes, but in all cases this moment of identification where the manipulation of the icon in a certain sense is a manipulation of the object itself is crucial to the possibilities of solving the constraints and the success of the experiment. One could counterargue here: yes, but it is precisely to avoid the sidetracks of intuition in this imaginative moment that we bind science to formal calculi — cf. Hilbert's formalist idea of bracketing intuition entirely while manipulating the formal symbols. But here a Peircian will answer: formal calculation *also* requires this imaginative moment; it may not disclose for me a very large and sensuous picture of its object, but it still, thanks to the syntax employed, can never be completely deprived of an iconic link to its object. And, what is more, it permits us to interpret Husserl's version of the *adequatio rei ac intellectus*: the iconic ecstasy only lasts for a moment, and after the experiment it becomes possible to see if the iconic result is in fact pertinent for (some partial behaviour of) the object it was supposed to depict. If not, another diagram may be invoked, a modification of the diagram present, maybe to erect a new subclass for the object not entirely grasped, etc. The diagrammatic movement through this imaginary moment alternates continuously between on the one hand the icon-and-object-is-one supposition of the imaginary moment and on the other the split consideration of diagram and the more or less spontaneously conceived object, the *Widerstreit* of Husserlian *Bildbewusstsein*. The aesthetic possibilities in the hypothetical character of this imaginary moment are also suggested in Peirce. For even if all of mathematics is hypothetical, not all hypothesis is (explicitly, anyway) mathematical:

> It cannot be said that all framing of hypothesis is mathematics. For that would not distinguish between the mathematician and the poet. But the mathematician is only interested in hypotheses for the forms of inference from them. As for the poet, although much of the interest of a romance lies in tracing out consequences, yet these consequences themselves are more interesting in point of view of the resulting situations than in the way they are deducible. Thus, the poetical interest of a mental creation is the creation itself, although as a part of this a mathematical interest may enter to a slight extent. Detective stories and the like have an unmistakeable mathematical element. [*NEM* IV: 268].

Given this difference between mathematics and poetry, one could add that they share a similarity in so far as both, in fact, are interested in the result of hypothetical reasoning, not the very steps leading there; this interest is rather the matter for the logician and the literary critic, respectively (all or some of whom may of course be incarnated in the same empirical person). As is evident, this rendering of the imaginary moment in icon contemplation has its counterpoint in Husserlian *Bildbewusstsein*, whose eidetic variation to a large extent plays the same role as the diagrammatic experimentation here, and it is no small consequence of Peirce's concept of iconicity that it permits mathematics, logic, and art to be understood as different practices in relation to this imaginary moment of thought. Furthermore, as a rendering of *Bildbewusstsein* or the more diffuse imagination, this is not conceived of as a separate and thereby ununderstandable faculty of the mind ("phantasy"), but is seen as a specific phase in a well-described diagrammatic and more generally iconic process of interpretation.

VII The Problem of Evidence

Still, a uncomfortable peculiarity remains. Is it not strange that icons so to speak "hide" certain similarities whilst on the other hand they are supposed to be the very source of evidence? As we saw, the most crucial property in them is their ability to enclose hidden insights, making it possible for experiment to 'discover unnoticed and hidden relations among the parts' (*CP*: 3.363). It is possible to give a receipt for the construction of an icon without revealing all of its possible similarities. A most striking example of this is the simple process of digitalizing a picture. Seeing a row of 1's and 0's does not immediately display the similarities inherent in the picture, even if the information in question is in some sense available with the right system of transformations, the right means of interpretation. Of course, in these wordings, a perceiver of some kind is implied, a subject (albeit not necessarily a human being) for whom certain similarities may be hidden. And even if we may not construct the icon digitally, there will always be more information in it than it is possible to exhaust. In some sense the information already lies in the digital sequence, but only if it can be processed, not only by some instance processing the icon onto a screen, but also by some instance able to, by some kind of *Bildbewusstsein*, to see the icon as an icon of some object. In the most simple icons, these hidden similarities are almost non-existent. If I contemplate a patch of a certain shade of the color red, I contemplate an icon, but the only experiment I may venture here is varying the color to see when it changes or varying the form and size of the patch to see when it disappears. Not a very promising experiment, but as soon as we reach an icon with the (still not very high) complexity of a circle, it is ripe with hidden properties (just think of the relation between its diameter and its periphery ...). In mathematics, an object as simple and intuitive as the natural numbers are (after Gödel's incompleteness theorem) ripe with truths (Goldbach's conjecture, Fermat's last theorem, *etcetera, etcetera*) which are not only hidden from immediate appreciation, but which may in many cases be formally undecidable. In a painting are many enigmas which the painter himself has never contemplated (and since the sheet of the painting is continuous, the number of possible similarities is at the very least infinite, which means that he was never even able to contemplate them all in finite time — so much for the biographical method) — what is, for instance, the precise distance between the main characters, which geometric figure do the persons describe if we draw lines between them, what is the sum of the height of all the trees depicted, and why does the woman look like one I know in Århus? These examples go to show that almost all of such hidden information is of course completely useless; the trick of the analyst is to make his experiment somehow find significant information. I remember for instance a tour-de-force analysis by Erik Fischer of an altar piece by Eckersberg, in which he drew the perspective lines of Judas' empty chair at the last supper, only to find that this chair was skew — probably as a symbol for the peculiarity of the missing person.[16] Principally conceived, the reason for these "hidden similarities" in the icon has several sources. One is that the icon does not have to be very complex in order to be unable to be "perceived in a glance". This goes not only for very large paintings from which it is impossible to get at a sufficient distance to be able to synthezise them in one gaze (a feature deliberately used by the abstract expressionists as a means of calling forth awe in the viewer), but also sufficiently complicated predicate structures in a text, in a mathematical problem, in a building, etc. But even if a very competent observer (or hard work on the part of a less competent one) makes it possible to "see it all in a glance", there's still all the possible relations between the parts to be worked out, relations between relations between the parts, etc. We need hardly stress that the amount of relations between elements grows proportionally to the square of the amounts of elements, and that the higher order relations, in turn, grow exponentially with order — amounts which in turn must be multiplied with the set of possible interpretation systems for these relations. Of course, this is why analysis is necessary, an analysis which in all these cases consequently cannot be anything but diagrammatical — including all the features mentioned above. These kinds of "hiddenness" are of course due to the

---

[16] Personally, I did not hesitate to draw the perspective lines of the objects standing on the (presumably horizontal) floor to find the horizon — only to find that our Saviour, positioned behind a table, must either possess abnormally long legs or be in a process of levitation …

"finitude of man", so central to the critical tradition in epistemology. Yet, one might loosen this fact from mankind's special *Dasein* and its destiny by stating that *any* physically instantiated analytical apparatus whatsoever will have to be finite and hence possess some limit for the size and complexity of the iconic structures it may process. Human language generally cuts any *Sachverhalt* into pieces involving no more than three or four actants (three being for Peirce the highest irreducible relation, so it is an advantage for us that we are not biologically limited to two),[17] but there is no principal reason for not admitting computers able to work with iconic syntaxes with far higher valencies. Another even more objective reason for the "hiddenness" is that the icon in question may appear in various versions, not similarly difficult to detect. The obvious example is Duchamp's painting that is to be seen between a hole in a door, an artwork which may appear simple until you discover the hole — but the solvability of a problem in general depends highly on how it is posed. Of course, this is also dependent upon the means available for the interpreter, but not only so. Here, one might propose a generalized use of Husserl's idea of *Abschattung*; the icon may so to speak display itself from several sides, and even if the same amount of information may principally be available from all versions, it might take much more computation to derive it from one icon than from another, analogous to Bennett's concept of logical depth. An addition on page 1 saying "It was the butler" of course takes less computation than reading all of the following 399 pages, collecting evidence all along. Conceived of at a great distance, in some way it remains an enigma why it is that icons exist with this intriguing property of hiding similarities, luckily a prerequisite to art as well as science; if gods exist, then they probably see everything directly — not *per speculum in aenigmate* — and hence would know neither icons nor indices nor symbols. In Peirce as in Kant, the various ways of the human mind are due to the fact that we do not, maybe unlike the gods, possess immediate "intellectual intuition".

But, unrejectable as the hidden-similarity hypothesis remains, it is strange how the icon may at the same time be the sole guarantee for evidence, sensually as well as logically:

> Each Icon partakes of some more or less overt character of its Object. They, one and all, partake of
> the most overt character of all lies and deceptions — their Overtness. Yet they have more to do with

---

[17] This problem of the reducibility of relations entails an enormous and still unfinished discussion. Löwenheim and Quine has, each in their own way, tried to show that all logical propositions may be reduced to dyads, but the general validity of their results are still doubted. We shall return to this.

the living truth than have either Symbols or Indices. The Icon does not stand unequivocally for this or that existing thing, as the Index does. Its Object may be a pure fiction, as to its existence. But there is one assurance that the Icon does afford in the highest degree. Namely, that which is displayed before the mind's gaze — must be *logically possible*. [*CP*: 4.531].

The icon has the undeniable quality of showing something possible — it cannot, unlike symbolic speculation, yield neither Husserlian *Unsinn* nor *Widersinn*, the first being only possible through the breakup of iconic syntax, the other only by constructing a contradictory predicate. We may talk and wonder about the round square, the rational square root of 2, or the married bachelor, etc., but no icon can display it. But when this principle applies to the icons at stake in logical reasoning, it has very strong results:

Now necessary reasoning makes its conclusion *evident*. What is this "Evidence"? It consists in the fact that the truth of the conclusion is *perceived*, in all its generality, and in the generality the how and why of the truth is perceived. What sort of a Sign can communicate this Evidence? No index, surely, can it be; since it is by brute force that the Index thrusts its Object into the Field of Interpretation, the consciousness, as if disdaining gentle "evidence." No Symbol can do more than apply a "rule of thumb" resting as it does entirely on Habit (including under this term natural disposition); and a Habit is no evidence. I suppose it would be the general opinion of logicians, as it certainly was long mine, that the Syllogism is a Symbol, because of its Generality. But there is an inaccurate analysis and confusion of thought at the bottom of that view; for so understood it would fail to furnish Evidence. It is true that ordinary Icons, ‐ the only class of Signs that remains for necessary inference, ‐ merely suggest the possibility of that which they represent, being percepts *minus* the insistency and percussivity of percepts. In themselves, they are mere Semes, predicating of nothing, not even so much as interrogatively. It is, therefore, a very extraordinary feature of Diagrams that they *show* ... that a consequence does follow ... [*NEM* IV: 318].

Evidence thus comprises as well the sensuous making overt a quality in the object as the evidence *that* some proposition follows from certain premisses; in both cases icons are responsible. But this raises once more the crucial question of how the same figure may be responsible for evidence and for hidden similarities. I think there are two reasons for this. The first lies in the process of iconic reasoning: evidence is what takes place *when* the experimentation reveals new aspects of the icon. Of course, the other parts of the predicate must as icons be evident themselves, but this evidence is backgrounded while the newly revealed quality is foregrounded and adds itself to the evidence already present. But this implies a thorough reformulation of the whole category of evidence: the fact that something is evident, does not imply that it may not conceal hidden aspects. A problem may be perfectly clear to me without me knowing how to detect the solution. To use a Husserlian metaphor which is not perfectly apt: the sight of one side of the object does not tell us how the back side looks. The metaphor is deceptive, for in the problem case the front side does in fact in some scrambled way contain the information necessary to reconstruct the back side. The other reason is that any object fails to portray its object with final precision; this possibility is only asymptotically open for the community of researchers. This, of course, is Peirce's answer by means of continuity to Kant's *Ding-an-sich*, it may be reached, but only in an indefinite future. But this implies that given any present icon, it is always in principle possible to find an even better icon which will then yield more evidence than the first one. Thus, as a consequence of both these reasons, iconic evidence is always relative.

But still, is it not a dubious idea to make icons the source of evidence? Husserl would say that evidence is constituted by the act in which the object is given in "anschauliche Fülle" — be it sensuous objects or logical truths, and that consequently evidence cannot be the product of any "Zeichenbewusstsein" *(Ideen)*; this would lead to an infinite regress, for in which *bewusstsein* should the *Zeichen* now be constituted? — and so on. Ergo, he argues, evidence must lie outside of the *Bild*- and *Zeichenbewusstsein*. Is it not the case that the icon as evidence locks us up in a Piranesian prison of icons of icons of icons of icons ... from which we are never able to escape in order to ascertain true evidence? It seems to me that Peirce's theory of evidence provides an answer to this objection: evidence in the Husserlian *anschauliche-Fülle*-version actually has two sources: one is the Peircian index-consciousness of something being given with the force of haeccity, the evidence *that* something exists. The other is evidence that something *is as it is*, and this part is always dependent on icons with the relativity just mentioned: iconic evidence is dependent upon the continuous shift between icon-consciousness (to construct a Peirco-Husserlian bastard) and meltdown between the two sides of the iconic sign during the moment of imagination.[18] It is this very process which makes it possible to reflect upon the object and ascribe it still more qualities; it is this process that makes it possible for the object the be given (seen from one side,[19] it is true) as

---

[18] Maybe this would also provide an answer to Husserl's problem in *Ursprung der Geometrie* about how original evidence might be transferred through history by means of symbols not containing this evidence ...

[19] The whole problem of the synthesis of the various profiles of the object is another, even if it possesses interesting analogues to the diagrammatic conception of the object. One profile of the object already contains hidden similarities in Peirce's conception.

evidence once and for all. This is a strong consequence of Peirce's theory of the icon: evidence is always potentially problematic — which is not a skeptical claim, for the contrary is true as well: problems are always potentially evident.

The strength of the Peircian concept of iconicity is thus that it permits the comparison of objects normally very far from each other: mathematics, logic, diagrams on the one hand, epistemology, phenomenology and the psychology of perception on the other, and language, semiotics, and aesthetics on the third — if we for a moment imagine an icon of ourselves with three hands.

References

Hempel, C. 1982. 'The Empiricist Criterion of Meaning.' In *Philosophy of Mathematics*. Benacerraf and Putnam (Eds.). Cambridge, MA:Cambridge University Press.

Eco, Umberto. 1976. *A Theory of Semiotics*. Bloomington: Indiana University Press.

—. 1989. *Foucault's Pendulum*. New York and London: Harcourt Brace.

Goodman, Nelson. 1968. *Languages of Art*: London: Oxford University Press.

Greimas, Algirdas Julien & Courtez, J. 1979, 1986. *Sémiotique - Dictionnaire raisonné de la théorie du langage* (Vol. I-II). Paris: Hachette.

Hofstadter, Douglas. 1985. *Metamagical Themas: Questing for the Essence of Mind and Pattern*. New York: Basic Books.

Husserl, Edmund. 1980a. *Logische Untersuchungen*. Tübingen: Max Niemeyer.

—. 1980b. *Phantasie, Bildbewusstsein, Erinnerung : zur Phänomenologie der anschaulichen Vergegenwärtigungen: Texte aus dem Nachlass*. (*Husserliana*, Vol. 23). Dordrecht : Kluwer.

—. 1980c [1913]. *Ideen*. Tübingen: Max Niemeyer.

—. 1985 [1939]. *Erfahrung und Urteil*. Tübingen: Max Niemeyer..

Peirce, Charles Sanders. 1931-1958. *Collected Papers*. Cambridge: Harvard Universsity Press.

—. 1976. *The New Elements of Mathematics*. Vol. I-IV. Carolyn Eisele (Ed.). The Hauge: Mouton.

Stjernfelt, Frederik. 1992. 'Letterforms, Categories, and the A Priori Stance.' *Culture and History* 12: 109-142.

—. 'Peirces begreb om kontinuet' ("Peirce's concept of the continuum"). Unpublished paper. Copenhagen.

Iconicity in the Ecology of Semiosis

Göran Sonesson

In the sixties and the seventies, while young people were trying to free the world, semioticians and philosophers, such as Eco and Goodman, were involved in a more important struggle: they wanted to liberate iconic signs, more particularly pictures, from their iconicity, and more generally, to deliver the world from all meanings which were not conventional. This issue later went out of fashion and was ignored by many semioticians and philosophers for that very reason, while others continued to take the result of the earlier demonstrations for granted, without any further discussion. Meanwhile, empirical findings in the psychology of perception and in ethnology clearly showed that the claims made by Eco and Goodman were unfeasible.

In my earlier work (Sonesson 1989, 1991, 1994a, b, c, 1995), I have quoted this evidence from psychology and ethnology, but, more importantly, I have showed that the arguments against iconicity were mistaken, mainly because they construed language, pictures, and, in particular, the world of our experience, in a fashion which is incompatible with our empirical knowledge, i.e. with that which we have good reasons to believe to be true about the world. Here, I want to review the argument, with a slight shift of emphasis: while continuing to insist on the foundational character of the Lifeworld, the "world taken for granted", I will consider some new problems which result from conceiving iconicity within the framework of a science of the Lifeworld, which, in my secularised version, I will call an *ecology of semiosis*.

I The Notion of Iconic Sign

Within semiotics, the term icon is rarely used in its most common religious and art historical sense, to refer to a pictorial representation of persons or events derived from the sacred history of Christianity, particularly as used as an aid to devotion, although the only extant semiotic monograph concerned with a single pictorial genre is in fact about icons in this sense (Uspenskij 1976). Nor is the term normally used to refer to all things visible, or to everything whose elements are graphically disposed, as in the jargon of computer programming, or in cognitive psychology (e.g. Kolers 1977). In semiotical parlance, which is derived from Peirce, an icon is a sign in which the "thing" serving as expression in one respect or another is similar to, or shares properties with, another "thing", which serves as its content. In fact, if we follow Peirce, there are two further requirements: not only should the relation connecting the two "things" exist independently of the sign relation, just as is the case with the index, but, in addition, the properties of the two "things" should inhere in them independently.

Thus, icons in the religious sense are not particularly good instances of icons in the semiotical sense, for they are, as Uspenskij has shown, subject to several conventions determining the kind of perspective which may be employed, and the kind of things and persons which may be represented in different parts of the picture. Contrary to the icons of computer programs and those of cognitive psychology, iconic signs may occur in any sense modality, e.g. in audition, notably in verbal language (not only onomatopoetic words, but also in the form of such regularities and symmetries which Jakobson 1965a,b terms "the poetry of grammar") and music (cf. Osmond-Smith 1972), and not all visual signs are iconic in the semiotic sense; indeed, many icons found in computer programs are actually aniconic visual signs.

Many semioticians, in particular those who deny the existence of iconic signs, apparently believe pictures to be typical instances of this category. There are several reasons to think that this was not Peirce's view. Pure icons, he states (1.157), only appear in thinking, if ever. According to Peirce's conception, a painting is in fact largely conventional, or "symbolic". Indeed, it is only for a fleeting instant, 'when we lose the consciousness that it is not the thing, the distinction of the real and the copy', that a painting may appear to be a pure icon (3.362; cf. 1989, III.1.).

It will be noted then that a pure icon is thus not a sign, in the sense that the latter term is commonly understood (although Peirce will sometimes state the contrary). At first, it may seem that although the icon is not a socially *instituted* sign, i.e. not something which is accepted by a community of sign uses, it could at least, for a short time span, become a sign to a single observer. But even this is contrary to the very conditions described by Peirce: he specifically refers to the case in which the sign loses its sign character, when it is not seen as a sign but is confused with reality itself (which could actually happen when looking at a picture through a key hole with a single eye, producing what Husserl dismisses as a "Jahrmakteffekte"), when, as Piaget would have said, there is no differentiation between expression and content.

Indeed, it would seem that, at least sometimes, the pure icon is taken to be something even less substantial: an impression of reality, which does not necessarily correspond to anything in the real world, for 'it affords no assurance that there is any such thing in nature' (4.447). Thus, it seems to be very close to the "phaneron", the unit of Peircean phenomenology (itself close to the Husserlean "noema"), which is anything appearing to the mind, irrespective of its reality status (cf. Johansen 1993: 94ff). In this sense, the Peircean icon is somewhat similar to that of cognitive psychology, for it involves "sensible objects" (4.447), not signs in any precise sense: however, it still comprises all sense modalities.

In most cases, when reference is made to icons in semiotics what is actually meant is what Peirce termed *hypo-icons,* that is, signs which involve iconicity but also, to a great extent, indexical and/or "symbolic" (that is, conventional, or perhaps more generally, rule-like) properties. There are supposed to be three kinds of hypo-icons: *images,* in which case the similarity between expression and content is one of "simple qualities"; *diagrams,* where the similarity is one of "analogous relations in their parts"; and *metaphors,* in which the relations of similarity are brought to an even further degree of mediation. Diagrams in the sense of ordinary language are also diagrams in the Peircean sense, e.g. the population curve which rises to the extent that the population does so. The Peircean concept is however much broader, as is the notion of metaphor, which would, for instance, also include the thermometer. Moreover, no matter how we choose to understand the simplicity of "simple qualities", the Peircean category of images will not include ordinary pictures (which would actually appear to be metaphors of metaphors), although Peirce sometimes seems to say so: if anything, a Peircean image might be a colour sample used when picking out the paint to employ in repainting the kitchen wall.

Contrary to the way in which icons have been conceived in the later semiotic tradition, diagrams, rather than pictures, are at the core of Peircean iconicity; at least, they are of most interest to Peirce himself. Indeed, mathematical formulae and deductive schemes, which are based on conventional signs, are those most often discussed in his work.

II The Ground as a Principle of Relevance

Conceived in strictly Peircean terms, iconicity is one of the three relationships in which a representamen (expression) may stand to its object (content or referent) and which may be taken as the "ground" for their forming a sign: more precisely, it is the first kind of these relationships, termed Firstness, 'the idea of that which is such as it is regardless of anything else' (5.66), as it applies to the relation in question. At the other extreme, iconicity has been variously conceived as a similarity, or identity, between the expression and the content of a sign, or as a particular variety of conventional coding.

To many semioticians, the study of iconicity amounts to an inquiry into what Peirce "really said" on the matter. Semioticians taking a more empirical stance will argue that whatever Peirce wanted to tell us, more recent experiences and analyses may force us to conceive of iconicity differently. Yet it could be suggested that some of the usages to which iconicity are nowadays put are fairly different from the one intended by Peirce, and that something has been lost on the way. In particular, since large parts of recent semiotics has been concerned with rejecting the very notion of iconicity, it seems unfortunate that this critique has often begun from a very shallow understanding of Peirce's theory, and that the authors of this critique have hardly bothered to inquire into the possibility of adapting this notion to the present state of semiotic theory.

Considerations of iconicity must take as their starting point the iconic "ground", or what has been described as the "potential sign-vehicle" (Bruss 1978: 87). The ground is a part of the sign with the function of picking out the relevant elements of expression and content. It would appear that, in Peirce's view, two items share an *iconic ground*, being thus apt to enter into a semiotic function forming an iconic sign, in the parts of expression and content, to the extent that there is some set of properties or another which these items possess independently of each other, which are identical or similar when considered from a particular point of view, or which may be perceived or, more broadly, experienced as being identical or similar, where similarity is taken to be an identity perceived on the background of fundamental difference (cf. Sonesson 1989a, III.1-3.).

In one of his well-known definitions of the sign, or rather the sign-vehicle, Peirce (2: 228) describes it as something which 'stands for that object not in all respects, but in reference to a sort of idea, which I sometimes called the *ground* of the representation'. According to one of his commentators, Greenlee (1975: 64), the ground is that aspect of the *referent* which is referred to by the expression, for instance, the direction of the wind, which is the only property of the referential object "the wind" of which the weathercock informs us. On the other hand, Savan (1976: 10) considers the ground to consist of the features picked out from the thing serving as *expression,* which, to extend Greenlee's example, would include those properties of the weathercock permitting it to react to the wind, not, for instance, its having the characteristic shape of a cock made out of iron and placed on a church steeple. In one passage, however, Peirce himself identifies "ground" with "abstraction" exemplifying it with the blackness of two black things (1.293). That, of course, would be an iconical ground; an indexical ground, in a parallel fashion, would then be whatever it is that connects the properties of the weathercock as a physical thing to the direction in which the wind is blowing. If so, the ground is really a *principle of relevance,* or, as a Saussurean would say, the "form", connecting expression and content (cf. Sonesson 1989a: 205ff).

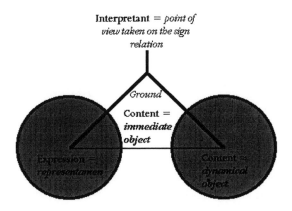

Fig. 1.

Generally put, an *indexical ground,* or indexicality, would then involve two "things" that are apt to enter, in the parts of expression and content ("representamen" and "object" in Peircean parlance), into a semiotic relation forming an indexical sign, due to a set of properties which are *intrinsic to the relationship between them,* such as is the case independently of the sign relation. This kind of ground, which is a relation, is best conceived in opposition to an *iconic ground,* which consists of a set of two classes of properties ascribed to two different "things", which are taken to possess the properties in question independently, not only of the sign relation, but of each other, although, when considered from a particular point of view, these two sets of properties will appear to be identical or similar to each other. This is the sense in which indexicality is Secondness, and iconicity Firstness.

III   Iconicity and Other Grounds

Contrary to the indexical ground, which is a relation, the *iconic ground* thus consists of a set of two classes of properties ascribed to two different "things", which are taken to possess the properties in question independently, not only of the sign relation, but of each other. Indexicality as such involves two "things", and may therefore be conceived independently of the sign function. Since iconicity is Firstness, however, it only concerns one "thing". Indeed, as Peirce (3.1.; 3.362; 4.447) never tires of repeating, a pure icon cannot even exist: it is a disembodied quality which we may experience for a fleeting instant when contemplating a painting out of awareness. Perhaps, then, to use some of Peirce's own examples, the blackness of a blackbird, or the fact of Franklin being American, can be considered *iconicities;* when we compare two black things or Franklin and Rumford from the point of view of their being Americans, we establish an *iconic ground;* but only when one of the black things is taken to stand for the other, or when Rumford is made to represent Franklin, do they become *iconic signs* (or *hypo-icons,* as Peirce sometimes said). Just as indexicality is conceivable, but is not a sign, until it enters the sign relation, iconicity has some kind of being, but does not exist until a comparison takes place. In this sense, if indexicality is a potential sign, iconicity is only a potential ground.

Since the iconic ground is established on the basis of properties the two items possess only because of being what they are, the standard of comparison must be something like similarity or identity. Signs based on similarity have been distinguished before in semiotic theory, by Degérando, for instance, in terms of analogy. Indeed, Peirce also says that an icon (more exactly, a hypo-icon) is 'a sign which stands for something merely because it resembles it' (3.362) or 'partak[es] in the characters of the object' (4.531, my insert). This point of view was pursued by Charles Morris (1946: 98ff), who considered that a sign was iconic to the extent that it had the same properties as its referent. According to this conception, iconicity becomes a question of degrees: a film is more iconic of a person than a painted portrait, but less so than the person itself. Abraham Moles (1981) has elaborated on this proposal, constructing a scale which comprises 13 degrees of iconicity going from the object itself to the zero degree epitomised by a verbal description. Such a conception of iconicity is problematic, not only because distinctions of different nature appear to be involved, but also because it takes for granted that identity is the highest degree of iconicity, and that the illusion of perceptual resemblance typically produced, in different ways, by the scale model and the picture sign, are as close as we can come to iconicity short of identity. Although Peirce does mention paintings and photographs as instances of iconic signs, he much more often refers to abstract properties.

The same confusion is found in other semiotic theories involved with iconicity. Umberto Eco's (1968: 1976) critique of iconicity is almost exclusively concerned with pictures. In pictorial semiotics, both as conceived by the Greimas school and

64

in the version of Groupe μ, iconicity is supposed to account for one of the two semiotic functions of the picture sign, the one giving the illusion of seeing something depicted in the sign, opposed to the plastic function, which is concerned with the abstract properties of the pictorial surface. However, if a circle, as in one of Groupe μ's (1979) examples, is taken to stand for the sun on the iconic level, and on the plastic level for roundness, which, in turn, as we know from psychological tests, may signify softness, etc., then, what is called here the plastic language is at least as iconic, in Peirce's sense, as the iconic layer: for roundness is certainly a property possessed both by the circle representing the sun in this hypothetical drawing and by the circle prototype; and, beyond that, there must be some abstract, synaesthetically experienced property which is common to the visual mode of roundness and the tactile mode of softness (cf. Sonesson 1994).

When conceiving iconicity as engendering a "referential illusion" and as forming a stage in the generation of "figurative" meaning out of the abstract base structure, Greimas & Courtés (1979: 148, 177) similarly identify iconicity with perceptual appearance. However, not only is iconicity not particularly concerned with "optical illusion" or "realistic rendering", but it does not necessarily involve perceptual predicates: many of Peirce's examples, like those of Degérando beforehand (cf. Sonesson 1989: 204ff), have to do with mathematical formulae, and even the fact of being American is not really perceptual, even though some of its manifestations may be.

IV   Beyond the Critique of Iconicity

During the renewal of semiotic theory in the sixties and seventies, most semioticians were eager to abolish the notion of iconicity, again taking pictures as their favoured example, while claiming that pictures were, in some curious way, as conventional as linguistic signs. Bierman, Goodman, Lindekens, and Eco have all argued against using similarity as a criterion in the definition of iconical signs and/or pictures; and even Burks and Greenlee have introduced some qualifications on Peirce's view which serve to emphasize conventionality. Some of these thinkers, such as Bierman and Goodman, were mainly inspired by logical considerations, together with a set of proto-ethnological anecdotes, according to which so-called primitive tribes were incapable of interpreting pictures; Eco and Lindekens, in addition, wanted to show that pictures, conforming to the ideal of the perfect sign, as announced by Saussure, were as arbitrary or conventional as the sign studied by the most advanced of the semiotic sciences, general linguistics. Saussure himself never went to such extremes:

in his unpublished notes he recognises the motivated character of both pictures and miming, but at least in the latter case he argues that the rudiment of convention found in it is sufficient to make it an issue for semiotics.

The most interesting arguments against iconicity were adduced by Arthur Bierman (1963), and were later repeated in another form, notably by Nelson Goodman (1970). According to one of these arguments, which may be called the *argument of regression* (cf. Sebeok 1976: 128), all things in the world can be classified into a number of very general categories, such as "thing", "animal", "human being", etc., and therefore everything in the universe can refer to, and be referred to, everything else. Thus, if iconicity is at the origin of signs, everything in the world will be signs. This may not be so far from what Peirce thought: at least Franklin and Rumford are, as we know, potential signs of each other. It is certainly a conception of the world common in the Renaissance, as well as among Romantics and Symbolists. In the case of more common iconical signs, however, like pictures and models, a conventional sign function must either be superimposed on the iconic ground, or the iconic ground must itself be characterised by further properties. Even in the former case, however, iconicity is still needed, not to define the sign, but to characterise *iconic signs* (cf. Sonesson 1989: 220ff).

Differently put, if Peirce meant to suggest that there are three properties, iconicity, indexicality, and symbolicity, which, by themselves and without any further requirement, trigger the recognition of something as a sign, then the argument of regression will create trouble for his conception. On the other hand, if he merely wanted to suggest that something that was already recognized as being a sign could be discovered to be an iconical sign, rather than an indexical or symbolic one, by means of tracing it back to the iconic ground, then the argument of regression will have no bearing on it.

According to another argument, which has been termed the *symmetry argument* (Sebeok 1976: 128), iconicity cannot motivate a sign, for while similarity is symmetrical and reflexive, the sign is not. Pigments on paper, or carvings in a rock, could stand for a man, but not the reverse; nor will they, in their picture function, stand for themselves. This argument is based on an identification of the commonsensical notion of similarity with the equivalence relation of logic. No doubt, the equivalence relation, as defined in logic, is symmetric and reflexive, and thus cannot define any type of sign, since the sign, by definition, must be asymmetric and irreflexive. But to identify similarity with the equivalence relation is to suppose man to live in the world of the natural sciences, when in fact he inhabits a particular sociocultural Lifeworld. *Similarity*, as experienced in this Lifeworld, is actually asymmetric and irreflexive. That this is true of ordinary comparisons in verbal language and in metaphorical visual displays has now been experimentally demonstrated (notably by Rosch 1975; and Tversky 1977; cf. also Sonesson 1989, 220ff, 327ff): indeed, according to common opinion, Korea is much more similar to China than the reverse — simply because China makes more sense (is more well-known, more important, more powerful, etc.) as a standard of comparison. If we generalise this finding to the case of signs, there is every reason to suppose that a three-dimensional object, rather than some lines on a surface, would count as a natural standard of comparison.

While this relationship between three-dimensional and two-dimensional objects may well be a universal, it is easier to show the principle at work in cases which vary cross-culturally. Among numerous apocryphal stories of tribes failing to recognise pictures as such, there is one verified case in which the group (the Me' studied by Deregowski) had never seen paper, and was therefore led to focus on the material *per se*. When pictures where instead printed on cloth, the Me' immediately recognised the sign function and perceived the pictures. To these people paper, being an unknown material, acquired such a prominence that it was impossible for them to see it as a vehicle for something else; on the other hand, it is precisely because paper is so trivial a material to us that we have no trouble construing instances of it as pictorial signifiers (cf. Sonesson 1989: 251ff).

It thus becomes necessary to posit a kind of taken-for-granted hierarchy of prominence among the things of the Lifeworld. For something to be a sign of something else, it must be ranked relatively low on the scale of prototypicality applying to the "things" of the Lifeworld. Such a scale would be similar to the basic metaphor underlying ordinary language which Lakoff & Turner (1989: 160ff) call "The great chain of being". Indeed, these regularities of the Lifeworld, together with the similar laws of environmental physics, formulated by James Gibson, stand at the origin of an even broader domain of study, which we have called the *ecology of semiosis* (cf. Sonesson 1993, 1994a, b).

Contrary to the argument of regression, the symmetry argument may thus be warded off, without introducing a supplementary sign function and without amending the definition of the iconic ground.

V Non-pictorial Iconic Signs

Goodman also argues that a painting is actually more similar to another painting than to that which it depicts. However, similarity should not be confused with identity: indeed, between two pictures (two canvases, etc.) there is *identity*, according to a principle of pertinence, and on the basis of this property a picture, just as any other object, may be used as an *identity sign* or an *exemplification* (as, for instance, in an art exhibition, or in front of the artist's workshop; cf. Goodman 1968). On the other hand, there is similarity only on the basis of a fundamental dissimilarity. It is certainly not in their "important" properties, if that means the attributes defining them as "selves", that the picture and its referent (or content) are similar. In fact, the hierarchically dominant categories of the picture and its referent must be different; for a picture which is just a picture of the picture-of-X is indistinguishable from a picture of X (cf. Sonesson 1989: 226ff).

Although the sign relation is thus not needed in order to render similarity asymmetric and irreflexive, it is required in order to distinguish similarities which are signs from those which are not. At this stage, then, it would seem that the picture could be defined by the sign relation, together with similarity; but Eco rightly observes that, on closer inspection, there is really no similarity between the painted nose and the nose of a real person. The same observation is even more obviously valid in the case of the stick-figure, whether it is drawn on paper, or carved in rock. However, it has no bearing whatsoever on iconic signs which are not picture signs, and the argument really shows the confusion between pictures and iconic signs in general: indeed, the Americanness of Franklin and Rumford is identical, as far as this goes, as is the roundness of circles and other round things, and the pattern and colour of a tailor's swatch and the cloth it exemplifies. In the case of the picture sign, it may really be necessary to construe similarity as a result, rather than a condition, of the emergence of iconicity, but that is an issue which concerns the analysis of a specific variety of iconic signs, the picture, not iconicity in general.

The alternative analysis in terms of conventionality suggested by Goodman, Eco, and others is conceived to take care of the case of pictures, but paradoxically, it seems that it would really be needed, not for pictures but for some other iconical signs which rely on identity. Goodman's and Greenlee's contention that the referent of each picture is appointed individually and Eco's proposal that the relations of the picture are correlated with those of the referent are incompatible with what psychology tells us about the child's capacity for interpreting pictures when first confronted with them at 19 months of age (as demonstrated in a famous experiment by Hochberg). On the other hand, we do have to learn that, in certain situations, and according to particular conventions, objects which are normally used for what they are become signs of themselves, of some of their properties, or of the class of which they form part: a car at a car exhibition, a stone axe in the museum showcase or a tin cane in a shop window, an emperor's impersonator when the emperor is away, and a urinal (if it happens to be Duchamp's "Fountain") at an art exhibition. There is never any doubt about their pure iconicity, or about their capacity for entering into an iconic ground — but a convention is needed to tell us they are signs.

When Man Ray makes a picture of a billiard table, we need no convention to recognise what it depicts. However, if Sherrie Levine's (real, three-dimensional) billiard table is to represent Man Ray's picture, there must be a label inverting the hierarchy of prominence of the Lifeworld. This shows that among the properties determining the probability of an object functioning as the expression of an iconic sign is to be found three-dimensionality rather than the opposite.

If anything, present-day technological development has accentuated this difference between potential signifiers, and potential signifieds: the hologram may be three-dimensional, but it lacks solidity and perdurability; and while it may be true that the traditional photograph, unlike the film, has sufficient thing-character to suggest a fetishistic usage, as Metz (1990) claims, this no longer applies to photographs stored on CD-ROM. The realm of signifiers becomes ever more elusive.

VI   The Criterion of Independence

Apart from the reasons mentioned at the beginning of this essay, there is another sense in which pictures are far from being central instances of icons. As was noted above, the fact that an object serving as the expression of an icon and another object serving as its content possess, in some respects, the same properties should not be a result of one of them having an influence on the other. In the case of an icon (contrary to the case of an index), 'it simply happens that its qualities resemble those of that object, and excite analogous sensations in the mind for which it is a likeness' (2.299). Since both Franklin and Rumford are Americans, Peirce claims, one of them may serve as a sign of the other; but the fact that Franklin is an American is quite unrelated to Rumford's being one. But there is at least one sense in which this is not true, not only in the case of a photograph (which Peirce often pronounces to be an index), but also in the case of a painting or the image on a computer screen: in each case, the "thing" serving as the expression is expressly constructed in order to resemble the "thing" serving as the content, although a direct physical connection only exists in the first instance. Leonardo painted the canvas known as Mona Lisa in order to create a resemblance to the wife of Francesco del Giocondo, and, although the resemblance is of a much more abstract kind, the same is true of Picasso painting Gertrude Stein or Kahnweiler. And it is as true of a synthetic computer picture showing a lamp correctly illuminated from above right as of a photograph with the same subject.

Peirce's claim that the properties of expression and content pertain to them independently seems more relevant to identity signs (like Franklin representing Rumford) than to pictures. On the other hand, in another sense pictures are far more iconic than, for instance, objects representing themselves: they require far less indexicality and convention. From this point of view, and contrary to what has been suggested by Morris (1946: 98ff), and is often repeated in theatre semiotics, an object is not its own best icon.

When used to stand for themselves, objects are clearly *iconical:* they are signs consisting of an expression which stands for a content because of properties which each of them possess intrinsically. And yet, without having access to a set of conventions and/or an array of stock situations, we have no possibility of knowing either *that* something is a sign or what it as sign *of:* of itself as an individual object, of a particular category (among several possible ones) of which it is a member, or of one or another of its properties. A car, which is not a sign on the street, becomes a sign at a car exhibition, as does Man Ray's iron in a museum. We have to know the showcase convention to understand that the tin can in the shopwindow stands for many other objects of the same category; we need to be familiar with the art exhibition convention to realise that each object merely signifies itself; and we are able to understand that the tailor's swatch is a sign of its pattern and colour, but not of its shape, only if we have learnt the convention associated with the swatch (cf. Sonesson 1989, II.2.2. and 1994).

Convention is thus needed, not only to establish the sign character, but also the very iconicity of these icons. Since iconicity can be perceived only once the sign function, and a particular variety of it, is known to obtain, the resulting icons may be termed *secondary* (Sonesson 1994). This also applies to "droodles", a kind of limiting-case of a picture exemplified by Carraci's key, in which a triangle above a horizontal line is discovered to represent a mason behind a stone wall once we are told so; as well as the manual signs of the North American Indians, which, according to Mallery (1881: 94f), seem reasonable when we are informed about their meaning.

In these cases, knowledge about the sign function already obtaining between the two "things" involved is clearly a prerequisite to the discovery of their iconicity. The opposite case, in which it is the perception of iconicity which functions as one of the reasons for postulating a sign relation, would seem to be more germane to Peirce's conception of the icon. Such a *primary icon* is actually realised by the picture sign. Indeed, we know from child psychology and anthropology that no particular training is needed for a human being to perceive a surface as a picture. The possibility of this feat remains a mystery: the properties possessed in common by the picture and that which it represents are extremely abstract. Again, picture perception may only be possible because there is a taken-for-granted hierarchy of things in the world of everyday life which makes certain objects and materials more probable sign-vehicles than others (Sonesson 1989; 1994c, d).

VII The "World Taken for Granted"

Ecological semiotics will be my term for what Husserl and his followers, Schütz and Gurwitsch, have called the science of the Lifeworld, as well as for Gibson's "ecological physics" and Greimas' semiotics of the "natural world" (cf. Sonesson 1989, 1994a, c, d). It may seem strange to put together ideas and observations made by a philosopher, a psychologist, and a semioticians; yet these proposals are largely identical. Husserl, Gibson, and Greimas all invented this science because they realised that the "natural world", as we experience it, is not identical to the one known to physics but is culturally constructed. Like Husserl's Lifeworld and Gibson's ecological physics, but unlike Greimas' natural world, semiotic ecology will suppose this particular level to be a privileged version of the world, "the world taken for granted", in Schütz's phrase, from the standpoint of which other worlds, such as those of the natural sciences, may be invented and observed (cf. Sonesson 1989, I.1.4, I.2.1, and *passim*).

It is a basic property of the Lifeworld that everything in it is given in a *subjective-relative* manner. This means, for example, that a thing of any kind will always be perceived *from a certain point of view,* in a perspective that lets a part of the object form the centre of attention. What is perceived is the object, though it is always given through one or more of its perspectives or *noemata,* which themselves are unattended. Gibson observes that when we are confronted with the-cat-from-one-side, the-cat-from-above, the-cat-from-the-front, etc., what we *see* is all the time the same invariant cat. To Husserl, this seeing of the whole in one of its parts is related to *the etc. principle,* our knowledge of being able, at any one point, to turn the dice over, or go round it, to look at the other sides.

Everything in the Lifeworld is given in "open horizons", that is, reality is not framed off like a picture, but goes on indefinitely, however vaguely indicated. Beginning with the *theme,* or centre of attention, the experienced world gradually fades away, without there being any definite limits, and we only have to change the centre of attention in order to extend the field of distinct experience. Every object has an *outer horizon,* i.e. the background field of other, nearby objects, and an *inner horizon,* the parts and attributes that are presently out of view or just unattended. To both the horizons, the etc. principle applies.

The *temporal* organisation of the Lifeworld is similar to the *spatial* one. In the consciousness of each moment lies embedded the consciousness of the immediately following moment and the consciousness of the immediately preceding moment, called the *protention* and the *retention,* respectively. Each protention, in turn, contains its protentions and retentions, as so does each retention. They may be general and vague, like the expectancy that life will go on, or that something will change, or more definite, like the expectancy that the dice will turn out to have a certain number of eyes on the hidden sides. This model of time consciousness was used in theatre semiotics, and in literary semiotics, by members of the Prague school, notably by Mukařovský. However, it is much more general, underlying all schemes of expectation.

VIII   Regularity and Abduction

Every particular thing encountered in the Lifeworld is referred to a general *type.* *Typification* applies to all kinds of objects, even to human beings: according to Schütz, other people, apart from family members and close friends, are almost exclusively defined by the type to which they are ascribed, and we expect them to behave accordingly. 'In perceptual experience, the spatial shapes of things are determined only as to type − a margin of latitude is left for variations, deviations, and fluctuations' (Gurwitsch 1974: 26). Thus, there are no circles in the Lifeworld, only things with "roundish" shapes, with "circular physiognomy". Indeed, the "good forms" of Gestalt psychology, and the prototypes of Rosch's theory, are clearly typifications (see Sonesson 1989, I.2.1.).

Closely related to the typifications are the *regularities* which obtain in the Lifeworld, or, as Husserl's says, 'the typical which in which things tend to behave'. In fact, once an object has been assigned to a particular type, we know more or less vaguely what may be expected, or rather protained, from it in the future, and we can then learn to manipulate desirable changes ourselves. Many of the "laws of ecological physics", formulated by Gibson (1982: 217ff), and which are defied by magic, are also such 'regularities [that] are implicitly known': that substantial objects tend to persist, that major surfaces are nearly permanent with respect to layout, but that animate objects change as they grow or move; that some objects, like the bud and the pupa transform, but that no object is converted into an object that we would call entirely different, as a frog into a prince; that no substantial object can come into existence except from another substance; that a substantial detached object must come to rest on a horizontal surface of support; that a solid object cannot penetrate another solid surface without breaking it, etc. Some of the presuppositions of these "laws", such as the distinction between 'objects that we would call entirely different', are also at the basis of what we have called the Lifeworld hierarchy, and the definition of the sign function.

The Husserlean description of regularities fits in with the notion of *abduction,* which Peirce puts alongside the more familiar procedures of deduction and induction, and which reasons from one particular instance to another, not, however, exclusively on the level of individual facts, for the facts, Peirce tells us, are mediated by certain "regularities", principles that are tentatively set up or taken for granted. Peirce wondered how it was possible for so many abductions to prove right, postulating a natural instinct as an explanation. Actually, there are an infinite number of ways to relate facts, but most of them would seem to be humanly inconceivable. The limited number of alternative abductions really proposed may be due, not to a natural instinct, but to the commonalty of the most general organisational framework of the Lifeworld.

Contrary to what is often believed, children spontaneously believe in non-magic (Gibson 1982: 218); indeed, it is on this background that magic becomes pertinent, as a kind of rhetoric of the "natural world". The "terrestrial environment" of all animals has continued to possess certain simple invariants during the millions of years of evolutionary history, such as the earth being "below", the air "above", and the "waters under the earth" (Gibson 1966: 8ff). The ground is level and rigid, a surface of support, whereas the air is unresisting, a space for locomotion, and also a medium for breathing, an occasional bearer of odours and sounds, and transparent to the visual shapes of things by day. As a whole, the solid terrestrial environment is wrinkled, structured, at different levels, by mounts and hills, trees and other vegetation, stones and sticks, and textured by such things as crystals and plant cells. The observer himself underlies the consequences of the rigidity of the environment and of his own relationship to gravity. Also linguists trying to explain the existence, in all languages, of a set of small words designating the spatial and temporal dimensions of the environment, have found it necessary to postulate a basic framework of the experimental world, determined, in part, by gravity (cf. Miller & Johnson-Laird 1976).

IX The Lifeworld Hierarchy of Things

Inside "ecological physics", in Gibson's sense, there must be some kind of "social physics", not exactly in the Durkheimian sense, but on the micro-level. Schütz and Mead have talked about the array of "things" of the human world which are peculiar in being "at hand", occupying the "manipulatory sphere"; and Wallon has discussed the "ultra-choses", which are outside this sphere, but are seen from there. Even these humble things do not only have a use, but are also there, as Lévi-Strauss would have said, to think with. In this sense, I have referred above to the hierarchy of prominence of Lifeworld things, and I have in fact been using such a scale in two different, but complementary, ways. On the one hand, objects, such as the human body itself, in particular the face, but also common objects like chairs, must be so central to the human sphere that they will be recognized with only scant evidence, even though the invariants embodied in a particular picture are found in other objects as well. In this case, the objects at the highest levels of the scale stand the best chance of being selected. On the other hand, I have argued that only objects low down on the scale will be recognized as susceptible of embodying a sign function, without being particularly designated as such, which in our culture is true of a sheet of paper or a canvas.

One may wonder whether the same scale, with the same ordering, would be involved in the two cases. This is not clear at present. However, a human being, a shape which is easily recognized as such with very scant indications, is perhaps also that object which is most difficult to see as a mere signifier of something else if he is not explicitly so designated, as in the theatre or in a ceremony. On the other hand, the human face, which is probably that object which is most easily identified of all, serves at the same time as support for conveying other signs, the expressions of feelings and attitudes; but then again, it is not the face but its movements which are signifiers of these other signs. It is just that, unlike that of the Cheshire cat, the human smile cannot exist independently.

It will be remembered that, according to Peirce, Franklin and Rumford are iconical signs of each other. But we have just seen that very special circumstances must obtain in order for a human being to function as a mere signifier. A convention would be needed for Franklin to represent Rumford, or the opposite. This may happen if Rumford appears on the stage playing the part of Franklin, or the reverse; it may even suggest itself spontaneously to the someone acquainted with Franklin but not with Rumford. The latter would be a case of prominence by familiarity, as when we compare the identical twin being presented to us with the one we knew before.

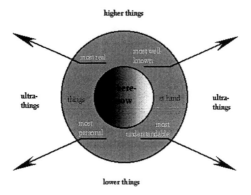

Fig. 2.

Even so, the case seems strange because the iconic ground is supposed to reside in the common Americanness of Franklin and Rumford, which is not in itself a property which can be seen. The ambassador more officially and clearly represents Americanness, but he does not represent any particular other American. The case of any blond girl being made to represent Marilyn Monroe is much more straightforward: blondness is iconic, but still a convention is needed, since it is also endemic. The iconicity of Franklin and Rumford, as well as of the ambassador, is not visual or even sensual: it is a case of a shared abstract property. But since it is a very common property, the two parts entering into the sign relation must be determined by convention or habit.

X The Night of all Iconicities

But Peirce's example may be interpreted in quite a different way: the iconicity obtaining between Franklin and Rumford may well be symmetric, and it may actually involve the general category of Americanness. This means that not only are Franklin and Rumford signs of each other, but they are also signs of all other Americans which have ever existed and which will exist, and each one of these is equally a sign of all the others (and possibly also of themselves). This cannot happen in our sociocultural Lifeworld; it can probably not be the case in any actual Lifeworld; but it is certainly true of the Neoplatonic conception of the world, as expressed, for instance, by Ficino during the Renaissance; and it was true more recently in the art and literature of Symbolism.

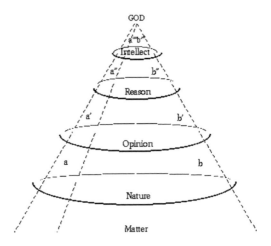

Fig. 3.

Gombrich (1972: 170) describes the Neoplatonic conception in the following way: 'The microcosm as well as the macrocosm must be envisages as a series of concentric circles surrounding the ineffable unity in ever widening distance. Thus a relationship which is palpable below is more contracted and condensed nearer the centre. The proportion a:b will equal a':b' and a'':b'' in each of the spheres, but in the centre all are one and all are equal. God, in the famous words of Nicolaus Cusanus, is a *coincidentia oppositorum.*' The concentric circles of Neoplatonism constitute a particular interpretation of the terrestrial environment, with its upwards and downwards directions. Gombrich considers the particular case of diagrammatic iconicity, but the same could be said about "simple properties" like Americanness (which, although simple in itself, may determined an extensive set of lower-order properties).

In the literature of the Middle Ages it is possible to encounter the nightmare dreamt by Bierman and Goodman, where everything might be a sign of everything else because of general properties they have in common. In "The Quest of the Holy Grail" (c. 1125), meaning is often iconic: the sun is shining just like Christ, the tents are round just like the world; the black knights represent sin, the white knights virtue, etc. Even in the Grail world, however, there is a rudiment of a hierarchy of prominence: as Todorov (1971) observes, it is normally the ordinary, trivial acts, e.g., events such as sitting down to eat, which signify higher values, not the reverse (asymmetric iconicity). On the other hand, some adventures from the Grail story are symmetric: the passion of Christ represents the Grail story, and vice-versa, and the three tables, that of the Lord's Supper, the Grail table of Joseph of Aramathea, and King Arthur's round table, all refer to each other.

Over and over again in the Quest, a knight having an "adventure" will ask a hermit to explain to him "what it means". This is explicitly presented as something different from the causes and intentions behind the event (that is, different from the meanings discovered in Ricœur's hermeneutics, or even in psychoanalysis). In one case, a hermit explains the combat between white and black knights to Lancelot in the following way: it took place in order to decide which of the warlords had the greatest number of knights as followers (a cause clearly situated at the level of the Lifeworld); the meaning was the fight between earthly and heavenly knights, between mortal sin and virginity (a meaning located in the celestial sphere). Lancelot's decision to fight on the side of the black knights (which on the Lifeworld level seems the just choice to make, since there were fewer combatants on the black side), meant that he choose sin.

Unlike some "visions" which are also found in the Quest, these "adventures" have no spatial and temporal borders to ordinary reality. They are continuous with the Lifeworld itself. For instance, when Bors sees the Phoenix nourishing her offspring with her own blood, he does not understand the meaning of the apparition, but 'he knew sufficiently to understand that it was a sign of great importance'. This scene is clearly at another level than the reality in which Bors' moves: it is set off from the Lifeworld. Even Bors, who does not understand it, realises that it has a character of unreality — or "other-reality" — which singles it out as a sign.

In contrast, the "adventures" do not have this sign-character: they are segments of reality; embedded in the Lifeworld, enmeshed in the continuous chains of causality that make up our lives. How, then would it be possible to distinguish a signifier from something which is not? Apparently nothing in the properties of the signifier itself would justify such a distinction.

XI From the Holy Grail to the Internet

One may wonder whether anybody really lived in the Grail world: is it a cultural text — or is it only a meta-text about a cultural text? Literary texts give a framework, single out certain parts as being of relevance, which reality could not do itself without a hierarchy of prominence. Such a system of relevance may serve to pick out certain iconic traits of reality, starting out from the signified instead of the signifier: thus, white and black being identified with virtue and sin and the celestial realm, all things in the Lifeworld which are white and black are susceptible to serve as sign vehicles. Like the symbolic play of the child, this interpretative net thrown on reality may even be able to survive for shorter moments of time.

Starting out from my notion of a Lifeworld hierarchy, Anders Marner (1996) claims to discover a double discourse in Surrealism: on the one hand, Breton and his disciples follow a "via ascensus", which takes us upwards from the terrestrial environment, the objects at hand, to the ultra-things above; on the other hand, Bataille and a few others start out from the "via descencus", which goes downwards from the manipulatory sphere to the ultra-things below, or rather, to unorganised matter. Between them, Breton and Bataille rediscover the Neoplatonic cross-section, each carving out a part for himself: everything potentially iconic of "high" or "low things" respectively will then be able to serve as a signifier.

Marner rightly concludes that nobody could really live in the surrealistic Lifeworld — which is tantamount to saying it is not really a Lifeworld. The Grail world may have had more reality, because it relies on a much wider social consensus. If the Grail world was, in some sense, historically real, we would have to conclude that it was more indirect, more of a life at a distance, than our own "imploded" information society, contrary to what is suggested by the prophets of postmodernity. For a person looking at television, itself shown on his television set, or using a computer which is simulated on another computer, there must still be one screen, and an environment in which it is placed, which is a zero-level world, a world which is not indirect, at least not as indirect as the other parts. Even the person who claims to lead a life which is as real as the other one on the Internet, in some MUD-MOO or the like, is certainly mistaken, because he has access to the net-world through his computer, which is unmistakably located in the Lifeworld, while the opposite is not true.

There is never any doubt that what is seen on the screen is a sign of something else (i.e., a signifier), not the reverse. In contrast, in the Grail world, everything might turn out to be a signifier. Not even the knights and the hermits are necessarily zero-level. In the adventure with the black and white knights, Lancelot himself is a signifier of sin. And in another adventure, one of the hermits giving a interpretation turns out to be the devil and his interpretation becomes a false one, which is then interpreted by a true hermit ⁻ which makes even the last true hermit somewhat precarious.

References

Bierman, Arthur K. 1963. 'That There Are No Iconic Signs.' *Philosophy and Phenomenological Research* 23: 2: 243-249.

Bruss, Elisabeth. 1978. 'Peirce and Jakobson on the Nature of the Sign.' In *The Sign - Semiotics Around the World*. Bailey, R.W., Matejka, L. & Steiner, P. (Eds.). Ann Arbor: Michigan Slavic Contributions.

Eco, Umberto. 1968. *La struttura assente*. Milan: Bompiani.

‐. 1976. *A Theory of Semiotics*. Bloomington: Indiana University Press.

Gibson, James. 1966. *The Senses Considered as Perceptual Systems*. Boston: Houghton Mifflin Co.

Gibson, James. 1982. *Reasons for Realism. Selected Essays of James J. Gibson*. Reed, E. & Jones, R. (Eds.). Hillsdale, New Jersey, and London: Lawrence Erlbaum Ass.

Greimas, A.J. & Courtés, Joseph. 1979. *Sémiotique: Dictionnaire raisonné de la théorie du langage*. Paris: Hachette.

Gombrich, E.H. 1972. *Symbolic Images. Studies in the Art of the Reanaissance*. London: Phaidon.

Goodman, Nelson. 1968. *Languages of Art*. London: Oxford University Press.

—. 1970. 'Seven Strictures on Similarity.' In *Experience and Theory*. Foster, L., & Swanson, J.W. (Eds.). Cambridge, MA: University of Massachusetts Press.

Greenlee, Douglas. 1973. *Peirce's Concept of Sign*. The Hague and Paris: Mouton.

Gurwitsch, Aron. 1974. *Phenomenology and the Theory of Science*. Evanston: Northwestern University Press.

Jakobson, Roman. 1965a. 'À la recherche de l'essence du langage.' *Diogéne* 51: 22-38.

1965b. 'Poesie der Grammatik und Grammatik der Poesie'. In *Mathematik und Dichtung*, Gunzenhäuser, R, & Kreuzer, H. (Eds.). München: Nymphenburger Verlagsbuchhandlung.

Johansen, Jørgen Dines. 1993. *Dialogic Semiosis*. Bloomington: Indiana University Press.

Kolers, Paul. 1977. 'Reading Pictures and Reading Text.' In *The Arts and Cognition*, Perkins, D. & Leondard, B. (Eds.). London and Baltimore: Johns Hopkins University Press.

Lakoff, George & Turner, Mark. 1989. *More Than Cool Reason*. Chicago and London: University of Chicago Press.

Mallery, Garrick. 1972. *Sign Language Among North American Indians*. 1881. Reprinted: The Hague & Paris: Mouton.

Marner, Anders. 1996. 'La retórica en el doble discurso del surrealismo/Retoriken i surrealismens dubbla diskurs.' *Heterogénesis* 15: 13-28.

Metz, Christian. 1990. 'Photograph and Fetish.' In *The Critical Image*. Sqioers, C. (Ed.). London and New York: Routledge.

Miller, G.A, & Johnson-Laird, Ph. 1976. *Language and Perception*. Cambridge, MA: The Belnap Press 1976.

Moles, Abraham. 1981. *L'image - communication fonctionelle*. Bruxelles: Casterman.

79

Morris, Charles. 1971 [1946]. *Signs, Language, and Behavior.* 1946. Reprinted in C. Morris: *Writings on the General Theory of Signs.* The Hague: Mouton.

Osmond-Smith, David. 1972. 'The Iconic Process in Musical Communication.' *Versus* 3: 31-42.

Peirce, Charles Sanders, *Collected Papers I-VIII.* Hartshorne, C., Weiss, P. & Burks, A, (Eds.). Cambridge, MA: Harvard University Press 1931-58

Rosch, Eleanor. 1975. 'Cognitive Reference Points.' *Cognitive Psychology* 7: 4: 532-547.

Savan, David. 1976. *An Introduction to C.S. Peirce's Semiotics.* Toronto: Toronto Semiotic Circle.

Sebeok, Thomas A. 1976. *Contributions to the Doctrine of Signs.* Bloomington and Lisse: Indiana University Press/Peter de Ridder Press.

Sonesson, Göran. 1989. *Pictorial Concepts. Inquiries into the Semiotic Heritage and Its Relevance for the Analysis of the Visual World.* Lund: Lund University Press.

—. 1992. 'Le mythe de la triple articulation. Modéles linguistiques et perceptifs dans la sémiotique des images.' In *Signs of Humanity L'Homme et ses signes. Proceedings of the Fourth Congress of the International Association for Semiotic Studies, Barcelona/Perpignan, Mars-April 1989.* vol. 1. Balat, M., Deledalle-Rhodes, J. & Deledalle, G. (Eds.). Berlin: Mouton de Gruyter.

—. 1994a. 'Sémiotique visuelle et écologie sémiotique.' *RSSI* 14, 1-2, printemps: 31-48.

—. 1994b. 'Iconicité de l'image - Imaginaire de l'iconicité. De la resemblance à la vraisemblance.' In *Les États généraux de l'image. Actes du Premier Congrés de l'Association internationale de sémiologie de l'image, Blois, Novembre de 1990.* Constantini, M., (Ed.). Tours: Université Franéois-Rabelais.

—. 1994c. 'The Ecological Foundations of Iconicity' (to appear in *Semiotics around the World: Synthesis in Diversity. Proceedings of the Fifth International Congress of the IASS, Berkeley, June 12-18, 1994.*

—. 1994d. 'Pictorial Semiotics, Perceptual Ecology, and Gestalt Theory.' *Semiotica* 99 3/4: 319-399.

—. 1994d/1995. 'On Pictorality. The Impact of the Perceptual Model in the Development of Visual Semiotics.' In *The Semiotic Web 1992/93: Advances in Visual, Semiotics.* Sebeok, Th., & Umiker-Sebeok, J. (Eds.). Berlin and New York: Mouton de Gruyter.

Tversky, Amos. 1977. 'Features of Similarity.' *Psychological Review* 84: 4: 327-352.

Todorov, Tzvetan. 1971. *Poétique de la prose.* Paris: Éditions du Seuil.

Uspenskij, Boris. 1976. *Semiotics of the Russian Icon.* Lisse: Peter de Ridder Press.

Iconicity and Evidence

Erling Davidsen & Helle Munkholm Davidsen

> POLONIUS: *What do you read, my lord?*
>
> HAMLET: *Words, words, words*
>
> Shakespeare

I Iconicity and Similarity

One has many reasons to challenge similarity as the criterion for the definition of the iconic sign. One of the stronger ones lies in the difficulty in determining in which way, or in which sense, an icon looks like its object. Thus, the icon seems either to resemble "too little" or "too much"!

In accordance with this idea, Umberto Eco stresses in *La struttura assente* (1972) the lack of similarity between the icon and its referent by demonstrating that icons do not possess the basic qualities of the object referred to. In Nelson Goodman (1968) we have the opposite case. Here the problem is that the icon resembles "too much". A given icon may resemble too many things for the ground of the similarity criterion to determine which object the icon actually represents. Still, the problem is to be countered as do, say, Jørgen Dines Johansen og Svend Erik Larsen in their book *Tegn i brug* ("Signs in Action", 1994: 54, our translation) by arguing

> that there is only *similarity* proper 1) in *relation with implicit or expressed criteria* (i.e., that similarity only exists in relation to a descriptive language), and those criteria are themselves 2) selected on the grounds of their relevance to the aim of the presentation.

In other words, such relativization of the concept of similarity implies that a relation of resemblance only occurs when one has decided which similarity one wants to look for. The point of view or the interpretant (Peirce) is then the agency that transforms a phenomenon whose relations of similarity to other phenomena are virtual into a sign whose relation of similarity is realized in relation to one object.

Such relativization of the concept of similarity may at first glance appear plausible, but it is not satisfying for it still maintains the point of view that anything, in principle or virtually, resembles anything, and that any phenomenon could be realized as an icon. A portrait might, for instance, just as well be an icon of another portrait, rather than of the person it represents. Still, not even an art historian examining resemblances between a variety of portraits would be likely to consider a given similarity between two such paintings in terms of iconic representation.

Göran Sonesson (1992) seems at first glance to go beyond this relativistic view by giving up the criterion of similarity as a sufficient condition for the establishment of the iconic sign. Referring to George Lakoff and Mark Turner's (1989) "Great Chain of Being", Sonesson suggests the existence of a veritable "order of prominence" (*prominensordning*) in the world which organizes its phenenomena hierarchically (1982: 138ff). The point here is that a given phenomenon may serve as an iconic representation only of something of higher "prominence".

Still, even if the introduction of such an "order of prominence" might be taken to explain why an image of a man is the iconic representation of this man — and not the other way round —, and why our art historian does not spontaneously associate an iconic representation between two portrait paintings (of same the prominence), this does not contribute much more than to systematizing relativism. In our view, the assertation of the order of prominence does not change the core problem of the relativistic approach: that anything may be an icon for anything. It only introduces a — for that matter questionable — restriction which only aims at a systematization of this problem.

II   The Sign and Its Interpretant

The demarcation of the definition of similarity outlined above seems not to lead to the desired elimination of "irrelevant iconicity". Still, when all is said and done, this might perhaps be due not to the concept of similarity but to that of the icon?

Along with the symbol and the index, the icon belongs to the interpretant in the Peircean classification of the sign. If the iconic sign is identical in this manner with its "iconic point of view", then it is hardly possible to make the iconical sign the object of analysis. In this sense, one would not be able to determine whether the sign

CAT

is a symbolic, indexical, or iconical sign by taking into account the representamen only since this question addresses the interpretant (the point of view). In terms of analysis, or description, the classification of the sign therefore seems inappropriate:

i) the interpretant cannot be objectivized, and therefore the sign does not lend itself to analysis

ii) sign classification leads to misapprehensions

As for the latter, an example is to be found in Sonesson's Peircean analysis of Velásquez' painting *Las Meninas* (Sonesson 1992: 31, our translation, our inserts):

i) 'In its capacity as a picture (*bild*)' is 'an *iconical* sign' that contains 'other iconical signs: the pictures on the walls but also the mirror reflections [*spegelbilden*]'
...
ii) 'whereas a mirror reflection [*spegelbild*] is realized by the fact that an event shown in the mirror is located in its real [sic!] proximity, this is also an *indexical* sign'
...
iii) 'we see now that there are also conventional signs in the image, although they may be harder to distinquish from the other signs. Peirce himself indicated that all real [sic!] images in some way or another were conventional.'

In the very same passage, *Las Meninas* is taken for an iconical sign 'in its capacity of being a picture' (in *i*) and a conventional (symbolic) sign (in *iii*). The misapprehension here is due to the fact that the sign classification does not make it possible to distinguish one sign from another. The "mirror reflection" "S)" is in a similar sense iconic (in *i*) and indexical (in *ii*).

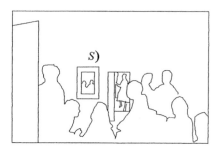

Fig. 1.

The interpretation of the mirror image as being an indexical sign (*ii*) is established with reference to the iconical sign's denotated "reality", i.e., the *referent*, or the "event shown in the mirror" and "is located in its real proximity". Such an interpretation is hardly consistent, for the "reflected image" remains precisely a *picture* (of a "reflection") however subtly we may approach it. A "symbolic exposition", i.e. that the "mirror image" is Velasques' signature) would in this sense not challenge the sign's (i.e. the representamen's) iconic pregnancy, that is if such concept makes sense at all. The latter will not be the case if signs only exist due to the mercy of the interpretant. In that case, the signs remain only as points of view leaving no trace in the representamen.

However, if one perceives a class of signs as a class of representamens — thus recognizing the formal relevance of classification although still substituting its object — the notion of iconical pregnancy then seems more plausible. Thus, the question of whether a given sign is an icon or a symbol is determined here not by the interpretant (i.e. the point of view) but by the representamen. In this sense it is no longer relevant to ask what kind of similarity a given interpretant may suggest between an icon and a natural object. The challenge now lies in addressing to the sign itself the question of similarity.

By perceiving the sign *sui generis* it becomes obvious that the question of similarity should be placed under the semiosis of the iconical sign; that is, under the relation between the expression and the content of the latter. By this move one immediately obtains a number of advantages. Firstly, one is relieved of the fruitless speculations on a given icon's similarity (or lack of similarity — which in fact amounts to the same here) to a natural object. For here the icon is no longer determined by similarity. Secondly, one avoids what we see as an arid relativism which lets anything resemble anything and thus serve as an icon for anything. On the contrary, the icon is now to be determined as a sign function in which the expression of a sign resembles its content.

We now think that we can say without offence that the sign

CAT

is not iconical in the sense that its expression does not resemble its content, but that the sign

Fig. 2.

is iconic since its expression does resemble its content.

84

Iconicity and Non-Sign

Eco observes quite early (1972: 176ff) that the signification of an icon is perceived spontaneously. He attributes this phenomenon to the codes of recognition which seem to derive from common experiences of perception. The icon does not resemble the natural object as we perceive it but rather its mental representations, Eco argues. Moreover, the codes of recognition is for Eco characterized by two features: 1) they rely on selection, and 2) they are general. Returning to the iconical figure of a cat above, it does seem obvious that, rather than resembling any natural cat, this icon represents features which we (in a given culture) see as being significant for not any particular (individual) cat but cats in general.

However, spontaneous signification is hardly brought about by any codes nor by our experimental knowledge of the latter. If that was the case, a symbolical sign's signification would be as spontaneous as that of the icon. The spontanous production of signification — or, as we would say, the evidence — in icons is instead tied up with the iconical expression's realization (*"gestalting"*) of those mental representations we have made of things, that is, with the iconical semiosis' simulation of things' *phenomenal gestalt*.

By this we wish to assert that 1) the icon is evident not simply by resembling a given thing but by looking like this thing's way of being a thing, and 2) that a given thing's way of being a thing, i.e., its *phenomenal gestalt*, is experienced as being evident by every common thinking being.

Things appear as being evident, for things are not signs. Things only lose evidence when a pragmatical use (i.e. intention, "culture", etc.) and its point of view turn them into signs. In our opinion, one gives up understanding the icon's specific function of *simulating* the evidence of things if one does not recognize the fundamental evidence of things. To us, this specific function, which characterizes the icon, both justifies and makes necessary its definition as a type, namely as a *sign which simulates non-signs*.

III Signa Evidentia

The icon is to be divided formally only into its expression and its content. In actual fact we are of course faced with great difficulties in distinguishing the two due to the fact that the icon's expression and content have "collapsed". The differential bar, which the symbol, i.e., the linguistic sign, establishes between the sign's expression and content as a precondition for its referential function, is suspended in the iconical sign. The effect of this suspension is the experience not of similarity, as Sonesson seems to argue

> ... the picture is a sign which in addition to signifying another object [föremål] gives rise to the experience of similarity between the sign's expression and content [1992: 135, our translation, our insert]

— but of evidence. The experience of similarity does depend on the articulation of difference. Still it is precisely this difference that constitutes the linguistic sign; a difference which is suspended in icons. The enunciation, or *modus* of icons are therefore not:

 'This resembles (but is not) a CAT'

— but rather:

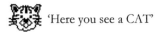 'Here you see a CAT'

The icon demands no natural referent in order to produce an effect of reality, but refers, if referring to anything at all, to itself. In a certain sense, the icon is auto-referential. As a sign, then, the icon appears as being neither arbitrary nor accidental, neither motivated nor necessary — but evident.

Signum evidens is a fairly disregarded sign phenomenon, and the reason for this is that it does not resemble a sign but a "thing". The "thing" and its evidence is without doubt a semiotic problem but hardly a semiotic phenomen. The assertation that the world appears intelligible for us as *phenomenal gestalt*, i.e., forms, must not lead us to assert that these *gestalts*, or forms, are representations. The *gestalted* forms signify here nothing besides that which "things" are when not being anything besides than what they in fact are.[1] Their evidence as being pheno-gestalt relies thus

---

[1] Phenomenology is, no doubt, able to go much further here, and perhaps also to contribute to the clarification of the concept of discreteness (*discrétion* in the French) which has been so urgent for semiotics (Gremas et al.). However, the recognition of our asserted affinity between pheno-gestalt and non-representation will confront semiotics with a number of new epistomological choices, and not least call for the courage to question the semio-ontological equation:

$$world = signifying\ world$$

on the non-representational relation outlined below:

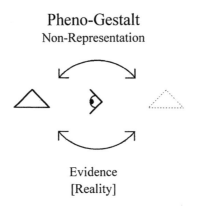

Pheno-Gestalt
Non-Representation

Evidence
[Reality]

Fig. 3.

The realization of this connection between non-representation and evidence may serve as a pivotal point for the clarification of the icon as a specific type of sign.

The icon then both stands for evidence and a relation of representation (*aliquid stat pro aliquo*). Therefore, we are immediately confronted with the following intricate question: how can something stand for something else (being different from it) while at the same time being evident? As far as the so-called symbolical sign is concerned, this question never comes up. It is true that the symbol refers to a relation of representation, but the symbol's signification is not evident. No matter how much we contemplate a symbol, it remains non-evident. Of course, this is due to the fact that the relation of representation in symbols relies on difference. In language, says Saussure, there is only difference without positive parts, and that is, in respect to the linguistic sign, an adequate assumption. Language, the symbol, or the linguistic sign is effective only due to the bar which is established as a differentiating relation between expression (*aliquid*) and content (*aliquo*), and which guarantees that in the expression of the linguistic sign no trace of the content of the latter is left. Thus, the bar is the condition for the arbitrarity of the linguistic sign; it determines its pragmatics, its efficiency, altogether.

On the other hand, the icon's effectiveness as a sign is determined solely by the success of the veritable *semioclacy* which is realized by the suspension of the bar between a sign's expression and content. Owing to this suspension, the iconical sign is articulated as a non-sign, whereafter it is attributed the very same ontological

87

status as any other thing. One might say that iconicity is not things-becoming-signs but signs-becoming-things. The precondition for this trick is not a natural relation of reference between icon and object, between icon and "thing", as outlined above, but the *isomorphy* one will find between the figurative gestalt of the icon and the phenomenal gestalt of the object, that is, between *icono-gestalt* and *pheno-gestalt*. It is such isomorphy which attributes the same phenomenal status to them:

Icono-Gestalt
Representation

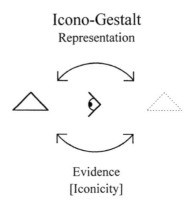

Evidence
[Iconicity]

Fig. 4

What, then, is the phenomenal status of the icon? Well, this is a question which today is more important to pose (and to formulate correctly) than to have answered immediately. This question challenges a number of the ontological truths in semiotics and has far-reaching consequences for its way of perceiving signification and the world.

Let us, by means of conclusion, attempt to render intelligible the scope of this question by returning to what we have designated above as the semio-ontological equation:

$$world = signifying\ world$$

If the so-called thymico-proprioceptive category

exteroceptivity versus interoceptivity

establishes differentiating semiosis in perception and thereby founds and stabilizes the difference between outer/inner, signifier/signified, apparancy/immanency, etc. — and it is assumed here that it does — it is then rather the *pheno-gestalt*, which also belongs to the level of perception — but beyond any arche-semic articulation — that makes these differences collapse in the icon.

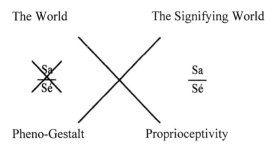

The World   The Signifying World

$$\frac{Sa}{Sé}$$

Pheno-Gestalt   Proprioceptivity

Fig. 5.

Still, the world does not fall apart only because of that! We are tempted to say that it is quite the reverse. This precisely *athymical* diffusion between inner/outer conditions not only common zest, but also, presumably, the common intercourse with the world. The proprioceptive bar between inner and outer is rather in peril of developing cyclothymy as far as the former (i.e., common zest) is concerned, and in respect to the latter (i.e., common intercourse with the world), an intemperate effort at interpretation, not unlike that of paranoia.

Semiotics is free to reject the proprioceptice articulation's realistic return to that world it articulates as being differentiating and significant — and that is precisely what it does (Greimas 1966: 8ff) — but in that case, such a rejection must be motivated by the wish to uphold a certain epistemology. Still, in that case, we are quite convinced that the icon will remain as semiotics' incessant challenge.

References

Eco, Umberto. 1972. *La struttura assente*. Paris: Mercure de France.

Goodman, Nelson. 1972. *Problems and Projects*. Indianapolis and New York: Bobbs-Merrill.

—. 1986. *Languages of Art*. London: Oxford University Press.

Greimas, Algirdas Julien. 1966. *Sémantique stucturale*. Paris: Larousse.

Johansen, Jørgen Dines & Larsen, Svend Erik. 1994. *Tegn i brug*. Aalborg: Amanda.

Lakoff, George & Turner, Mark. 1989. *More Than Cool Reason. A Field Guide to Poetic Metaphor*. Chicago and London: The University of Chicago Press.

Peirce, Charles Sanders. 1931-1956. *Collected Papers*. Cambridge, MA: Harvard University Press.

Saussure, Ferdinand de. 1985 [1916]. *Cours de linguistique générale*. Tullio de Mauro (Ed.). Paris: Payot.

Sonesson. Göran. 1992. *Bildbetydelser. Inledning till bildsemiotiken som vetenskap*. Lund: Studentliteratur.

Contexts

Grounding Iconicity

Per Aage Brandt

Iconicity in signs falls out of the Saussurean scope and seems to call for a Peircean view, at least of sign types. However, if the semantic triad of signs proposed by Peirce is accepted, a "system-oriented" approach then contrasts with phaneroscopic ordering: according to the latter, *icons* come first, *indices* second, and *symbols* third; whereas the systematic consideration proposes a code-based ordering, which must take *indices* as primitives (no codes at all), then *icons* (weak codes), and lastly *symbols* (strong codes) — "code" means, then, the sign's reference to an interpretive instance, and the ranking refers to an evolving or emerging autonomy of the structure of this instance.

None of these simple principles of classification seem to make us any wiser. Icons as firsts only remind us of their relation to seeing as prior to factual thinking, and to formal calculating; icons as systematic seconds remind us of the laws of perception and cultural apperception as their prerequisites.

Beyond the scope of such classifications, I prefer to think that a theory of icons or of iconicity must be realistically grounded, if we are to consider it as a contribution to knowledge, and I think that questions like the following must be admitted in the semiotic debate: *Where do icons come from?* When did they emerge in human evolution? How did we come to represent meanings by icons? In trying to answer such questions, we are seldom capable of more than stipulating scenarios, but even that is better than mere systemic or phaneroscopic speculation; the evaluation of hypothetic scenarios is at least as good a method in "grounding" research as it is in historiography.

I

For all we know, cave paintings did not precede the emergence of language in human evolution. These iconic manifestations[1] of the Upper Paleolithic are due to

---

[1] Cf. *Semiotica* 100, 2/4 (1994): Special Issue, *Prehistoric Signs*.

linguistically equipped Cro-Magnons (and perhaps not the Neanderthals). Some of the morphological conditions for language to emerge might therefore coincide with those of iconicity. Let me here propose a scenario for understanding or imagining what might have happened.[2]

Morphological conditions[3] include, I strongly suppose, the hairlessness of the Cro-Magnon body, the distribution of its fatty tissues allowing for swimming and diving, fishing,[4] and mirroring itself in the surface of the water, thereby providing it with a mimetic control of its gestures. Fishing becomes a female speciality, as opposed to male hunting, I also suppose. A particularly important aspect of this ecological and morphological development is the subsequent specialisation of expressive *facial* mimetics, which allows for refined gaze-following in communication, as well as for distinct emotional expressivity in the hairless human face, especially the female one. Body painting now becomes specialized as *facial painting*, relating graphic cosmetics to the idea of there being thoughts, feelings, representations, or wishes going on behind the decorated face of another human being. In this respect, body painting remains ritual, whereas facial painting suggests individual mental events, accessible by a specific face-to-face empathy evolving out of the mimetic competence thus obtained.

Such a *facial semiotics* still underlies modern cosmetic conceptions. It attunes inter-individual communication, both visually and phonetically, since phonation implies close facial imitation but continues inwards and eventually includes the control of lips, tongue, vocal cords, jaw, etc. Global utterance intonation remains associated with global facial expression and its natural "graphics" (vertical and horisontal extension, eye movements, etc.). Facial semiotics may well develop in slightly different ways in males and females, or by degrees that account for the woman's role in the epigenetic transmission of language in the late stage of nursing.

Now, if facial graphics as a cultural practice refers to mental events, and these events include mental representations, it is possible to interpret visual facial semio-

---

[2] This view is socio-culturally elaborated in P. Aa. Brandt's "Hvad nyt — 50.000 års modernisme. En evolutionær rapsodi." The Royal Danish Academy of Fine Arts, 1997 (to appear), a strongly revised translation of Brandt (1996).

[3] Biological and cultural changes are currently studied as interrelated; sexual dimorphism is a particularly interesting issue here: the early female gracilization in modern hominids, discovered by D. F. Frayer in the 1980's seems to be a crucial fact in the development of the gender based separation and division of labor that (according to my interpretation) might also have affected the species' semiotic and linguistic skills (cf. Soffer 1992).

[4] Cf. Cleyet-Merle (1990).

tics as a primitive *symbolic* practice of signs. If, by facially grounded empathy, humans are led to imagine the forms of mental life in individuals of the species — distinctly and differently from what they do when communicating with faceless domestic animals, or with gods wearing masks — , there might be a second development in the evolution of signs, when 1) mobile masks and shields take over the graphic support function, and when 2) stationary cave walls take over the support function as an instance, probably, of sacred, transcendent, impersonal intentionality interpreted as a "spirit" having the rock or the cave wall as its "face". We still speak catachrestically of the "sur-faces" of things. The stationary graphic support thus becomes an intending "face" in the hypothetic phenomenology of our ancestors. But as such a support does not reproduce more of the morphology of the human face than its convexity, or its outlined two-dimensional significance (by the significance, in fact, of horisontal versus vertical extension in mimetics), it makes it possible in return to unfold the idea of an intended and represented content more fully. The graphics thereby and therefore becomes *imaging*. This hypothesis — focussing on the displacement of the graphic support — would explain why human faces do not appear as the first imaging motives, and do not in fact occur before writing systems are developed, say, 40.000 years later (by 8000 B.C.). The explanation is, then, that the imaging support "is" a face, and that the graphic practice aims at its *meaning*, not at its appearance. The iconic activity then seeks to make the (facial) spirit think of and want to do something specific: send animals to the hunter, for instance. The magical force assigned to images is still in many cultures a semiotic fact.

If this is true, then iconicity develops out of early symbolicity. It also becomes clear why images represent "possible" states or things: what other people think are *possible* things, in the simple sense that I do not have to believe the same things when they are communicated to me by them; iconic representations given by linguistic descriptions and by shown images take the same modal value of possibility. They are intended by the other as more or less plausible, and I am free to reevaluate this plausibility, which will then at a minimum correspond to the value of pure "possibility in some made-up world". Images create mental spaces.

II

Iconic signs are then what we might call signs performing *thought-writing*, comparable with later signs of *speech-writing*. When the latter type appears, engraved on smooth stones, on clay tablets derived from pottery, on parchment, and so on,[5] the volume of the support comes eventually to represent the human facies *as a speaking face*, and then the situation is ripe for facial portraits, referring to the authors of the corresponding texts (as virtually pronounced by individuals with expressive "characters" of age, disposition, etc., marked on their faces). Modern coins are still good examples of this logic; heads showing portraits, tails showing readable figures, numerical and verbal: as the body-part terminology reminds us ("head" versus "tail"), the symbolic side remains subordinate to the iconic side, from where the authority flows that guarantees the validity of the nominal quantum. Modern books, whether of science, of philosophy or of poetry, often show facial portraits of their authors on the cover; these facial icons are evidently supposed to summarize or even authenticate in some way the tonality or intention of the texts. Speech-writing initiates the historical and *modern concept of symbolicity*, emancipated from the human skin — but never from the idea of an imaginable face as a minimal "signature" of the writ. Any implied author is an imaginable voice attached to an imaginable facial countenance (but not necessarily to a whole body; the same is true for deities). Imagine, by contrast, a masked author portrait on a modern book..., *Iconicity, this first form of symbolicity, becomes an accompaniment* of the written text, this second form of symbolicity. Only in scientific symbolization by diagrammatic modelling is the archaic, imaging symbolicity — the thought-writing form — still revered. Painting as an autonomous art form evolves out of the facial authentication of texts, and of mentally supportive illustrations of texts; still, the magical feeling related to the very *stroke* of the painted surface seems to be an essential resource of pictorial aesthetics, and is often feared, if not exploited, by religious minds. The stroke, in fact, takes the observer back to the facial grounding of iconicity. It must be strictly supervised by the artistic discipline, and any deviation is explosive, as the history of art tells us. Written art critique now controls it severely.

So, if the proposed scenario is followed, this time symbolicity is first, and iconicity is its first manifestation; later, iconicity becomes a lateral form, linked to speech-oriented symbolicity, and ends up as a mysterious resource 1) of aesthetic emotion, 2) of scientific thought, and 3) of seduction, manipulation, and other vile concerns.

If the hypothesis is valid, it also explains why contemporary cognitive research finds it possible to obtain knowledge about our mental structures — our semantic organizations, natural patterns of thinking and organizing meaning — by studying iconic representations, rather than speech-writing only. These studies aim at finding

---

[5] Cf. Schmandt-Besserat (1992). Reviewed by Watt (1994).

the schematic architecture of internal thought-writing (our "mental graphics", so to say) by reading external thought-writing (icons we live by) and comparing it to the results of linguistic semantics: what we say depends on what we can mentally see and feel that others can mentally see — by a sort of imaginary deixis drawing figures in the air while speaking to empathically given partners.

III

Computers and mass media are yielding a veritable renaissance for iconicity in contemporary culture. In a world of *screens*, the importance of the supports — still more sophisticated, ephemeral, immaterial — for the evolution of human semiotics becomes clearer than ever. A screen is still an intelligible entity by the force of the *face* as an attractor of intentional attention. People experience computers as human simulators with big heads and small bodies, turning those heads towards them and shining like human faces seem to do by emotional involvement. Writing or drawing on these luminous sur-faces is thus a natural thing to do. We know of course that some of the characters shown by such an active surface are due to causal processes; this is also the case with real human faces, marked by involuntary, unintentional tics or irrelevant routines, traces, scars, illnesses, etc. The programmes of a computer are, so to speak, its inherent illnesses, which we have induced into it in order to profit from its regular symptoms (we treat our industrialized domestic animals in much the same fashion); they react in interesting ways to our symbolic input, by mirroring it in deformed and processed versions, some of which we find intelligible and useful. The computer screen is normally placed at a distance from its user coming close to the proxemics of intimacy in human pragmatics. This fact further stimulates our symbolic fluency — and differently from the white sheet of paper on the table *under* our faces. Here is an artificial "square head" we can talk to or project our mental graphics onto, or playfully interact with, and use to mail human messages, as if it were a pronominal dummy for anyone, including ourselves, with whom we might want to exchange mental events. It exemplifies a rather evident semiotic fact about communication that earlier technologies have however hidden, namely that the two decisive properties of the face — 1) there is thought behind it; 2) it speaks — that gave rise to iconicity (cf. 1) and to (modern) symbolicity (cf. 2) both introduce a *temporal* dimension: icons lead to other icons, and (pure) symbols lead to other symbols *in the other*, and essentially by *causal* processes (cf. programmes, illnesses) that are out of our reach. In much the same way as a bomb shown on the screen notifies us of imminent, unwelcome events, or a written message informs us of a programme's immediate past and future, any human sign — iconic or symbolic — calls for two inferences as to non-present processes in the other person who is present: meanings will lead to new meanings, and signifiers to new signifiers. This is the *indexical* dimension of any semiotics.

Indices are simply the causal-temporal extensions of sign exchange. They are thus as facially grounded as icons and symbols. But whereas these are linked to *present* and intentional experience, indices are dependent on non-present knowledge, presently accessible to the communicating human subject of the inferences that any communication imply. Since no facial other, human or artificial, living or inert as a support, can be experienced as intending outside the present moment, and since the experiencer can never freely create the knowledge that triggers an inference, this indexical dimension of semiotics cannot be intended in itself; I would say that it is essentially involved in any communication as *the contribution of Reality to meaning*. Iconic indexicality is what we use the term "reference" for, meaning "substantial reference"; symbolic indexicality is a "formal reference". Epistemologically, *substantial reference* is correspondence, and *formal reference* is coherence. Neither of these types of reference can be presentically experienced by communicating subjects as intrinsic to communication; both are extrinsic, given by laws that "ground" the act of communicating in the world that communication is in and about. Reality intervenes by determining extrinsically what we cannot but infer about meanings and signifiers when communicating. C. S. Peirce saw this formal reference of symbols; George Lakoff and his colleagues have seen the substantial reference of icons when studying metaphors as inferencing mechanisms. The global result of these insights should now yield a semio-cognitive understanding of the double phenomenon of possibly interacting *iconic cognition* and *symbolic cognition*: of substantial, image-and-meaning-based inferencing as opposed to formal, signifier-based inferencing, naturally interacting in many semiotic practices, if also naturally separated in others. They are, I propose to think, necessarily interacting in all aesthetic practices, whereas they are separated in all scientific practices. Poetry procedes by shifting back and forth between semantic and non-semantic inferences. Painting procedes by shifting analogously between (semantic) *representation* by iconic 3D depth and (non-semantic) *presentation* by symbolic strokes on a 2D surface. Correspondingly, music shifts between the (semantic) harmonic representation of a mentally spatial motive and (non-semantic) presentative phrasing. As Freud saw, dreaming is a natural art form shifting between associations (inferences) by signifiers and associations by imaginary scenes.

By contrast, science in all forms necessarily develops formal ontologies (calculuses) as distinct from substantial ontologies (empirical). Empirical discovery and formal modelling are mutually challenging activities which problematize each other in the steady — if also bumpy — process of objective understanding of the world. Substantial truth and formal validity only coincide a posteriori and on special occasions — when findings and ideas merge into perfect bits of new knowledge; scientists will describe these moments in aesthetic terms.

It follows from this analysis that *indices are not signs*. They are only the causal-temporal extensions of intentional sign reading. They are, so to speak, substantial og formal metonymies. The mistake of believing that they are signs has caused great harm to the entire enterprise of semiotic theory. It has made it falsely plausible that the inferential, referential and hence indexical *import* of symbolization — iconic or not — is unconnected with it and with communication as an inter-facial exchange of signs. Inferential dynamics would then be characteristic of "indices", whereas icons and symbols would remain static and conventional, cut off from real-existential significance. Human interrelations would be temporally static, and only nature would infuse dynamics into our phenomenology.

IV

Primitive symbolization evolved into surface-based imaging, "thought-writing", and then into speech-writing. Two aspects of the human face were thereby generalized: its imagined "inside" and its expressive "outside". Two aspects of understanding were also unfolded: an "inner" understanding by causal-temporal extension of the *iconic* mental graphics (substantial inference), and an "outer" understanding by causal-temporal extension of the neo-symbolic phono-graphics (formal inference). The latter restimulated iconicity as a *neo-iconic* seeing by reading; art and scientific thinking were differently based on neo-iconic representations in their variable relationship to neo-symbolic presentations.

If we translate this account into Saussurean terminology, just for expository reasons, we arrive at something like the following chart:

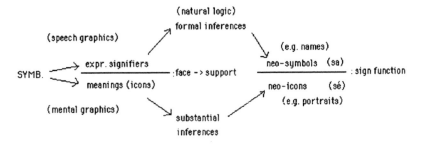

Fig. 1.

The modern sign function links syntactically controlled neo-symbols to semantically controlled neo-icons; the control instances are given by the inferential grounds on which understandings have to rely. Although these grounds are generally distinct by the nature of our phenomenology, they touch and channel impulses from one to the other under certain rather particular circumstances, and in three ways:

From formal to substantial inference: *performative communication*

From substantial to formal inference: *creative mental activity*

Both ways indistinctly: *dreaming and art*

The apparently mysterious Saussurean barrier between signifier and signified is then a descendant of the supposed first support, the human face. The well-known similes of the coin or the sheet of paper's recto and verso show that the support is now approached from behind as well as from "ahead" (cf. the cave walls). The evolution of symbolicity has probably affected our inferential structures even on a neural level, so that neo-iconicity, emancipated from iconicity's first religious or magical dependencies and thematic stereotypy (mainly animal motives), now only seems limited by the laws of our schematic imagination. These laws are therefore the major concern of current cognitivist, semiotic, and philosophical inquiry.

Substantial inferences have their own grounds in our bodily experience of the material world, framed as it is by the limited set of natural elements, or states of matter: light, temperature, pressure, motion inform us about fluids, solids, orientations, earth, wind, and fire, which we schematize universally in dynamic spatiotemporal forms. These forms seem to combine extensively into continuities that we can scale up and down rather freely (by a principle of natural metonymy); iconic and directly perceptual experiences can thus be shared by subjects with different scopes and perspectives on "the same things". Three *standard scopes* seem however to be

100

cognitively relevant: 1) an individual scope, 2) a socio-cultural average scope, and 3) an Olympic scope. Though the scaling of events differs, figurative schemata are reused from scope to scope. Since the meanings of events also differ, such reuse can carry them over — metaphorically — from domain to domain; this is a main resource of inference.

Formal inferences have their specific grounds in our expressive metrics: we choose accentual speed and intonational curves when directing the other's attention by speech; we attune our gazes, voices, segmentations and syntactic phrases to each other through facial signs by which we communicate whether or not we are following the expressive flow of the other, to whose metrics we then attune. Sentences are separated by "blanks for attunement". Linguistic communication seems to have needed constant attunement, since the sentential unity became such a strongly structured syntactic frame. If the available period of attention is short, the speaker must "make sense" in a hurry; focussing only on selected details of some time-space, leaving the rest to silence or pronominal compactness, the spoken sentence has a duration of a few seconds. We do not know where this *haste* comes from; my guess is that shared attention, even when it appears to be an auditive fact, is dependent on eye contact in the face-to-face situation, and such a situation is generically unstable ⁻ different from group routines and trained collective behaviour, difficult to maintain emotionally (cf. psychotic subjects' difficulties with all face-to-face relationships), and pragmatically complex: listening to another person speaking is a doing so radically distinct from other doings that languages have closed-class forms (first and second person; deixis; functional attunement and mode markers) regulating the "cooperation" at stake in what we peacefully call "dialogue". In human evolution, "dialogue" must have been a highly problematic, revolutionary, and dramatic new experience. It may also have been psychically and socially dangerous; misunderstandings and conflicts, insults and humiliations must have been unavoidable (since speakers must have been very unevenly skilled), and thus must have led to acts of violence (cf. also modern quarrelling, especially between male and female speakers, who do not use language in exactly the same way, or do not possess exactly the same linguistic competence). I suggest imagining the invention of poetry as a means of stabilizing and pacifying these new situations (cf. modern lexicographic practise, in which quoting literary authors is an acknowledged validation of tricky expressions).

However that may be, language universally takes a sententially framed syntactic form. The sentential frame is carpentered by an inner structure of cases, actants, and prefigured circumstants; its unity is rigid and discontinuous; it cannot extend (as images can), and can only yield shifts of semantic scale through embedding or

juxtaposition (conjunction, disjunction). The prototype of all abstract discretes —
composite wholes: states, events, actions — might be this propositional unit, the
basic element of what becomes Logic. Numbers refer to sentences as well: *one* is a
framed something in time and space, a whole (an "integer"), somewhat more resistent
to partitioning than, say, *five*; a part of *five* is an embedded whole. Mereology,
a probable cognitive source of mathematics, then springs from the sentential experience.
What we "count", what counts, is a *bounded sentence content*, something happening
or being there for some subject: a "sayable" something, a "closed" fact.

Writing begins with counting (imprinted animal figurines on pottery): each
character is a "sayable" something ("you owe me five cows"). Iconographic characters
become phonographic rather naturally, since substantial iconicity rejects framing
and closing. But *neo-iconicity*, inscribed in sign functions, accepts closing and
framing; it also accepts *counter-intuitive imagery*: it becomes a Hjelmslevian "form of
content", a syntactically controllable and partitionable whole, suitable for non-
stationary (mobile, abstract) uses, for being carried around on mobile supports and
exchanged (cf. playing cards); and for being counter-intuitively believed in — far-
fetched ideas, psychotic delusions, myths and miracles, 'impossible things', as Alice
says to the Queen... — , if there are "reasons" to do so. Cultures gather around
venerated "impossibles" and strengthen their social coherence by sharing them;
individuals culturally come to give up — sacrify, in fact — their natural, experienti-
ally based mental iconicity and to accept the induced "reasons" to believe in neo-
iconic imagery. The surprising semiotic thing is that modern humans *can* do this: the
phenomenon called belief works on functionally established neo-iconicity as well
as on primitive, unframed iconicity; believing defeats knowing, to a great extent.
Therefore, neo-iconic metaphors can and do deeply influence and shape our
thought. Neo-iconically based convictions are responsible for the wonderful, but
also frankly horrible phenomenon of what we could call the arbitrariness of intelligence in our species. They are manifested both by the most insane ideologies and
by the finest works of our sciences and arts. Neo-iconicity is the very essence of
human rationality as we know it.

And yet, painters cannot but feel that their canvas stares at them, and writers that
their white sheet glares upon their efforts. Now, our luminous screens take over the
archaic forms of supervision. But symbolicity still *faces* us.

References

Brandt, Per Aage. 1996. 'What's new? - 50.000 years of Modernism.' In *The Modern Subject*. S.
Meyer & O. M. Christensen (Eds.). Senter for Europeiske Kulturstudier, University of Bergen.

Cleyet-Merle, Jean-Jacques. 1990. *La préhistoire de la pêche*. Paris: Editions Errance.

Schmandt-Besserat, Denise. 1992. *Before Writing, Vol. I: From Counting to Cuneiform*. Austin: University of Texas Press.

Soffer, Olga. 1992. 'Social Transformations at the Middle to Upper Paleolithic Transition: The Implication of the European Record.' In *Continuity or Replacement. Controversies in Homo sapiens evolution*. G. Braüer & F. H. Smith (Eds.). Rotterdam and Brookfield: A.A. Balkema.

Watt, W. C. 1994. 'In the beginning.' *Semiotica*, 99-1/2: 221-234.

The Barrel Hoop and the Trinity
Some Ideas of Iconicity in the Middle Ages

Hanne Roer

In medieval texts one often meets the same examples again and again, due to the respect with which the *auctoritates* were handled. This has often been regarded as laboriousness, but is in fact a courteous way of introducing new concepts - without rejecting the tradition, as is the modern ideal. Accordingly the modern reader should study these examples carefully, and this is what I intend to do in order to trace some ideas of iconicity in medieval linguistic and literary texts.

One recurring example of iconic signs is the *circulus vini*, the circle announcing that here is a tavern where wine is available; the circle was actually a barrel hoop, thus indicating in an indexical and quasi-iconical way (Eco, Lambertini, Marmo, Tabarroni 1989: 23) the container of the wine. Another example is the *pannus rubeus*, the red cloth also used by the owner, *tabernarius,* to advertise the wine in his shop; according to Siger de Courtrai, the cloth signifies the wine and the red the colour of the wine (Sigerus de Cortraco 1977: 2).

Such signs were classified in different ways, as natural or conventional signs, as will be shown. Taking Augustine and Roger Bacon as starting point, I will proceed to the modistic grammarians and philosophers, Martinus and Boethius de Dacia and end up with Dante Alighieri. By tracing and analysing just one, apparently unimportant, semiotic topos I may seem to be using a marginal strategy, searching out marginal elements as clues to essential contradictions in the core of the theory.[1]

This is actually the case in the field of logic: the modistae neither classify signs nor try to define iconic signs, in spite of their central claim of a similitude between linguistic and ontological levels. In the Middle Ages there is, however, a general fascination with the power and reality of icons, images and pictures (the period has even been characterized as iconodule) and the Peircean notion of iconicity may thus be a fruitful approach to what is more vaguely called the symbolic attitude of the Middle Ages. This, indeed, central theme can be studied in the treatises and the

---

[1] As has been done by Eco and Marmo (1989: 3-41) on the *latratus canis*, the barking of the dog, another recurring example.

Divina Commedia of Dante Alighieri who, among other things, tries to create a synthesis of semiotics and the universal symbolism.[2]

I Augustine

Augustine is the founder of medieval semiotics. Although loans from Platonic, Aristotelian and Stoic terminology are considerable, Augustine differs from his predecessors by basing his linguistic investigations on the notion of the sign. Neither Aristotle nor the Stoics had clearly defined or distinguished the sign, $\sigma\eta\mu\epsilon\iota o\nu$ or $\sigma\eta\mu\alpha\iota\nu\omega\nu$, from, say, the symbol, $\sigma\upsilon\mu\beta o\lambda o\nu$ (Maieru 1981: 54-55). Augustine, however, yields a precise definition of the sign and makes it the starting point for his biblical exegesis. In order to present the right interpretation of the Trinity and the Incarnation Augustine was led to a new kind of semiotics, focusing on the *verbum*, the word, and furthermore adding psychological and social aspects to the study of language.

This is seen in *De Magistro* (389), a dialogue written a few years after Augustine's conversion; Augustine and his interlocutor, Adeodatus, discuss the possibilities of knowledge and of communicating knowledge, which of course was necessary for the future education of the wise Christian. Thus the first statement of the text is that the purpose of language is either to teach or to learn. The discussions in this dialogue can thus be understood as an introduction to the encyclopedic, Christian teaching that Augustine lays out in his later works. Two theses seem to structure the dialogue: the first claiming that we only reach knowledge of *res* through *signa*, especially linguistic signs, the second, introduced rather abruptly by Augustine (§38, Parodi 1996: 132), claiming that signs provide no knowledge at all and that we only understand signs, if we already possess an inner knowledge that we only have to recall. The concept of the interior master thus replaces the master of the exterior signs. At first sight semiotics seem to be rejected, but it is more correct to say that a certain non-dynamic semiotics is being refused, signs in the first part of the dialogue being understood simply as substitutions of things (Parodi 1996: 50):

---

[2] There are other important aspects of Medieval iconicity, e.g. discussions of the sacraments and of analogy, but surveying the examples of iconic signs and some implications of the importance of Trinitarian theology for semiotics is enough for one article...

Aug. Constat ergo inter nos verba signa esse.

Ad. Constat.

Aug. Quid? signum nisi aliquid significet, potest esse signum?

Ad. Non potest.

Aug. Quot verba sunt in hoc versu: Si nihil ex tanta superis placet urbe relinqui?

Ad. Octo.

Aug. Octo ergo signa sunt.

Ad. Ita est.[3]

However, the eight words of the quotation fra Vergil (Eneide 2, 659) cannot all be signs, as Adeodatus later concludes, since they do not all substitute things. But *nihil*, nothing, is in fact a kind of sign, designating a certain disposition of the mind (*affectio animi*, Parodi 1996: 52), explains Augustine. The same goes for the preposition *ex*; words like these refer to other signs in order to signify and do not lead to *res*, and this denotative function is what Agustine is trying to define.

Signs are double, they have a sensible phonetic aspect and an element of mental signification; furthermore, they have to be interpreted by a human subject. The semiosis is thus a *trinal* process, an important discovery in the history of semiotics. The borderline between signs and things is vague; everything can function as a sign, that is, signify something other than itself. The most important signs are linguistic signs, pertaining to the auditory sense, whereas visible signs (e.g., gestures, but also written words, Parodi 1996: 62) are of minor importance. Gestures or other visible signs, we would say indexical and iconic signs, do not lead more directly to the *res* than words; a fine example of this is that it is possible to show the meaning of the word *ambulare*, to walk, by the act of walking, but it is not possible to do so if one is asked while walking. One can walk faster, but that does not really give an understanding of the word (Parodi 1996: 58). Signs, and most evidently verbal signs, are arbitrary, but due to social conventions they can be decoded; thus the *verbum*, word, is equalized with *nomen*, name, (the argument being that they signify each other reciprocally) which is linked to the symbolic and to the treaty.

Augustine is the first to distinguish between an object language and a metalanguage (Parodi 1996: 27 and 118): some signs are signs for signs, as language, others for things that are not signs (acts, events, unintentional gestures, cf. Parodi 1996: 62).

---

[3] 'Aug: We agree on the fact that words are signs. Ad.: Yes. Aug.: Is it then possible that the sign is a sign if it does not signify something? Ad.: No. Aug.: How many words are there in this verse: *Si nihil ex tanta superis placet urbe relinqui*? Ad.: Eight. Aug.: Consequently there are eight signs. Ad.: So it is.'

The discussion of the first category is rather obscure. One important point is that although *res* and the truth are logically superior to the signs used to signify them, knowledge of signs is in no way inferior to knowledge of things (Parodi 1996: 112); the difference between *caenum*, dirt, and *caelum*, heaven, is just one letter, although they signify two immensely different things. Still, as signs they are of equal value. Augustine seems to have discovered the Hjelmslevan commutation test, implying that signification is produced in language by internal distinctions. This disquieting discovery may be the cause of the surprising "conversion" in §38 (but anticipated in the preceding paragraphs) where Augustine teaches (not without convincing protests from Adeodatus) that it is impossible to learn anything by means of language alone: the signification of words depends on the context in which they are being used and, furthermore, it is not possible to understand verbal signs without an inner knowledge of the truth (- *dixi vim verbi, id est significationem, quae latet in sono, re ipsa, quae significatur, cognita discimus, quam illam tali significatione percipimus* (Parodi 1996: 128).[4]

Words are ambigous, and only the "inner master" can escape the infinite process of signification, having the Christian faith that makes knowledge and communication possible. The dialogue seems to end in this paradox: all signs must be interpreted, an act that presupposes a knowledge that partly has been acquired by the means of signs, partly by visions. The memory of a divine wisdom is the *sine qua non* for all knowledge including the art of semiotics. This interior light makes it possible to recall copies, images, of the *res. Ergo ne hunc quidem doceo vera dicens vera intuentem; docetur enim non verbis meis, sed ipsis rebus deo intus pandente manifestis; itaque de his etiam interrogatus respondere posset* (Parodi 1996: 136).[5]

The dialogue is closed by Augustine putting a final emphasis on the utility of language, albeit inferior to inner visions, for the Christian wise. *De Magistro* is an open work, where the groundwork for the Augustinian semiotics is laid, and it shows the character of the semiotic questions raised by Augustine in a platonic, negative dialogue. Later, in *De Doctrina Christiana* and *De Trinitate*, his semiotics become systematic and fully integrated with dogmatics. Thus the first of the four

---

[4] 'I have said that we learn the power of a word, i.e. the signification, that is hidden in the sound after having acquired knowledge of the thing, that it signifies, rather than we acquire knowledge of the thing through the signification.'

[5] 'Although I say true things, I am only able to teach the one who sees things; he learns not through my words, but only through things that have been made manifest by the interior divine revealer; that is why he would be able to answer if he were asked about these things' (Parodi 1996: 136).

books of *De Doctrina Christiana* contains the dogmatic and moral truths that have to be uncovered as the result of the exegesis. The rules of interpretation, regulated by these truths, are put forth in the following books and were highly influential for centuries, since *De Doctrina Christiana* was the first and for a long time the only manual of biblical exegesis.

In book I, *De rebus investigandis in Scriptura*, it is established that every knowledge has as its object either things or signs and that things can be studied only through signs: *Omnis doctrina vel rerum est vel signorum, sed res per signa discuntur* (*De Doctr.* 1949: 182). Things like wood and stones are not used to signify something else, as signs are. It is, however, possible to study things and signs separately if one remembers these conditions, as it is possible to put forth the dogmatic truths that predetermine interpretation of the Scripture, remembering that God is beyond human language. The thoughts of God are to be found in Scripture, although it is composed by several human beings; hence the need for knowing the biblical languages and basic philological skills. Signs of the wisdom of the ineffable God are everywhere and teach in the same way as medicin cures, by using similarity and contrast (an example of similarity: mortality is cured by the death of Christ, *De doctr.* 1949: 196).

This leads to the definition of the sign (book II, *De signis interpretandis in Scriptura*): *Signum enim est res, praeter speciem quam ingerit sensibus, aliud aliquid ex se faciens in cogitationem venire.*[6] Many of the examples of signs that follow are often reproduced later on: traces show that an animal has passed, smoke that there is fire, the sounding war trumpet tell the soldiers what to do. Some of these are natural, other are intentional signs, *signa naturalia* or *signa data*. The natural signs are mostly indices (traces, smoke, *De doctr.* 1949: 238), it seems; the *signa data* belong to all senses, but most important are verbal signs, followed by visual signs. The gestures of actors and military signs are visual signs, almost visible words, says Augustine (*De Doctr.* 1949: 242), or hypo-icons in the terminology of Peirce (1965: 157). As in *De Magistro*, it is pointed out that letters have an iconic element intended to fix the meaning of the flowing verbal signs. Another interesting distinction is the one between *signa propria* and *signa translata*, literal and figural signs: the first kind designates the things intended, whereas the last designates some-thing else. Thus *bos*, ox, as a proper sign designates a certain animal, but in the figural sense one of the evangelists (*De Doctr.* 1949: 258).

Apparently there is also an iconic element implicit in the linguistic sign: *Appetunt tamen omnes quandam similitudinem in significando, ut ipsa signa, in quantum possunt, rebus quae significantur similia sint. Sed quia multis modis simile aliquid alicui potest esse, non constant*

---

[6] 'A sign is a thing that, apart from presenting a form to the senses, lets something else coming from itself enter the faculty of thought' (*De Doctr.* 1949: 238).

talia signa inter homines, nisi consensus accedat.[7] Iconic signs, statues, paintings or the figurative fictions of the poets, produce easily understandable distinctions that are necessary for the functions of human society. Again, iconic signs are efficient but much simpler and less precise than verbal signs (as actually walking in order to show the meaning of 'walking' in *De Magistro*) and of course potentially dangerous, offering the senses pleasure.

Finally in the *De Trinitate*, Augustine accomplishes his semiotics, understanding everything in the world as traces of the Creator, and the human capacity for decoding these signs as an imperfect imprint of the Trinity in the soul (*De Trinitate*, Vol. I, 1955: 498; man is, after all, created in the image of God, Gen. 1.26). The interpretation of signs is not infinite; there is one last, ineffable *res* that does not signify something other than itself and to which all signs refer. The images of the things that are recalled in the intellect, as proposed in *De Doctrina Christiana*, are considered as being ultimately *imagines Dei*, images of God. Christ is the perfect word, *incommutabilis*, unchangeable, in contrast to human language and other human signs. This being the case, humans can only understand the images of God through other images; Augustine quotes Paul: *In illa enim Trinitate summa origo est rerum omnium, et perfectissima pulchritudo, et beatissima delectatio. Itaque illa tria, et ad se invicem determinari videntur, et in se infinita sunt. (...) Qui videt hoc vel ex parte, vel per speculum et in aenigmate (I. Cor. XIII, 12), gaudeat cognoscens Deum -.*[8] The so called universal symbolism, characteristic of the Middle Ages, derives from Augustine and his extensive use of the words from Paul, which are to be quoted again and again, including the conclusion: at the end of time we shall see face to face (*facie ad faciem*), without intermediaries.

Until then, the human soul, the imperfect image of God, may lead to an interior, immaterial language (the word in the heart, *verbum in corde*), through a dialectic of triadic cognition. The concepts of mind, love and knowledge (*mens, amor, notitia*) combine into a triad whereby the soul recognizes itself. The soul, however, tends to forget itself and has to seek itself continually; it does so because of its memory

---

[7] 'Everybody seeks a certain similarity in signifying in order that the signs may be as similar as possible to the things they signify. But since something can be similar to something else in many ways, such signs are only be established if there is consent on their meaning' (*De Doctr.* 1949: 300).

[8] 'For in that Trinity is the supreme source of all things, and the most perfect beauty, and the most blessed delight. Those three, therefore, both seem to be mutually determined to each other, and are in themselves infinite. (...) Let him who sees this, whether in part, or 'through a glass and in an enigma', rejoice in knowing God — ' (*De Trinitate*, Vol. I, 1955: 498-500). All translations from *De Trinitate* by Haddan and Shedd (1988).

of itself being whole and because of a will to know itself and the outer world. Another triad emerges: memory, will and understanding (*memoria, voluntas, intelligentia*). Like the theological Trinity, the parts are equal and one substance.

Spontaneous perception by the senses of exterior things consists of a vision that by an act of will is directed at an object (a very imperfect triad, *res, voluntas, visio,* since the parts are not the same substance). By an act of will the exterior experience can be recalled as a memory to the inner vision, all in all creating a succession of triads (this and the following models are mine):

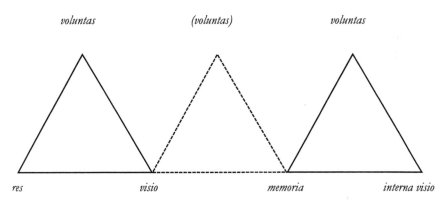

Fig. 1.

A third intermediary triad seems to be presupposed, as indicated in the model. These triads, however, are connected to sensibility and cannot be an image of God; this has to be searched for in that part of the soul which is directed towards the exterior world. This function of the soul is called *scientia*, in contrast to the *sapientia* that is the activity of the soul towards the eternal. The first triad of faith emerges, a triad that no longer presupposes the external world as the object for love:

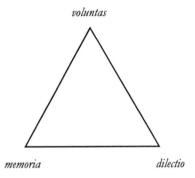

voluntas

memoria   *dilectio*

Fig. 2.

But this triad is temporal, imperfect in other words, since faith will cease to exist when we see "facie ad faciem". Only in the eternal soul is the image of God to be found; when the soul contemplates itself the highest trinity takes form:

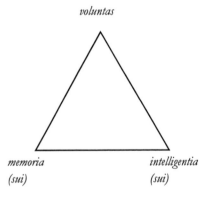

voluntas

memoria   *intelligentia*
(sui)   *(sui)*

Fig. 3.

In the soul's contemplation of itself the highest trinity emerges, and in this way we may understand the word: *Per hoc quando ad se ipsam cogitatione convertitur fit trinitas in qua iam et verbum possit intelligi: formatur quippe ex ipsa cogitatione, voluntate utrumque jungente. Ibi ergo magis agnoscenda est imago quam quaerimus.*[9] This contemplation is naturally only an image of God insofar as the soul recognizes that everything is created by God. Thus the relation to God is essential for the understanding of the Trinity. No intellectuel comprehension without faith...

In this last triad a word comes from the memory, a *verbum* which is the identity of the soul to itself. Hence it is analogous to the Verbum of the Gospel of John which sprang from the Father and became the Son without losing any of its immortality. This analogy is the very basis of Augustine's theory of the inner word (*verbum in corde*) which is an imperfect, of course, image of the divine Word. It is a precondition for the recognition of any object that an inner word is said before any spoken, or even intended, sound. Only when the inner word has to be actually pronounced, must it assume a sign, a sound or a gesture.

This interior word is an image of God, since it becomes corporal without being transformed to matter; the incarnation can thus be interpreted as a sort of emanation. Of course the inner word is just a reflection of the divine word, it can be false, it is unstable and mortal; hence, it is only possible for the soul to contemplate itself "per speculum et in aenigmate".

II   Roger Bacon

From Augustine we leap to the late Middle Ages, to the *De Signis* (ca. 1267) of Roger Bacon. This text begins with definitions and a classification of signs; the first sentence tells us that the sign belongs to the category of relations and says something about the thing it signifies. Everything may function as a sign: voices, the barrel hoop (the *circulus vini,* at last!) or an action, as long as it represents something other than itself and allows us to infer something about the signified. Signs are not identical to the signified things, but they add something to the thing in order to represent it.

A proper definition follows i § 2: *Signum autem est illud quod oblatum sensui vel intellectui aliquid designat ipsi intellectui, quoniam non omne signum offertur sensui ut vulgata descriptio signi supponit, sed aliquod soli intellectui offertur, testante Aristotele, qui dicit passiones animae esse signa rerum quae passiones sunt habitus ipsi et species rerum existentes apud intellectum, et*

---

[9] 'And hence, when it is turned to itself by thought, there arises a trinity, in which now at length we can discern also a word; since it is formed from thought itself, will uniting both. Here, then, we may recognize, more than we have hitherto done, the image of which we are in search.'

ideo soli intellectui offerentur, ita ut repraesentant intellectui ipsas res extra.[10] This definition emphasizes the relation between signs and the things outside the intellect and shows how Bacon shifts from an intensional to an extensional semiotics. As Eco and Marmo (1989: 22) put it: 'With Bacon the problem of the relation between words and things shifts totally. Thus the term *significatio*, which up until then had served to indicate the relation betweeen words and definitions or concepts (a purely *intensional* one), is used by Bacon to indicate the relation of reference (*extension*) between words and things or states of the world. The *vox* is *significativa rei extra animam*.' This explains why Bacon classifies the signs in an apparently non homogeneous way. He distinguishes between *signa naturalia* and *signa ordinata ab anima*, natural and intentional signs; the natural signs include three groups:

1.1 signs that allow us to draw certain or probable conclusions about the presence, past and future; so the crow of the cock tells us the hour of the night, the fact that a woman has milk tells us that she has given birth, etc.

1.2 signs that by a conformity and similarity to the signified thing make this knowable, as images and paintings.

1.3 signs that allow us to know their causes with absolute certainty, as traces tell us that a living being has passed and smoke that there is a fire.

Iconic signs are considered as natural; Bacon seems either to have forgotten or not to accept the Augustinian point of view, underlining the conventionality of the idea of similarity. But we do meet iconic signs in the second category as well, among the intentional signs:

2.1 deliberate and conventional signs like words, the barrel hoop and things for sale exposed in windows.

2.2 intentional signs that function "naturaliter", that is, spontaneously and involuntary, as the sighing of the sick and the voices of wild animals. The interjection is said to fall between 2.1 and 2.2.

Iconic signs, as well as animal language, appear in both categories; one of the reasons for this is that *natura* is used in four different meanings, as Bacon points out himself (§14), the two most important ones, however, being *natura* meaning *virtus*

---

[10] 'A sign is something which, after being offered to the senses or the intellect, designates something for the intellect, since not every sign is offered to the senses, as the common description of the sign presupposes. Some signs are offered only to the intellect, as Aristotle confirms saying that the passions of the soul are signs of things, and these passions are the very appearance and the forms of things, as they exist in the intellect, and so they are offered solely to the intellect in order to represent the very things outside to the intellect.'

agens (that goes for the category of natural signs) and in the sense of *principium operationis* (the intentional signs that function "naturaliter").

Another reason is the shift from intensional to extensional semiotics: the emphasis on the word-thing relation overshadows such problems as that of iconicity which is relegated to psychology. It is interesting, though, that Bacon maintains that signs represent something other than themselves by adding something to the things or passions signified — except for images, paintings, the external shape of colours, sounds, etc. (1.2) which designate without adding something but by imitating certain real forms existing in the mind of the artist. This intermediary instance, the mind, apparently mirrors forms of things or states of the world; it is, however, not treated further.

In 2.1 there appear again what we would term indexical or iconic signs: the barrel hoop outside the taverna, and bread and other forms of merchandise exhibited in the windows of shops, all classified as conventional signs on the same level as language because of Bacon's wish to show that they all designate something outside the mind. He does, however, distinguish between language and things when he says that the merchandise not only represent other things, but also themselves: — *res expositae venditionis in fenestris venditorum positae pro signis, non solum ad repraesentandum alia, sed se ipsa, ut panis in fenestra et cetera comestibilia* — (§7).[11] Apparently Roger Bacon's conclusion is that iconic signs function in two ways, by imitating existing real forms and thus independent of conventional forms or codes, or as conventional signs representing themselves and at the same time something else. The last group thus includes both iconic and indexical signs and not the least mixtures of them.

III The Modistae

Roger Bacon is often referred to as premodist because he belongs to the tradition of speculative grammar (as opposed to school grammar, the grammatica of the *artes liberales*) which culminates in the modistic theory, starting about 1270 and brought to an end by the *Destructiones Modorum Significandi* of Johannes Aurifaber about 1330. Speculative grammar was based on the theory of a universal grammar underlying the different actual languages, and this grammar was regarded as a stable structure representing an autonomous area of research in accordance with the new Aristoteli

---

[11] ' — things exposed for sale in shop windows are posed as signs, not only in order to represent something else, but also themselves, as for example the bread in the window and other eatable things — .'

an criteria introduced in the 12th century.

One finds this notion for example in the *Greek Grammar* of Bacon: — *grammatica una et eadem est secundum substanciam in omnibus linguis* —, 'grammar is one and the same according to substance in all languages' (Nolan 1902: 27). The idea of an universal, grammatical structure is not, however, turned into a coherent theory before the first generation of the modistae uses the concept of *modi significandi*, modes of signifying — the most important term in medieval linguistics — for analyzing it. Phonetic aspects were considered irrelevant, obviously differing in different languages, and semantic aspects became less important, as it became clear that a formal, functionalistic approach was the best way to describe the presupposed universal structure. Certain general traits of the signifying process necessary for the constitution of the grammatical categories were investigated; the most important of these were the relations to the *word classes*. The eight word classes — inherited from Priscianus — are thus central in modistic theory which, however, also includes a syntactical part on relational concepts. A main distinction of the parts of speech is the one between words which signify stable and immutable essences (that signify *per modum habitus et quietis*, through the mode of state and rest) and words that signify changing states (*per modum fieri et motus*, through the mode of becoming and motion).[12]

The modistae analyze the word as consisting of an element of expression, *vox* (literally a *voice sound*), and two levels of signification; one regarding the lexical meaning, the other the general traits, the *modi significandi* that determine the syntactic relations. The ancient notion of *impositio*, the application of a name to a thing, is interpreted as a deliberate coupling of expression and meaning that takes place in a twofold act: by the first application the expression, *vox*, is connected to a specific, lexical meaning (*dictio*); by the second application the words receive some general meanings or *modi significandi* that determine the grammatical categories of the word, most important its relation to a word class.

It is not discussed how the first naming, *impositio*, is possible or what exactly happens in this act. Generally the modistae define the relation between the element of expression, *vox*, and the object referred to as *ratio significandi*, and it is considered as the form (the Aristotelian form-matter distinction is applied to the whole theory of speculative grammar by the modistae) which transforms the element of expression, *vox*, into a *dictio*. The term *dictio* is usually translated by J. Pinborg (e.g. in Sigerus de Cortraco: xxii) as "lexeme"; C. Marmo, however, prefers "sign function" (as defined by L. Hjelmslev; Marmo 1994: 127) due to his interpretation of modistic

---

[12] This is based on a philosophical distinction from Averroes, as pointed out by Pinborg in the introduction to Siger de Courtrai (Sigerus de Cortraco: xxi).

grammar as a semiotic theory. I shall comment on this below; first we must note the fact that the essential dynamics of the *ratio significandi* that turns the expressive element into a *dictio*, as well as the *ratio consignificandi* of the second imposition that turns the sign function into a part of speech, is not satisfactorily explained. This must be due to another crux of the theory, namely, the lacking explanation of the relation between the three different levels: the *modi essendi, modi intelligendi* and the *modi significandi*, the modes of being, understanding and signifying.

These levels of modes are not identical with the Aristotelian triad (consisting of words, concepts and things) from *Perihermeneias*, but are rather a transformation of this into a dynamic process of signification. The modistae are realists and take it for granted that there is an objective structure that allows the transformation of *modi essendi* into *modi intelligendi* and finally into *modi significandi*; but they do not all explain this in the same way. According to the *De Modis Significandi* by Martinus de Dacia, these levels are simply identical: *Circa secundum notandum quod modi essendi et modi intelligendi et modi significandi sunt idem penitus quod patet ex dictis, differunt tamen accidentaliter.*[13]

This is the conclusion of Martinus' description of the way in which a thing is apprehended by the intellect to become a concept to which the mind, in order to communicate this concept to another, applicates an expression. The expression, *vox*, is a sign, and here we meet the barrel hoop again:

Ulterius intellectus volens alii conceptum suum significare, rei intellectae vocem imponit, ut eius conceptus scilicet res intellecta per vocem tamquam per signum exprimatur. Unde sicut tabernarius vinum significat per circulum, eodem modo intellectus rem intellectam exprimit sive significat per vocem, et post copulationem sive impositionem vocis ipsa res dicitur res significata, et omnes proprietates rei quae prius dicebantur modi essendi rei extra et modi intelligendi rei intellectae, iam dicuntur modi significandi.[14]

---

[13] 'As for the second question it must be noted that the modes of being, the modes of understanding and the modes of signifying on the whole are the same, as is obvious from what has been said above, although they differ accidentally.'

[14] (Martinus 1971: 5). 'As the intellect finally wants to signify its concept for another it applies an expression element to the thing understood in order to let the concept, or the thing understood, be expressed by the expression element, as if by a sign. For, as the innkeeper signifies the wine by the barrel hoop, in the same way the intellect expresses the thing understood or signifies it by the expression element, and after the cobling or the application of the expression element the thing itself is called the thing signified, and all the properties of the thing that before were called modes of being of the thing outside and modes of understanding of the thing understood, are now called modes of signifying.'

The modistae do not classify signs as for example Roger Bacon does, but some of the well known examples of signs show up again.[15] Apparently they have been incorporated in the theoretical texture; Martinus thus uses the classical example of an indexical-iconic sign to emphasize the close connection between language and things. This may be taken as proof for the hypothesis of C. Marmo: that the modistae accept the semiotics of the premodists since they do not argue explicitly against it.

The expressive element is certainly a sign of the concept and the thing, whereas the three modes are simply identical, not signs for one another, still according to Martinus:

> *Nec se habet modus significandi ad modum intelligendi et essendi sicut signum ad significatum ut quidam dicunt. Nam sicut vinum significatum per circulum non est signum vini in cellario, sed substantia circuli, eodem modo modus significandi non est signum modi intelligendi et modi essendi, cum nihil possit esse signum sui ipsius, quare penitus sunt idem, et ita unum non erit signum alterius, sed eorum signum est vox, quia vox significat rem et consignificat proprietates rei.* (Martinus 1961: 6-7).[16]

The barrel hoop is regarded here as a conventional sign that signifies something other, not itself, and the difference implied by the sign cannot describe the relation of the three levels of modes. The *circulus* is of course also used in this general sense of *sign* in the previous quotation (the *vox* as a sign of something other than itself); my interpretation of it as an iconical-indexical sign was in fact due to my extratextual knowledge of the classifications of Bacon. But when Martinus uses this and not one of the other classical examples it is hard not to explain it by his ultra (naive, some would say) realism.

The barrel hoop thus seemed to be used first as a sign that is similar or close to

---

[15] Nods and other gestures are mentioned as signs that the grammarian has to consider, although verbal language is the most important field of investigation (cf. Martinus 1961: 7). Apparently for the same reason as in Augustine: the verbal sign is a more efficient sign, *habilius signum*.

[16] 'And the mode of signifying does not hold the same relation to the mode of understanding and being as the sign to the signified, as some claim. For as it is not the wine signified by the barrel hoop that is the sign of the wine in the cellar, but the substance of the barrel hoop, in the same way the mode of signifying is not a sign of the mode of understanding and being, since nothing can be a sign of itself, because the modes are wholly the same, and thus one of them cannot be a sign of the other, but the expression element is a sign of them, because the expression element signifies the thing and consignifies its properties.'

its signified, later on as a symbolic sign, functioning in the same way as a verbal sign — in other words first to point to things, next to the character of the sign. So the use of the barrel hoop anticipates the solution of Boethius de Dacia[17], who splits the mode of signifying into an active and a passive mode, the former being the properties of the words and the latter the properties of things as conceived and signified. This is only an apparent solution and it may lead to an infinit series of modi, as pointed out by, for example, Pinborg:

> The difficulties of this explanation are the same as those which any picture-theory of cognition encounters, namely, how can properties of spoken words resemble modes of the intellect and through them properties of external objects?.....There is no tertium comparationis. (Sigerus 1977: xxvii)

The modes of being are never defined *an sich*, because they were invented as a counterpart to the modes of signifying.

Siger of Courtrai later uses the already quoted example of the red cloth (*pannus rubeus*, cf. supra), as an illustration of the two modes — the active and the passive — of signifying:

> *Modum autem signandi sequitur modus significandi sicut rem sequitur modus rei, qui etiam duplex est ob causam prius dictam. Modus autem significandi activus est ratio quaedam concessa voci ab intellectu secundum quod talis vox talem modum essendi significat. Modus autem significandi passivus est ipse modus essendi per vocem, mediante modo significandi activo, significatus, seu modus significandi relatus ad modum essendi; ita quod sicut vox, mediante modo significandi, significat ipsam rem, sic, mediante modo significandi activo significat modum essendi seu proprietatem rei, sicut pannus rubeus pendens ante tabernam: unde pannus significat vinum, unde rubeus, rubedinem vini* (Sigerus 1977: 2).[18]

---

[17] The *Modi Significandi* by Boethius most likely is written before Martinus' text, but the solution of Boethius is followed by the next generation of modistae.

[18] 'The mode of signifying follows the denoting mode like the mode of the thing follows the thing, and it is double of the reason already spoken of. The active mode of signifying is a procedure given to the voice sound by the intellect, according to which a given voice sound signifies a given mode of being. The passive mode of signifying is the mode of being itself signified through the voice sound, having the active mode as its medium, or the mode of signifying related to the mode of being ; thus in the same way as the voice sound, having the mode of signifying as its medium, signifies the thing itself, so it, having the active mode of signifying as its medium, signifies the mode of being or the property of the thing, as does the red cloth in front of the tavern: as cloth it signifies the wine, as red it signifies the redness of the wine.'

The barrel hoop is replaced by the red cloth in Siger's attempt to explain the relation of the three levels, because the cloth exhibits the same doubleness as the mode of signifying: it is at the same time symbolic and iconic (the mode of signifying is a sign of the thing, the active mode in particular is an iconic sign of a property of the thing). The active mode of signifying is placed in the intellect by Siger, and that raises another problem, i.d. how does it differ from the mode of understanding? Siger's "solution" seems to be another example of what might be termed as the rhetorics of realism.

The linguistic theory of the modistae was ambitious: their aim was to account for how physical words, meanings, and the world of objects were linked together (cf. Pinborg in Sigerus 1977: xxxiv). Although the modistic theory is restricted by the links to traditional grammar and the Latin language, this broad view of grammar — something other than logic — is of great interest today as well, as cognitive grammar makes similar claims. Hunting for statements on iconicity, hoping to approach a *tertium comparationis*, we therefore proceed to the interjection that according to Roger Bacon was semi-iconical. Martinus, however, does not find the interjection to be a more "immediate" linguistic expression: the interjection accompanies a verb expressing a fact that the speaker is impressed by. The interjection expresses the presence of this impression, or passion, in the speaker (Martinus 1961: 83-85) and many different kinds of expressions can work as interjections without necessarily having been fixed in an imposition. Boethius does not essentially depart from this but hints at an immediateness of the linguistic reaction to the passion in the soul:

Dicitur etiam interiectio significare tales affectiones mentis voce incognita, quia cum subito ex aliqua interiori causa vel exteriori occupat hominem timor vehemens vel admiratio vel etiam gaudium, subito homo sine deliberatione prorumpit in has voces has affectiones animi significantes dicendo 'attat' vel 'papae' acuendo ultimam syllabam (Boethius 1969: 296).[19]

But soon after, Boethius concludes that nothing can be expressed without having first been apprended by the intellect (Boethius ibid., cf. Marmo 1994: 253).

Thus the modistic picture-theory of cognition does not presuppose any verbal

---

[19] 'It is claimed that the interjection signifies these conditions of the mind with an unknown vocal expression because when suddenly due to some interior or exterior reason fear or admiration or even joy seizes a man, then he suddenly without further deliberation breaks out into such expressions that signify these conditions, saying *attat* or *papae* stressing the last syllable.'

mimicry of things. Onomatopoetics is only a parenthesis hinted at in this linguistic theory. In literature, especially poetry, these aspects of language are central in modern as well as in medieval poetry, as we will soon see in the case of Dante. There might, however, be other aesthetic criteria involved in the modistic grammar: I am thinking of the syntactic terms *congruitas* and *perfectio*. In order to obtain *congruitas*, well-formedness, certain rules must be followed: formally case, genus, number and person must correspond in an construction to be *congruus*, and semantically the construction must consist of words that make it understandable, make sense. The *perfectio* of a construction is defined as efficiency — it consists of the capacity to create in the mind of the listener a complex meaning (as Marmo puts it, 1994: 404). Formally the minimal, perfect construction consists of noun and verb, *suppositum* and *appositum*. According to the modistae, *congruitas* is a presupposition for perfection: well-formedness precedes the use of language for communication. This is a more rigid conception than that of the premodists, who considered figurative constructions, without semantic congruence, as ranking higher than plain language with an obvious literal sense (cf. Marmo 1994: 406). The modistic rigidness is an effect of their indifference to the context when dealing with the interpretation of verbal signs.

Well-formedness consists of the right proportions according to Martinus: *Primitus est notandum quod congruitas in grammatica non est aliud quam passio grammaticae ex proportione seu conformitate modorum significandi causata* (Martinus 1961: 108).[20] The words of a construction may have many different modes of signifying some of which are identical, others differing. A balanced distribution of these modes — proportion always means the right proportion — is the necessary condition for *congruitas*. According to Marmo (1994: 411), the generations after Martinus define proportion more precisely: of the two elements of a construction the dependent one must necessarily be "fullfilled" by a *modus significandi* in the *terminans*, the governing element, e.g. *homo albus,*where the *modus adjacentis* of the latter has the *modus habitus* of the former as its counterpart. This fits completely into the general medieval longing for harmoni and symmetry — a cosmological aesthetics to be applied to every detail of the universe, also to grammar, as confirmed by Martinus in his definition of *perfectio*:

> *Unde oratio dicitur perfecta, quando anima quiescat super ipsam. Sed si proferatur suppositum solum ut* homo vel homo albus *vel dicendo* si Socrates currit, *fluctuat anima et vacillat et non quiescit, quia suppositum est nullius termini determinanti in hac oratione. Licet enim sit per se stans absolute, tamen per comparationem ad animam, ut*

---

[20] 'First we must note that congruence in grammar is caused by nothing other than a grammatical phenomenon of proportion and conformity.'

anima super aliquod perfectum quiescat, debet habere appositum, ut per ipsum finitetur et quiescat anima super orationem (Martinus 1961: 114).[21]

IV Dante Alighieri

Dante does not want to let the soul of his reader rest upon well-formed constructions of his — or rather he wants to provoke his reader and at the same time let him experience cosmological harmony in his poetry. His writings, thus, are a long investigation of the emergence of poetical language and its effects upon the reader. One might say that Dante focuses on the transformation of a universal deep structure into a material, communicative language. To put it in the terms of the critics: in the allegorical frame of universal symbolism Dante investigates the possibilities of the phonetical material and its ethical potentials. It is possible to find quite a few general statements on language and they are consistent from the perspective of Dante's poetics, though not following any specific tradition.

Dante defines the linguistic sign in his poetics of the poetical vernacular, *De Vulgari Eloquentia* I, 3: *Hoc equidem signum est subiectum nobile de quo loquimur: nam sensuale quid est in quantum sonus est; rationale vero in quantum aliquid significare videtur ad placitum* (DVE 1978: 40).[22] Dante here clearly follows Augustine, and the distinction recalls the distinction natural / artificial previously made by Dante in DVE I, 1. Thus the sign is defined as sensual-natural and rational-conventional (as noted by Mengaldo, DVE 1978: 41) and since natural is the quality that distinguishes the vernacular from Latin, it is hardly surprising that the poetics of DVE is predominently a poetics of sound.

Different sounds are commented upon in Dante's survey of the Italian dialects and the nomination of the Bolognese dialect as the most beautiful dialect (though not to be identified as the utopian noble vernacular, the *vulgare illustre*) reveals something about the aesthetic norms of this text: *Si ergo Bononienses utrinque accipiunt, ut*

---

[21] 'Hence a construction is called perfect when the mind comes to rest upon it. But if only a subject is pronounced e.g. *man* or *white man* or the expression *if Socrates runs* then the mind fluctuates and vacillates and does not come to rest, since the subject does not belong to a determining term in this construction. It is possible for it to stand alone, yet as far as the mind is concerned that it might come to rest upon something perfect, it must have a predicate so that it finishes itself, and the mind might come to rest upon the construction.'

[22] 'This sign is the noble subject of our discourse: for in as far as it is sound it is rational, and in as far it signifies something that you want to signify, it is rational.'

dictum est, rationabile videtur esse quod eorum locutio per commixtionem oppositorum ut dictum est ad laudabilem suavitatem remaneat temperata: quod procul dubio nostro iudicio sic esse censemus (DVE 1978: 122).[23] The mixture of soft, melodious and harsh sounds provide the necessary dynamics of Dante's poetical, ideal Italian and lets it come alive before the eyes of the reader of Dante's poems. No doubt that Dante's interest in the linguistic surface — which could not be neglected by a vernacular poet — made him aware of the historicity of language, a consciousness shared by very few others, among whom Roger Bacon. The mutability of languages after Babel, usually lamented upon as the loss of the perfect Adamic language, is in *De Vulgari Eloquentia* treated as a deplorable loss due to the sinful character of humans, but also as the possibility for the artistic creation of a new ideal language, one that is both historic-material and universal.

In the second book of DVE (the beginning of the instructive part of the poetics, left unfinished after a few pages), sounds are classified after supposedly inherent qualities: some are childish, some are feminine, some masculine; some are rustic, some urban. This may seem in conflict with the view of language as conventional (*ad placitum*), but Dante needs naive realism in order to account for the significance in poetry of usually overheard verbal phenomenons. Of the urban words some are combed, some slippery, and some are hairy, some bristling (*pexa - lubrica, yrsuta - reburra*, DVE 1978: 190), and the combed and the hairy ones are the grandiose words suited for the noble vernacular. The metaphors of cloth and hair are common in medieval poetics and rhetoric (cf. *Poetria Nova* by G. de Vinsauf 1967: 83; for other references se Mengaldo ad loc.). Thus the cloth, the *pannus* or rather *panni* we meet in Dante (e.g. in *Al poco giorno e al gran cerchio d'ombra*, v. 36, one of the *rime petrose* from 1296) probably have nothing to do with the sign classifications of the philosophers. It is, however, obvious that Dante does not accept the rhetorical dichotomy of content and form, which reduces language to the clothing of thoughts, but constantly emphasizes the importance of the "form" in the signifying process. The *io* of Dante's poems often refers to the trembling of his voice, which is a topos in earlier love poetry, related to the psychological state of the lover. In Dante it is metapoetical and is reinforced by sound patterns such as alliterations, by onomatopoetical words, and by unusual metrical patterns (cf. Roer 1996). One of

---

[23] 'If the bolognese receive from both parts, as it has been said, it seems reasonable that their language from the mixture of opposites in the way already spoken of results in a well tempered and praiseworthy sweetness: and in our judgement it is beyond doubt that this is the case.' The Bolognese dialect has the softness of the Imolese and the harshness of the Lombards, which Dante describes immediately before describing the bolognese dialect.

numerous examples from the *Divine Comedy* is the stuttering of the pilgrim when he meets the master poet Vergil, who in his answer echoes the trembling voice of the younger poet: *'Miserere di me' gridai a lui / 'qual che tu sii, od ombra od omo certo!' / Rispuosemi: 'Non omo, omo già fui,...'* (Inferno I, 65-67).[24] The elder poet converts the stuttering into an elaborate figure, an elliptic chiasm.

At the end of the long poem the pilgrim finally reaches the point from which the whole poem springs, like the Verbum of Augustine —i.d. the vision of the Trinity:

Ne la profonda e chiara sussistenza
de l'alto lume parvermi tre giri
di tre colori e d'una contenenza;
e l'un da l'altro come iri da iri
parea reflesso, e 'l terzo parea foco
che quinci e quindi igualmente si spiri.
Oh quanto è corto il dire e come fioco
al mio concetto! e questo, a quel ch'i' vidi,
è tanto, che non basta a dicer 'poco'.
O luce etterna che sola in te sidi,
sola t'intendi, e da te intelletta
e intendente te ami e arridi!
Quella circulazion che sì concetta
pareva in te come lume reflesso,
da li occhi miei alquanto circunspetta,
dentro da sé, del suo colore stesso,
mi parve pinta de la nostra effige:
per che 'l mio viso in lei era messo.[25]

---

[24] "'Have pity on me" I shouted to him, "whoever you are, shadowman or living man!" / He answered me: "I am not man, man I once was..."'

[25] 'Within the profound and shining subsistence of the lofty Light appeared to me three circles of three colors and one magnitude, and one seemed reflected by the other, as rainbow by rainbow, and the third seemed fire breathed forth equally from the one and the other. O how scant is speech, and how feeble to me conception! and this, to what I saw, is such that it is not enough to call it little. O Light Eternal, who alone abidest in Thyself, alone knowest Thyself, and, known to Thyself and knowing, lovest and smilest on Thyself! That circling which, thus begotten, appeared in Thee as reflected light, when my eyes had dwelt on it for a time, seemed to me depicted with our image within itself and in its color, wherefore my sight was entirely set upon it.' Paradiso XXXIII, 115-132. Translated by Singleton.

The Trinity is described as three circling circles — everything is active in God — of three colours and still in one form, as the dogma of the three persons in one prescribes. One, the second circle, seems reflected by the first (118-119), just as the second person of the Trinity, the Son, is begotten from the father. The third, i.d. the Holy Ghost, is made of fire, which refers to the love and the pentacostal verbal multiplicity (the tongues of fire in Cor.I, 12-13). Thus Dante does not differ essentially from the Trinitarian theology known from Aquinas and Augustine,[26] but it is striking how he emphasizes the materiality of the face said to be *painted* on the second circle (translated as *depicted* by Singleton) in v.131. This *our image* is the second person of the Trinity, Christ, the Verbum made flesh, and the mystery of how exactly mortal flesh can be part of the trinitarian God and how it fits into it is the main interest of the poet — and it is focused on in the rest of the poem (as noted by Singleton in his commentary, 1975: 583). According to Arbery (1989: 39) the painting of the human exterior of Christ is both apart from man and God, and Jesus is, in grammatological terms, the "supplement" both to God's divinity and to man's humanity — the addition, the substitute, the divinity, the intrusive sign. This "bad" writing on the perfect mathematical form of God (still according to Arbery) is however also by Dante considered as good writing: the possibility of imitating the eternal motions of the Trinity in the poem. The inner Word that Dante receives and understands in a flash (140-141) cannot exist as such in the soul, it is already a sign — and the possibility of this infinite progress, frightening for the theologian, is the promise of a never ending poem. Thus in the final verses of the comedy Dante the pilgrim is is left circling among the stars.

References

Augustine

De Brouwer, D. 1955. *La Trinité. Œuvres de Saint Augustin*. 2 vol. Paris.

Schaff, P. (Ed.). 1988. *A Select Library of the Nicene and Post-Nicene Fathers of the Christian Church. First Series*, Vol. III. Edinburgh and Michigan.

Parodi, M. 1996. *Sant'Agostino. Il Maestro*. Milano: BUR.

---

[26] Freccero (1993: 187-188) stresses that the interchangeability of theological and poetic coherence, characteristic of the Christian Middle Ages, is particularly apparent in Augustine. Freccero makes use of Kenneth Burke's term "logology", presupposing that theological principles are derivations from verbal systems: 'Divine Justice was like a poem with variable meter, death like phonemic silence, even God's relationship to the world was thought of as the embodiment of a speech act, the incarnation of a proferred word.'

Roger Bacon

Fredborg, K.M., Nielsen, L. & Pinborg, J. 1978. *An Unedited Part of Roger Bacon's "Opus Maius": De Signis. Traditio. Studies in Ancient and Medieval History, Thought, and Religion*, XXXIV: 74-136.

Nolan, E. & Hirsch, S. A. 1902. *The Greek Grammar of Roger Bacon and a fragment of his Hebrew Grammar*. Cambridge.

Modistae

Boethius de Dacia. 1969. *Boethii de Dacia Opera. Modi Significandi sive Quaestiones super Priscianum Maiorem*. Corpus Philosophorum Danicorum Medii Aevi IV, Pars I. J. Pinborg & H. Roos (Eds.). Copenhagen.

Martinus de Dacia. 1961. *Martini de Dacia Opera*. Corpus Philosophorum Danicorum Medii Aevi II. H. Roos (Ed.). Copenhagen.

Sigerus de Cortraco. 1977. *Summa Modorum Significandi Sophismata*. New edition by J. Pinborg. Amsterdam and Philadelphia.

Dante Alighieri

Dante. 1978. *De Vulgari Eloquentia*. In *Dante Alighieri Opere Minori*, Tomo II. A cura di P. V. Mengaldo. Milano-Napoli.

—. 1975. *Paradiso, Vol. I: Italian Text and Translation*. Transl. by C. S. Singleton. Bollingen Series LXXX. Princeton.

—. 1990. *Inferno*. A cura di N. Sapegno. Firenze. First Ed. 1955.

Geoffrey of Vinsauf

of Vinsauf, Geoffrey. 1967. *Poetria Nova of Geoffrey of Vinsauf*. Transl. by M.E. Nims, Toronto.

Modern Literature

Arbery, G. 1989. 'Adam's First Word and the Failure of Language in Paradiso XXXIII.' In *Sign, Sentence, Discourse*. Wasserman and Rovey (Eds.). USA.

Eco, U. & Marmo, C. (Eds.). 1989: *On the Medieval Theory of Signs*. Amsterdam and Philadelphia.

Freccero, J. 1993. 'Introduction to Inferno.' In *The Cambridge Companion To Dante*. Cambridge.

Maierù, A. 1981. '"Signum" dans la Culture Médiévale.' In *Sprache und Erkentniss im Mittelalter. Miscellanea Medievalia* 13:1, Kluxen (Ed.). Berlin and New York.

Marmo, C. 1994. *Semiotica e linguaggio nella scolastica: Parigi, Bologna, Erfurt 1270-1330. La semiotica dei modisti*. Roma.

Peirce, C.S. 1965. *Collected Papers*. Vol. II. Cambridge, MA.

Roer, H. 1996. "Stemmen og røsten." *Passage* 23: 67-91.

All translations are by the author of this article, apart from the translations of the quotations from

De Trinitate, which are by Haddan and Shedd in Schaff (1988), and from the *Paradiso* of *Divina Commedia*, translated into English by C. Singleton.

Toward a Meta-Rhetoric of Pictorial Media Specificity, Pictorality and Compound Signs

Troels Degn Johansson

I The Problem of Specificity

What does specificity of visual media mean as concerns semiotic theory of signification today? Not much, apparently. Whereas in the text analytic semiotics of the
Sixties and Seventies, media specificity was seen as a dominant "code" which therefore was to be given primary focus and which gave rise to specialised semiotics of
"Cinema", "Theatre", "Architecture", etc., this seems later to have been given up
and replaced with a general semiotics of culture, that is of culture as a semiotic
system. Hence today it makes little sense as well to maintain the traditional separation in semiotic studies between general and so-called special semiotics.

I shall not venture into an exhaustive explanation of why this is so, but it probably has to do with profound *cultural reasons*. As far as critical art is concerned, nobody would probably challenge the assertion that today, what matters is not the mast-
ery of a specific art form but of art as concept, that is of conceptual art as such.
Accordingly, artists are now giving up the "slavery of the technique" to be able to
contribute more freely with ideas to the societies and traditions of which they form
part. As concerns the study of media, we are experiencing a similar degradation of
especially those media that used to belong to the muses of the Fine Arts. What is
important is no longer the medium in its ideality but their actual use in societies and
by individuals. So, for the student of media it seems now less relevant to focus on
specific media as isolated phenomena in this sense than to identify and analyze *media
cultures*.[1]

Now does all this mean that the specificity of visual media is no longer relevant,

---

[1] Cinema, which first — after decades of efforts by dedicated critics — was celebrated as
an art form, but later on — and for good reasons — became particularly interesting to
mass media studies, is exemplary here. Still, this also holds good for other popular and
technically reproductive "art forms", or media such as photography, the short story, and
the poster.

or necessary to discuss when analyzing actualized signification, or "texts" (to the extent that it is still possible to speak of the text as an isolated, cultural phenomenon, or "message")? Of course not, and what is often overlooked in contemporary semiotics is in my view the rather simple fact that specific visual media still facilitate specific technical and discursive operations,[2] and that these operations may have a significant effect as for how "messages" in these media are organized semiotically. Owing to its temporal nature, cinema is for technological reasons a "natural" medium for the representation of movements and for particular discoursive forms, most notably the narrativity of feature films. Photographs, when compared to paintings, seem particularly natural as for a particular, descriptive thematization of the referential world, and computer media are again inseparable from hypertextual interactivity, that is when compared again to painting, photography, and cinema when the latter are not subjected to computer mediation. I do not say that actual specificity is reducible to such crude categories; still it certainly seems difficult to reject that these three examples, owing to their specific technological character, are characterized by distinctictively different themas, and that "stories", the "referent", and "interactivity" have been key concepts for the understanding of cinema, photography, and computer media respectively. Much of this is of course old hat to semiotics; still we realize now that semiotics have a problem when we are to account for the importance of the part played by media specificity in the organization of signification. On the one hand do we no longer accept that media specificity makes necessary a strong ontological separation of the field of pictorial semiotics, so that it is necessary to speak of special semiotics of cinema, photography, computer media, etc. On the other hand does it seem evident that specific media still organize signification in distinct ways.

I admit that notions of technology often are misleading when we are to characterize particular properties of individual media. Much confusion regarding precisely such popular concepts as "interactivity" in computer media, or the "referent" in photography is probably due to too vague or narrow definitions. However, not only pictorial semiotics but also a number of studies from other disciplines have approached this question systematically in *semiotic terms*, and especially by setting off from Charles S. Peirce's triadic sign categories, viz. the icon, the index, and the

---

[2] I distinguish between media discouse and technology to emphasize the difference between discursive form (i.e., narration, argumentation, and description) and the vehicle of those forms, i.e. technology.

symbol (i.e. sign relations that are characterized by similarity, contiguity,[3] and convention respectively). Pictorial media have often been laid out in these terms as *iconic* mediations of a primordial lifeworld of perceptual experience which in turn may be conceived of in terms of *indexicality*, i.e., an open set of entities that are characterized simply by being close to each other (i.e., contiguity), or forming part of a given totality (i.e., factorality) (Sonesson 1989a: 30 ff. 1992:163 ff.). In this conception we assume, or in Peirce's terms, *infer* by means of *abduction* that the world referred to in the image somehow continues "outside" the pictorial frame. Common photographic kinds of representation are of course particularly instructive when we are to understand this notion of pictorality. The concept of iconicity captures here the "idea" of similarity that *grounds* the actualization of the picture's iconic character. If this idea is evoked in intuitive experience, one may say that it is relevant to speak of an iconic sign relation. Due to the fundamental asymmetrical and hierarchical organization of iconic sign relations (cf. Stjernfelt and Sonesson above), the image will always be taken for "secondary" or derivative from the world. However, since pictures also form part of the lifeworld as objects and artefacts, one may argue that pictures also belong to the indexicality of this world of images. As for *pictorial objects*, one may say that they may be "found again" as part of the world they represent, say as paper photographs in a photo album. *Pictorial artefacts*, which are characterized by their thematization of their own production as pictures, are not only objects but also entities that seem to form part of the world "before" it is to be rediscovered as an object. In this sense, media have also been characterized in terms of indexical mediation (Sonesson 1996a). This goes especially for "Photography", which according to a very persistent wing of critics, is considered particularly "indexical" since the so-called "chemical" nature of photography "guarantees" some kind of contiguity between the picture and its referent.[4] Compared to this, figurative painting and also digital photography are supposed to be more "iconic" since these media are taken

---

[3] I maintain here Göran Sonesson's (1992) systematical definition of indexicality as either contiguity or factorality, i.e. sign relations that in linguistic terms resembles either metonymic or synecdochical figures.

[4] Following Barthes' *La chambre clair* (1980) one may argue that a picture in this conception should be seen as an indexical mediation of pure perceptual qualities such as emotions, thoughts, and colors, which are themselves in Peirce to be seen as iconic properties (e.g., the "blackness" of a blackbird). Thus Barthes finds that certain photos "incarnate" untamed sensations such as eroticism, melancholy, etc. I shall however not pursue this notion further here.

to lack their indexical theme.[5] I shall not pursue these questions here;[6] still, recognizing the actual application of Peirce's triadic sign categories to the problem of media specificity and the organisation of pictorial signification I will maintain this approach here but in the general perspective of pictorial semiotics.

Although semiotic concepts in this sense seem to have been employed with success to cover media's specific "technical" properties, specificity is perhaps most urgent to discuss from an intuitive approach to signification in media. One may say that the technical aspect of specific media is only relevant to the extent that it is *thematized*, that is, in as much as it is evident as a present pictorial theme to the intuitive perception of significiation. When accounting for the signification fact in a given text, or in respect of an object by means of semiotic analysis of signifying forms (i.e. in a so-called "Greimasian" approach), or of logical sign relations (i.e. a "Peircean" approach), it does prove relevant to concentrate on the intuitive level of the actual experience of signification. In pictorial semiotics this relevance is a starting point for both the phenomenologically orientated text analysis (Barthes, Metz, et al.) and the contemporary system analysis of intuitive signification (Sonesson and to some extent also Eco). It is especially on the intuitive level that it is difficult to ignore the part played by the specific medium as for how signification is organized and experienced, that may again be in terms cinema, photography, and computer media. For instance, a photographical image will, when forming part of the film strip of a common feature film, inevitably be dominated by a relatively "strong" narrative organization which, as Christian Metz notes, make the picture 'vanish before the plot it has woven ... so that the cinema is only in theory the art of images' (1964a: 42). The experience of moving images is in this respect usually the experience of story.[7] However, when seen as a still image the same picture may possibly

---

[5] This has at least been asserted by the critics of post-phototography, e.g. Lars Kiel Bertelsen (1995).

[6] Sonesson (1989b) provides a systematic semiotic critique of those theories of photography that sets off from the notion of photography being a particularly "indexical" medium. In my forthcoming article, 'Det nye billede' ("The New Image", Johansson (2000)) I have approached this issue more specifically with special reference to the temporal dimension of photographic representation and with address to the debate on post-photography, or digital photograhy — which, in the rearview mirror of more recent contributions to pictorial semiotics, perhaps seems a bit rigid and unresolved.

[7] This passage in Metz has given gise to much criticism since Metz at this stage does not account for the fact that such intuitive impression is largely due to a particular, yet dominant representational system, namely classical Hollywood montage. On the other hand, although Metz may be in error as for his argumentation, his "metaphysical"

thematize more strongly the referential world which in turn may be experienced as "absence", a "sense of loss", etc. (cf. Barthes 1981). Finally, when subjected to the hyperstructural environment of computer media, the very same picture may again form part of an interactive communication design which perhaps primarily thematizes choice. Although this example should be taken for no more than a simple supposition, it still does sketch out how a "picture" may possibly be formed, or mediated in various, specific ways, and that specificity thus is relevant to consider when studying the organization of signification in pictorial media. Specificity does at least *lend itself to thematization in the intuitive experience of signification*, and it is on this level that we may realize fully the findings of especially the phenomenological tradition in pictorial semiotics.

However, when laying things out like this we also problematize the concept of *pictorality* which especially in Sonesson has become crucial as a concept for the object of study in "pictorial semiotics" as he has it (instead of "visual semiotics"), for is it really possible at all to have actualized before us such "neutral pictorality" beyond any specific pictorial mediation? Of course not, but this notion of pictorality may still help us to discuss what (specific) pictures are without having recourse to ontological elaborations, and pictorality is indeed necessary as concept for the understanding of pictorial semiotics of visual media.

II   Specificity and the System Analysis of Pictorial Media

In this paper I shall try to unfold further the problem of specificity in terms of pictorality *qua* iconic mediation of indexicality in respect of the intuitive, or experimental dimension of signification in pictorial media. I find Göran Sonesson and his so-called "Sweden School" of cultural semiotics particularly interesting and relevant here since it on the one hand treats culture as a sign system — hence the methodological notion of system analysis — while on the other hand maintaining an intuitive approach to the study of actualized signification. Thus, compared to "Greimasian" text analysis, Sonesson's system analysis of signification maintains the phenomenological approach while substantiating for the signfication fact on a genealogical notion of system; a notion which in the text analytic tradition is less acceptable than the notion of "code" which is thought of rather as a theoretical

_____

identification of the "nature" of cinema as the narrativity of feature films is a conceptual model that — however reductive it may be — is well established in film studies even today.

construction. My point is here that, whereas textual analysis fundamentally attributes a great deal of importance to the specificity of the visual media as for how significaction is organized in various texts, this aspect seems not established in Sonesson's system analysis. On the other hand, one could argue that although especially Metz in length discusses aesthetic specificity in his vain attempt to found a semiotics of the cinema, he never really tries his theoretical work in the context of text analysis. Barthes' text analyses could on the other hand be said to be constantly obsessed with the significance of especially photographic representation as such (1964a, 1970), or even with 'an ontological desire'as he has it in *Le chambre claire* (1980:13). Here, Barthes may in turn be criticized for being perhaps irrelevantly "deviant", in as much as his analyses often ends up being more concerned with theoretical questions of another kind — that is precisely with desire and other subject theoretical matters — rather than simply with the organization of signification in pictorial texts. In this respect, Sonesson's system analysis does in my view make out a preferable starting point in as much as one should attempt to establish something *systemic* about pictorial media. Still a dialogue with the linguistic tradition is considered necessary since Sonesson does not really say much about specificity. I will take this dialogue between text and system analysis a bit further in the first part below (i.e. Part III). To develop the current perspective, this methodological dialogue seeks to identify the basic characteristics of system analysis' notion of relevance and objectivity in intuitive signification.

The problem is then whether the specificity of pictorial media *proves relevant* in the system analysis, that is, whether it should be taken for included in that set of cultural grounds that determine the so-called *principle of relevance* in Sonesson's semiotics of culture (cf. Sonesson 1992: 145 ff.). I shall try to make evident that this will be the case if one reconsiders critically first his theoretical elaboration on Groupe μ's visual rhetoric (1992) — which plays a large part in his work after his great systematical critique of the heritage of pictorial semiotics (Sonesson 1989a) — and secondly, Sonesson's ecological cosmology of pictorial media which sets off from the realist conviction that pictorial media in semiotic terms should be taken for mediations of a lifeworld hierarchy of iconicity (cf. his article above, and Sonesson 1996a, 1996b, 1997). My basic objection against Sonesson's import of Groupe μ's visual rhetoric — with its suggestive order of pictorial tropes — is that these tropes in Sonesson seem to end up attaining universal status irrespective of their actual, specific pictorial mediation, i.e. that *these tropes are supposed to function in more or less the same way be they mediated by cinema, still photography, or any other pictorial medium.* Groupe μ's visual rhetoric is of course an important contribution to pictorial semiotics inasmuch as this theory finally manages to disclose a significant formal and discrete level on the level of expression in pictures. Still, Groupe μ's pictorial tropes may — when studied in the context of at least some pictorial media — not always be "strong enough" to determine finally the organization of signification in a given text. I will argue that this classification of tropes — when taken for systemic nature — applies to a general, or ideal, notion of pictorality but not to actual and specific media in which pictorality may be mediated in various ways. Cinema, photography, and hypertextual computer media may again be taken to demonstrate this point in much as these media — following our preliminary supposition — mediates pictorality in a way that often "overdetermines" the organizational function of pictorial tropes and reduce them to less abstract entities. As I shall demonstrate by means of an example in Part IV below this holds good as for the common feature film. Here I try to make evident that this problem pertains fundamentally not only the concept of pictorality and specificity but also the status of the compound sign (in Swedish: *sammansatt tecken*) which in Sonesson's account make possible abstract meanings in pictures.

However, recognizing the great theoretical potential in the *rhetorical notion* — which in Sonesson's recent work serves as a model to understand the relationship between the lifeworld and its pictorial mediation as for how single elements interrelate in the picture and in the world, — I go on in the fifth and final part by arguing that a rhetorical viewpoint might indeed be a fruitful starting point, not as much as for how "things" interrelate in the picture but also, and perhaps more importantly, as for *how pictores interrelate with the life-world and with each other* to the extent that this dimension happens to be thematized in the picture. Along with this I hold that what should be considered the fundamental organizational problem in such perspective is not the compound sign but pictorial media in their specificity since specific pictorial media in Sonesson are seen precisely as the breaking of a lifeworld normality. Thus I suggest the notion of a "meta-rhetorics" to capture a general rhetorical function on the *macro-level* of pictorial signification, a level that may be opposed to the rhetorical functioning in compound signs at the *micro-level*.

III   System Analysis and Text Analysis

According to Sonesson, system analysis should be distinguished from text analysis and other kinds of analytical methods in semiotics in that it concerns the object of study (*studieobjekt*) in semiotics as such, that is the system. Text analysis, on the other hand, is in this conception occupied with the *studied object (det studerade objektet)*, that is the text. (Sonesson 1992: 63). This means that whereas text analysis in principle seeks to draw conclusions as for the nature of the system on the grounds of induction, system analysis deals in a deductive manner with the system as such, that is, somehow in accordance with textual phenomena. However, as an inductive method, common text analyses, say those classical ones performed by Barthes, are of course special in the sense that they study only one particular text and that they constantly reflect and compare their findings with an established notion of system.[8]

In this sense, text analyses are usually realized as a gradual integration of textual and systemic knowledge, thus achieving still "deeper and deeper" levels of meaning, as it were.[9] Barthes' emphasis on the interpretive process of this method and its subjective dimensions are of course important here. However, along with this it should be admitted that some text analytical approaches sometimes draw upon a larger textual material. This is for instance the case in those works that seeks to establish a system of classification, say precisely Groupe μ's classification of rhetorical figures. Here however, texts are approached for the sake of classification only, that is without the traditional interpretive orientation. Nevertheless, one could already conclude that the phenomenological dimensions in text and system analysis respectively are fundamentally different since each approach finds its horizon of initial naturalness on entirely different levels. Textual analysis is first and foremost a phenomenology of the text, whereas system analysis in turn may be characterized as a spiritual, or conceptual phenomenology. This goes at least for Sonesson's system analysis, and the objective of this article is likewise to establish something systemic of specificity from a phenomenological viewpoint. One should perceive our preliminary supposition precisely in these terms. Along with this it should it be noted that whereas in text analysis, the "system" (or more correctly the "code") is taken for a construction which is to be derived from the analysis of the text, the system analysis approach sees the system as something which is "there already". So, system analysis does not in this sense contain the same moment of positivism as textual analysis.

In contrast to the typical Barthesian text analysis, system analysis sets off from intuition, that is not only as for its treatment of the system but also as concerns the seeking of accordance, or evidence in the text. The so-called "principle of relevance" (*relevansprincip*), which is crucial for the understanding of Sonesson's system

---

[8] Sonesson (1992: 63 ff.) notes that when text analyses assume a classifying purpose, several texts will be necessary as the semiotician's studied object.

[9] Or perhaps rather "higher and higher" if one puts it in Barthes' (1964b:130 ff.) own terms, that is with reference to his famous diagrammatic distinction between, sign, denotation, and connotation.

analytical approach, stands here as a discriminating principle as for what accords to the system, and what does not. The problem here is how accordance, or evidentially is achieved. One could distinguish between at least three distinctively different strategies in this respect, namely *intuitive analysis, experimental analysis, and the demonstration of exemplarity.*

Intuitive analysis seeks to achieve evidentially in the text by setting off from the identification of what a particular text "means", that is, its "point" as it were, the point of its particular, pictorial abstraction. From this initial move (— this could be done simply by formulating in verbal language this point in a single sentence), one returns to the system analysis approach in trying to recognize how this point is unfolded, or organized in terms of signs, or rhetorical figures. It goes without saying that the intuitive analysis is essential to Sonesson: One could rightly say — as does Sonesson — that intuitive analysis grounds experimentally the principle of relevance in the system analysis of intuitive signification. It follows that system analysis is not confined to the metaphysics of the text, which as far as cinema is concerned implies some serious problems that are pertinent to deconstructive analyses (cf. Johansson 1994). On the other hand, it seem obvious that intuitive system analysis has some obvious limitations, for instance as concerns the analysis of art since art usually does not deliver its "meaning" *en bloc* before the intuitive apprehension. This does not mean that art should not be approached intuitively, but that "good" art is rarely exhaustive to such approach, that is, perhaps unless one is gifted with the genious of an artist. Supposedly, the imagery of advertisements should on the contrary be exhaustive to intuition. Sonesson's system analysis seems in any case particularly apt when dealing with popular and commercial genres of pictorial communication. System analysis seems conceived of as an approach to the level of immediate communication.

Experimental system analysis is less characteristic of Sonesson than of Barthes' close companion in the linguistic environment in the Sixties, Christian Metz. Although Metz is usually considered part of the text analytical tradition, he could as well be taken for a system analyst inasmuch as his project mainly consists in establishing the cinema as a semiotic system (or "code") irrespective of any particular filmic text. Metz' method in his founding papers for a semiology of the cinema (1964, 1971) is very much a conceptual phenomenology of cinema rather than a proper text analytic enterprise. On the other hand one could argue that Metz is not a real system analyst in Sonesson's sense since his systemic interest is never tried in connection with an actualization of signification on the level of text. Metz' problem could in this sense be said to be an irrelevant giving too much attention to the question of specificity compared to other aspects in the organization of signification, hence his overall objective of establishing a special semiotics of the cinema. Then again, this leaves us to perform a dialogue between Metz' work on systemic specificity and proper system analysis in accordance with the principle of relevance. This is however not the aim of this paper.

The *demonstration of exemplarity* is often employed in Sonesson, not least as for his elaboration on Groupe μ's rhetorical figures. The potential problem here is that a matter, which originally derived from a *text analytic classification*, fundamentally is considered part of, or taken for a *systemic nature,* i.e., that for instance those figures should be considered part of that set of fundamental laws, or principles that organizes pictorial signification. Along with this, when one returns to a textual material in order to find those principles exemplified one runs the risk of not refering to what a particular text actually means but only to the recognition of a particular formal figure. In those cases one could say that the work does not accord to the principle of relevance. As I shall try to make evident in the following part, this happens in Sonesson when certain rhetorical figures are found in media in which rhetorical figures are secondary to, or "weaker" than say a given narrative organization. On the other hand this problem leads us to concentrate on the relevance of specificity, and subsequently to assert something systemic about specificity on the ground of intuitive analysis.

IV   Specificity, Compound Signs, and Intertextual Referentiality

I have already suggested that cinema and other pictorial media make us problematize the function of specificity in Sonesson's import of Groupe μ's theory of visual rhetoric (1992) in respect of the over-determination of discoursive or technical properties in the organization of signification. Pictorial tropes may for instance be over-determined in the narrative experience of feature films since the discoursive "force" of this particular medium even makes "images vanish" in favor of the story. This problem does not concern Groupe μ since their aim is primarily to classify formal figures, or tropes. So, although this question may seem somehow beside the point as for Groupe μ's work as such, it does seem to prove relevant to the concept of pictorial sign that founds the conception of visual rhetoric, that is, at least to the extent that this has been developed in Sonesson. More specifically, cinema *qua* feature films clearly challenges the status of the compound sign because of the naturalizing function of diegesis. However, as we have pointed out initially we may also think of other kinds of pictorial mediations as organizational functions that are "stronger" than rhetorical tropes.

According to Sonesson, compound signs are fundamental to any rhetorical figure in as much as they conjoin absolute signs on the level of expression in order to establish a contextual implication which is abstract to the content of each absolute sign when seen "separately", that is, when out of context. This abstraction makes out the *rhetorical breaking of a norm*. The notion of norm refers here to the normality that would "otherwise" have been inferred from the absolute sign. This idea suggest that rhetorical figures are constituted by our ability to maintain a double attention in pictorial communication: We are able to focus on the context of pictorial appresentation while at the same time inferring an imagery of normality on the grounds of distinct elements in the picture. In Sonesson, normality is regarded to be grounded on the lifeworld that a pictorial appresentation may mediate and thus divert, or abstract in various ways. It should be noted here that, rather than utilizing the common linguistic concepts of connotation, synecdoche, or metonymy, Sonesson suggests the term contextual implication to stand for a compound sign which is given by a conjunction of absolute signs on the level of expression. Connotations are, on the contrary, characterized by a sign conjunction on the level of content.

I shall not go into details by introducing Groupe μ's classification of pictorial tropes in its disclosure of a "general visual rhetoric". In short, this classification is founded on three general oppositions, namely (1) pictorality versus plasticity, (2) presence versus absence of particular pictorial features (i.e. *in praesentia* versus *in absentia*), and (3) the conjunction versus disjunction of pictorial features. The classes of tropes consist of all possible combinations of these oppositions, e.g.: A disjunction/conjunction *in praesentia/absintia* on the level of pictoriality, plasticity, or both. A popular example of one of these combinations is a particular frame in Hergé's Tintin album *The Crab with the Golden Claws*[10] (cf. Fig. 1 below) which shows Haddock with bottles instead of eye pupils. Combining the figural categories of "conjunction" (i.e., of bottles and Haddock) and "in absentia" (i.e., lack of pupils), this figure infers a contextual implication on the level of content, which suspends indexical abduction in favor of an abstract meaning (i.e. "dangerous intoxication" or "delirium tremens" due to heavy drinking).

---

[10] Original version, *Le crabe aux pinces d'or*, published in black-and-white in 1941.

Fig. 1. A frame from the Tintin album ,The Crab with the Golden Claws *(1941).*

Seemingly, what happens in feature films is that the abstract content of formal rhetorical tropes inevitably becomes reduced to a primary iconic level of content given by the determinant discursive form which is specific to this medium, namely diegetic narrativity. Here, pictorial signification is first and foremost determined by the indexical abduction of a continuous and infinite perceptual world, or "life-world". Still, it would be more correct to state that in the cinema compound signs in the proper sense cannot be realized, for in compound signs it is indeed the abstract contextual implication that grounds and determines the absoluteness of signs conjoined on the level of expression. And, whereas abstract contextual implications are impossible in principle, so are compound signs with a conjunction on the level of expression. In this sense, it seems as though pictorial rhetorical tropes simply are not possible in the cinema (while plastic figures probably are, just think of the possibility of establishing and breaking norms of rhythm in montage). Seemingly, we may thus give up a pictorial rhetoric for the cinema, and maybe also for other temporal pictorial media that are dominated by narrativity. In this sense, owing to the persistence of diegetic time and space in the common feature film, what cinema makes evident in a rather simple manner is that the formal figures of visual rhetoric are not universal to all pictorial forms as for their abduction of contextual implication.

Thus, by setting off from a clear contradiction of what one may take as a universality in the conception of visual rhetoric, one may proceed by defining whatever qualifies, or disqualifies, in specific media the possibility of effective visual rhetoric, that is, not only a reproduction of formal rhetorical figures from the catalogues of systematic classifications but indeed a rhetoric, which is to be recognized by the

140

principle of relevance in the system analysis of intuitive signification. In my view, we should always ask ourselves not whether a particular figure is to be identified as a rhetorical one or not but first and foremost what those figures mean in the text, and how they bring about signification — say, on the grounds of stronger or more fundamental structures of organizations such as narrativity that may be specific in respect of certain pictorial media.

Now, to perceive the problem suggested above, one only has to imagine an animated version of that frame in Tintin that shows Haddock with bottles instead of eye pupils. In such version, the formal trope is re-naturalized as an integral part of that indexicality which is made out by Tintin's and Haddock's "world", and which is abducted from the iconicity of the animated film. Still, one only recognizes here the horror that Haddock's eyes really do look like bottles! If one insists that these bottle eyes do possess a connotative effect, one must admit that in this sense this is hardly due to any proper rhetorical trope but to *the diegetic scene in its totality and "naturalness" however grotesque that may appear!* Such fantasized imagery is perhaps not that far fetched as it may seem — it has in fact been realized in an original way by one of Hergé's admirers, René Pétillon, in his contribution to the memorial tribute album to the master which followed Hergé's death in 1983.[11]

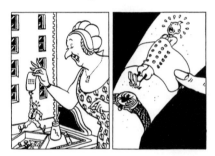

Fig. 2. Selected frames from René Pétillon's tribute strip to Hergé: 'Tintin Dreams'.

In his two-page strip, 'Tintin Dreams', Pétillon displays a grotesque dream sequence scenario by mixing figures and scenes from a number of well-known albums with the band-aid episode from *The Calculus Affair*[12] as the central *leitmotif*. In this manner Pétillon takes off Hergé in a manner that seems distinctively alien to the

---

[11] *(A suivre) Hors serie special Hergé.* Paris: Casterman.

[12] Original version, *L'Affaire Tournesol,* published in 1956.

original style while at the same time pointing the fact that the "Haddock trope" of 'The Crab …' *actually does occur in a dream sequence*: After having got lost in a desert and eventually also having lost consciousness, Tintin is dreaming deliriously about Haddock, the alchoholic captain of the ship Karaboudjan, whom he only just met for the first time in his life. In this sense, one may argue that the exemplary frame in Groupe μ and in Sonesson is separated from its actual context: They both focus on this particular frame with no reference to the sequential order of the album nor the desert/dream sequence of which it forms part. However, Pétillon also develops a "surreal" vein in Hergé's work which has later on been taken up by other comics artist and which further weakens the impression that abstract rhetorical tropes are especially characteristic of Hergé's work and the art of comics and cartoons in general.

Still, cinema may be pointed out as a medium that is *distinctively non-abstract* since this medium definitively cannot realize proper compound signs. Cinema seems in this respect to resemble dreams inasmuch as it cannot establish proper contradictions. In dreams, events take place as a matter of course however grotesque or chocking they may be. Here, things and persons make up contexts that are characterized by conjunction rather than contradiction. Although one may take cinema in this sense as a presence of separate pictorial elements (*Gestalte*), it would be wrong to identify a compound of these elements for "pairings" in the sense suggested by Groupe μ, i.e., as the rhetorical trope "conjunction in praesentia". In dreams as well as in cinema conjunctions are "natural": They make out a "norm of conjunction" which cannot be broken. The point is, I suppose, that, contrary to the rhetorical tropes, pictorial elements do not lend themselves to reflexivity. For instance, one cannot in principle state that a given element is there in the picture instead of something else (i.e. conjunction *in absentia*). Everything is always naturally there. However, here relays of reflexivity are to be identified rather on the very level of experiencing cinema or dreams. Hence expressions such as 'this may seem real, still it is only a dream', or '…still this is only cinema'. I am referring here to a general reflexivity of fiction whose nature is that of phantasy. As French psychoanalyst Octave Mannoni has pointed out, fantasy may be characterized by the similar saying of "I know very well that this is not really so, still…".

So, to return to my initial observation, the imaginary example of the animated Haddock trope does seem to stress the assumption that cinematic pictorality and other "matters of course" suspends contextual implication by which compound signs are reduced to an integral, or non-reflexive scene. Such reduction of compound signs means that appresentation first and foremost - but in various ways - is limited to the indexical abduction of a represented or referential space (cf. Sonesson 1992: 183-5). It is only on the grounds of indexial abduction that something like a contextual implication can be realized. Contrary to the tropes in the visual rhetoric, diegetic "implication" cannot be realized on the grounds of a compound sign owing to the impossibility of the latter. Whereas in the cinema, "implication" principally starts from diegesis, any connotation effect finds its expression in independent scenic signs. Surprisingly this is much like in verbal language whose rhetorical tropes, metonymy, synecdoche, etc., all are independent signs that operate on the level of content. In this sense, rather than "contextual implication" the concept of "connotation" actually seems to be a more appropriate term in this respect. Another, perhaps even better concept is that of "intertextual referentiality" which is usually intended for the postmodern avant-garde cinema. When director Lars von Trier in his feature film *Element of Crime* (1984) shows a horse with a carriage filled with apples, he is indeed showing a horse with a carriage with apples although at the same time he is clearly referring to a scene in a film by Russian director Andrei Tarkovsky. In this manner, the von Trier film draws upon the universe of Tarkovsky by means of an index factorality which may seem identical to those to be found in compound signs in still pictures. However, as we have claimed, cinematic referentiality is first and foremost bound to the indexicality of diegetic space.

The semiotic function of intertextual referentiality probably also grounds the Gevalia coffee commercials for cinema and television, "Which coffee would you serve for unexpected visitors" (in Swedish: 'Vilket kaffe skulle du bjuda på om du fik oväntat besök?'), although these are also referred to in Sonesson to examplify visual rhetoric. The typical Gevalia commercial plot is usually about the "collision" of contrasting worlds and scales, e.g., the asian jumbo jet captains that get lost with their air-craft on the landing ground and ends up knocking on the door of some person in a cosy cabin who in turn is taken by surprise and offer them fresh Gevalia coffee. Whereas it is true that the still-picture versions (for magazines, billboard posters, etc.) seem to function by means of compound signs (cf. Sonesson 1992: 178), one should not forget that they also, and perhaps more primarily refer to the version made for television and the cinema by means of intertextual referentiality. If this is so, also still-picture versions may be characterized by the autonomy and naturalness of a cinematographic version, not least because of their dependence of the story told in the latter. In this sense, still-picture versions of the Gevalia coffee commercials are taken for an index (:factorality), *not of a primordial life-world but of the fictional, cinematographic world of Gevalia commercials*. It is obvious at this stage to question again the very possibility of the rhetorical breaking of established norms in the cinema.

V   Re-Framing Pictorality: Specificity and "Meta-Rhetoric"

Pétillon's Tintin and the Gevalia commercials both seem to indicate that a visual rhetoric of compound signs are exposed to a "rhetoric" of a "higher" order, namely that of the medium. I suggested preliminarily that my notion of pictorality could be taken for a rhetorical one since we are referring to it generally as the breaking of a life-world normality. Sonesson defines Groupe μ's visual rhetoric precisely these terms, still Sonesson's general notion of pictorality seems to accord just as well with this conception. However, the scope of application must be much broader as far as such a "meta-rhetorical" approach is concerned, since this organizational order is both stronger and more general than that of the compound sign.

So far, I have been subscribing to a *general notion* of pictorality to capture the iconic mediation of a common life-world of indexicality. Moreover have I outlined a notion of *specificity* to designate media's specific pictorial life-world mediations. Is this a contradition in terms? I think not — still I should at this stage re-consider what is meant by pictorality. It follows from my argumentation so far that whereas it is no longer relevant to maintain decisive ontological demarcations of the field of (pictorial) semiotics to found special semiotics of "Cinema", "Photography", etc., it is still helpful to operate with a general notion of pictorial semiotics since signification in some respect seems to be organized in a special way in images. Accordingly, it does prove necessary to maintain a concept of pictorality as Sonesson (1989a: 295 ff.) is careful to point out. Sonesson deals in lengh with a general notion of picture and how pictorality in this sense may actualize sign relations in a systemic way. This aspect is formulated in terms of pictorial semio-genesis.

Thus, the concept of pictorality is used to cover the general matter of a pictorial semiotics. However, this concept should not immediately be taken for an ontological one either: What is important is certainly not to advance a strict ontological definition of "what images actually are" but to establish a theoretical foundation that may help us to understand how actual signification is generally organized in images. Following Sonesson, this means on the one hand that I attribute systemic, viz. genealogical substance to the concept of pictorality, and that I, on the other hand, employ this concept to think of images in general terms. In this sense one may assert that my concept of pictorality is of a *cognitive nature*, and that it may lead to a cognitive study of pictorial media which is pertinent to other domains in cognitive semiotics.

Now, what does specificity amounts to in these terms? Following my examples above I am led to conclude that specific pictorial media seem to mediate the life-world in distinct ways, and that specificity in some respect seems to over-determine compound signs as an organizational order of signification. Still, what has so far been referred to as the "life-world" stands out more and more as a rather vague and reductive concept. And, furthermore, what my examples seemed to suggest was not as much that specific media are representing the world distinctively different than "normal life-world perception": — What seemed important was indeed that specific media are representing things differently compared to a given "pictorial normality", say the typical Gevalia television commercial or the distinct comics universe of Hergé's Tintin. It is true that my concept of life-world is necessary for our understanding of how we generally infer the existence of a continuous world "outside" the picture. Still, my notion of specificity seems in fact to pertain less to the mediation of the life-world than to *that of a given pictorial normality*. In this sense, specificity may be found rather to be the (meta-)rhetorical breaking of a *pictorial norm*, and perhaps ultimately, to *pictorality as such,* a concept which in this article has been thought of precisely as a general and indeed an ideal one. In this sense, my notion of specificity captures in a sense the *actualization* of pictorality.

Sonesson's concept of prominence (1992: 138) is important when one is to distinguish pictorial "normality" from rhetorical diversions in such terms. Pictorial normality is by definition more prominent than its diversion. Any specific rhetorical diversion is in this sense organized in a general hierarchical order of prominence which is referred to by Sonesson above in terms of the Great Chain of Being (cf. Lakoff & Johnson's original notion). In my example above, the order of prominence is at play in Pétillon's Tintin. Pétillon shows that the "Haddock trope" is truly alien to Hergé (although it may still be found as a "surreal vein" in Hergé's work), and that such "alienation" in turn may lead to the development of a new, yet less prominent "pictorial language". In another contribution to the memorial tribute album to Hergé, Enki Bilal shows us in a single frame another rhetorical diversion of Hergé, namely a 3D-rendering of Tintin and Snowy which stands out more like a painting than a frame from a strip. Here, Bilal breaks rhetorically a pictorial norm of "flatness" and comics strip narrativity which is established locally by Hergé's particular style (Fig. 3 below).

Fig. 3. Enki Bilal's tribute to Hergé's Tintin. By rendering Tintin and Snowy in 3D, Bilal breaks rhetorically a pictorial norm that is established locally in the flatness of Hergé's particular style.

Apparently, *pictorial framing* becomes a crucial object of study for those who want to venture further into these matters. Obviously, the interrelation of pictures with the life-world is often thematized precisely by means of the frame. Similarly, rhetorical diversions of pictures is likely also to thematize a change in these terms. In Bilal's example, the existence of a field "outside" the frame is stressed significantly in the 3D rendering. The characteristic "Hergé doodle" which usually adds a sense of motion to his characters, appears in Bilal rather to be a spatial entity which emphasizes this outside field dramatically by spiraling off to the left behind Tintin's foot. In fact, both Tintin and Snowy appear in this version motionless, or "stiff", Snowy hanging somehow mysteriously above the ground. Hergé's Tintin style usually does not dramatize the outside-field in such a radical fashion, in fact the outside-field in Hergé is entirely constituted by narrative montage.

One recalls this aspect in Barthes (1980, 90 ff.), who distinguishes photography from the cinema in similar terms. Whereas the outside-field *(hors-champ)* of the cinema is considered as being that of the diegetic space, outside-fields in photography may for Barthes be of a more subtle and abstract kind *(hors-champ subtil)*. Commenting on this distinction, Pascal Bonitzer found the outside-field of feature films to be a "strong" one *(hors-champ étoffé)* (Bonitzer 1980: 6). I shall not elaborate further on this discussion here, a discussion which unfortunately has led to some rather rigid ontological definitions of cinema as well as photography. Suffice it at this final stage to realize that the thematization of the outside-field may be a fine indicator of a rhetorical diversion of pictorality, and that such thematization may be

146

relevantly described in terms of "abstraction" and "strength" (or "force"), i.e., terms which have also proven helpful in this article in my analysis of compound signs and their functional suspension by meta-rhetorical over-determination.

VI Conclusion

In this article I have approached the problem of media specificity in semiotics from a so-called "meta-rhetorical" approach and with special reference to the system analysis of Sonesson. Setting off from a brief discussion of what specificity may amount to in semiotics today, I outlined preliminarily a general notion of pictorality by having recourse to Sonesson's pictorial semiotics and earlier attemts to define spcificity in terms of Peirce's triadic sign categories. This led me first to undertake a methodological inquiry in order to distinguish the system analytical approach to that of text analysis. This step was considered necessary since specificity traditionally has been perceived on the grounds of text analycal semiology, that is, the linguistic tradition in semiotics. I then ventured into a more detailed analysis of the compound sign and its possible over-determination by higher organizational orders of discoursive and technology. This discussion was motivated by the observation that especially the pictorial compound signs of Groupe μ's visual rhetoric seem to function differently in feature films that is, when exposed to a strong narrative organization of signification. After this I returned to a more general perspective to reconsider the concept of pictorality as a general mediation of a primordial life-world. I concluded here that pictorality — following our preliminary outline — could be taken for a rhetorical function of a higher order than that of the compound sign, and that the rhetorical function of pictorality should be seen as the rhetorical breaking of established pictorial norms rather than some general life-world normality, which in my account only helps us to understand why we are able to infer so-called outside-fields in common pictorial representations. It may be argued at this final stage that I have reduced specificity to style, still my notion of specificity both implies a technological and a discoursive dimension. In this sense, the concept of style is much too narrow in its scope to capture the meta-rhetorical function outlined above. It may also be argued that I have reduced specificity to a *relative phenomenon,*still our discussion has managed so far to avoid the pitfalls of relativism so common to the study of iconicity and images. Specificity should in this sense no longer be thought of in terms of essence, uniqueness, purity, etc., but of relations — just like we think of signs and in fact most other matters in semiotics.

References:

Barthes, Roland. 1964a. 'Rhetorique de l'image.' *Communications* 4: 40-51.

—. 1964b. 'Éléments de sémiologie.' *Communications* 4: 91-135.

—. 1970. 'Le troisième sens: Notes de recherche sur quelques photogrammes de S.M. Eisenstein.' *Cahiers du cinéma* 222: 12-19.

—. 1980. *La chambre clair*. Paris: Gallimard.

Bertelsen, Lars Kiel. 1995. 'After Photography.' *Siksi* 4: 14-17.

Bonitzer, Pascal. 1980. 'Le hors-champ subtil.' *Cahiers du cinéma* 311: 5-8.

Groupe µ. 1992. *Traité du Signe Visuel*. Paris: Seuil.

Johansson, Troels Degn. 1994. *The Subject of Cinematography. On the General Possibility of Deconstruction in the Linguistic Semiotics of the Cinema*. Department of Film & Media Studies, University of Copenhagen.

—. 1998. 'Points of Departures. Modern Film Theory and its Postmodern Psychoanalytic Critique — with Roland Barthes.' In Rene Rasmussen (Ed.) *Civilisationens ubehag. Psykoanalysen i kulturen*. Aarhus: NSU Press.

Metz, Christian. 1964. 'Cinema: Langue ou Langage?' *Communications* 4: 52-90.

—. 1970. *Langage et cinéma*. Paris: Larousse.

Sonesson, Göran. 1989a. *Pictorial Concepts*. Lund: Lund University Press/ARIS.

—. 1989b. *Semiotics of Photography. On Tracing the Index*. Rapport 4 från Semiotik-projektet. Lund: Institutionen för Konstvetenskap.

—. 1992. *Bildbetydelser. Innledning till bildsemiotiken som vetenskab*. Lund: Studentlitteratur.

—. 1996a. 'Indexicality as Perceptual Mediation.' In Christiane Pankow (Ed.) *Indexicality: Papers from the Third Biannual Meeting of the Swedish Society for Semiotic Studies.'* Gothenburg University. SSKKII Report 9604.

—. 1996b. 'An Essay Concerning Images. From Rhetoric to Semiotics by Way of Ecological Physics.' *Semiotica* 110.

—. 1997. 'The Multimediation of the Lifeworld.' In *Semiotics of the Media. Proceedings from an International Congress*, Kassel, March 1995. Winfried Nöth (Ed). Berlin & New York: Mouton de Gruyter.

Cognitive Semiotics

Schemas and Symbols

Svend Østergaard

I Introduction

In the following it is my aim to comment on the relation between cognitive schemas, which seem to be determining our conceptual understanding of the world, and
symbolic representation as it appears in language. The idea is that on a primary level,
which will be specified later, the cognitive schema represents some inherent properties of the world to which the speaker refers. This is not to say that the schema is
an objective and one-to-one representation; the fact that different languages conceptualize a given situation by means of different schemas shows that this is not the
case, but certain types of schemas are always *motivated* by external topological and
dynamic properties. On the other hand, any expression of the schematic content
requires a procedure of lexicalization, unless the expression can appear as a holo-
sound, as for example in the case of animals. That is, the schematic content is
represented through a string of symbols constituting a syntactic construction. But
the symbolization is only possible if there is a *mental space* of a specific kind in which
the presentations of the external space are represented, and the existence of this
mental space paves the way for the subject's possibility of conceptualizing alternative views of the world.

Through the mental space the subject can take different *possible perspectives* on the
external space, and this faculty is reflected in language by the fact that syntax offers
different possibilities for the speaker to construe a representation of a given scenario. The option of the speaker is not necessarily related to any property of the
external space, but it can be an intrinsic property of the mental space. We see it in
the following way: there is a dynamic interaction between perception and mental
representations which makes it possible to construe a representation of the world
as a *possible* world. For example, it is possible to make inferences about absent
participants from what is perceived. Ultimately, this dynamic relation is responsible
for the emergence of the elaborate linguistic forms we know; that is, the emergence
of the different syntactic constructions.

Most linguists agree that one cannot separate the semantic and the syntactic
levels. The disagreement concerns the level at which one should proceed with a

formalization. The syntax seems to open the way for a formal "algebraic" representation of the syntactic structure, but here the linguists run into the problem of there being no one-to-one correspondence between the lexematic and the semantic units. Another approach would then be to examine the schematic level on its own and see how it is reflected in the syntactic structure; in this case we get an "image-schematic" representation in the style of, for example, Langacker, which is difficult to formalize in a coherent way (this is not the ambition of Langacker, either).

Although one cannot make a strict separation between semantics and syntax, it nevertheless seems reasonable to make a distinction between at least two different semantic levels, and therefore also between two different schematic levels. The schematic structure which is determined by the intrinsic properties of the external space constitutes the first semantic level: the semantics of the world, so to speak. We will denote this level sem_1. As an example of such a first order semantics, we can mention the existence of force-dynamic schemas in language, as analysed by Talmy (cf. Talmy 1985).

The different syntactic options that the speaker has for putting different perspectives on a representation of the external world constitute the second semantic level, *if* these options are independent of the external forms. Therefore, this level requires a high degree of grammaticalization, and a description of the semantics of a given sentence will always require a reference to some mental state of the speaker of which the external space is independent. We will denote this level sem_2. As an example, we can mention Eve Sweetser's analysis of conditionals which stresses the interplay between mental space and the "real" content world, (cf. Sweetser 1990). It is clear that in both schematic levels we have a mental representation, so one can perhaps stress the difference by qualifying the semantic forms of the first level as iconic, that is, they are attuned to the structure of perception. Another way of phrasing it would be to say that the first level is related to what Sweetser calls a *content world*, whereas the structure of the second level of semantics has its origin in the epistemic and speech-act worlds. However, this does not quite cover the situation and therefore the most general description would be to define the semantics of the second level as due to the speaker's selection of a perspective independent of the content world. Following this, it is more precise to say that the second semantic level embeds the first one, so that in any case we have a structure of the form sem_2 (sem_1).

In certain cases sem_2 can have zero-value: namely, when we have an unmarked, prototypic representation of the schematic structure of an event, as for example "George opened the door". If sem_2 is non-zero we have a syntactic construction where the schematic form of the basic event can be maintained, but at the same time a semantic element is added which can only be described by referring to a choice in the mental space of the speaker. For example, the passive construction "the door was opened by a butler" represents the full schematic form of the active version, but the passive form selects a perspective on the event which is only motivated by the speaker, for instance, because "butler" is a unit which has not been introduced in discourse prior to the formulation of the sentence and therefore cannot take the place of the subject.

In a "naive" way we can say that if we have a semantic content from the basic level represented in a string of symbols, then it is possible to make manipulations on the string. The reality of the mental space can then be expressed through "formal" operations on the syntactic strings. These operations can be *negations, embeddings*, for example, of a metalinguistic comment on the basic string; *raising from object to subject*, as in a passive construction; *procedures of generalizations*, in which basic semantic forms become abstract entities and therefore can be used in metaphoric constructions, etc.

To the extent that the semantic forms from the first level can be schematically represented by means of geometric and topological forms, we can say that they have an *iconic* basis. In the case of the dynamic schemas, we have to use more abstract representations consisting of dynamic curves in a force-dynamic topology; probably this corresponds to what the Peircian tradition calls a diagram, which is a special form of the icon. However, the semantic forms which have their origin in the second semantic level stem from the possibility of making formal operations on the forms from the first one. For example, if we perceive a number of gestalt forms framed in some way, then we can collect the forms in larger groups in a number of different ways. It may be the case that one of the groupings is more naturally selected, commensurate with adjacent rules governing perception. But that is irrelevent to the fact that it is still possible to regroup them otherwise. That is, there is a combinatorial reality which can only be found through calculation and therefore has no iconic basis.

In the same line, negations, embeddings, and certain types of abstractions are not iconic,[1] but they have their origin in a mental space which constitutes an *epistemic* reality parallel with, but different from, the *ontic* reality of the first semantic level. In the following we will take a more detailed look at the relation between the two levels.

---

[1] In a sense abstraction is never iconic if we distinguish between abstraction as an operation and the result of the abstraction; the result can be iconic although the operation is not.

II Saliency

There is no obvious reason for not adopting a realistic perspective on the *emergence of meaning*. This perspective induces us to assume that structures of meaning have their origin in structures of *salient discontinuities* in the world. On the other hand, the salient structures which catch the attention of the animal are those which are already imbued with meaning. Therefore, we seem to end in a circular argument which can only be avoided by adopting a dynamic viewpoint. The individual interacts *dynamically* with the world, and it is the salient discontinuities playing a role in this interaction which cause a conceptual understanding of these saliencies to emerge. That is, neither perception nor meaning is primary, but the dynamic structure in which the individual is embedded makes the two emerge jointly. In the terminology of René Thom one can say that it is the dynamic properties of the saliencies which imbue them with pregnancy. In the case of animals, the dynamic structure is determined by fear, hunger, and sexual desire, (cf. Thom 1988).

In general, however, the terms *pregnancy* (in french: *pregnance*) and *dynamics* are not well-defined. On the individual level, we can define them in the following way: any saliency is pregnant if it causes some activity of the individual; by activity we include mental response, for example a recollection caused by an external form. The activity itself can be qualified as dynamic. On the level of the species, any form is pregnant which plays a role for its organization. The distribution of individuals in such a higher order organization, as for example an ant colony, can be described mathematically in dynamic terms as soon as one can separate the appropriate parameters determining the behaviour of the individual. The dynamics, which depends on these parameters, then generates a morphology of the collective behaviour on a level higher than the individual. In the case of humans, we will not, of course, be able to describe such a dynamic system in detail because we do not have a finite and small list of determining parameters, that is, we do not have a finite inventory of pregnant forms. *Any* form might serve *some* purpose, therefore any form might be pregnant and thus cause a dynamic response. In fact, any salient form in its immediate surroundings serves *some* dynamic purpose: the table supports the books, the chair my body, the lamp produces light, etc. Exceptions to this are aesthetic forms. It seems as if there is a desire to double the dynamics of the world by representing it, perhaps because representation at least represents a weak form of mastering the phenomenal world.

In the description we have made so far we have two levels. On the one hand, a structure of salient discontinuities pertaining to the external world; this is an "objective" structure which can be subjected to a geometric determination. On the other hand, a dynamics which on a higher level organizes a morphology whose stability ensures the survival of the species, but where significant changes in the parameters determining the dynamics can mean extinction. The dynamic structure is of course unique for each species, probably having developed through evolution. It is through the implementation of the dynamics into the existing salient discontinuities that a conceptual structure emerges. *Concept* and *meaning* are therefore primarily dynamically determined; they cannot be grasped through the notion of mapping from an objective external world onto an inner conceptual structure, as an objectivistic philosophy would claim, (cf. Lakoff 1990).

The conceptual structure which emerges from this primary dynamics seems to be organized in three layers. Firstly, we have the concepts which are bound to gestalts, figures on a ground, but figures which cause the perceiver to perform some dynamic action. These gestalts need not only be spacial but can also be temporal, so gestalts are typically objects and simple events. Secondly, a higher degree of conceptual organization emerges from the ability to pack gestaltic units into scenic wholes, that is, a scenario consists of different gestalts which may or may not be causally connected to each other. This is essentially due to what Thom calls diffusion of pregnancy, by which he means that if a salient form causes a dynamic reaction, then this dynamic response can be activated by elements in the immediate surroundings of the form. This is shown in Pavlov's famous experiment: the serving of the meat is accompanied by the ringing of a bell; the two salient forms are then packed into a whole so that later the ringing of the bell alone can cause a dynamic reaction from the dog, production of saliva, etc. It is also known from the structure of memory: a scent can cause a recollection of a previous experience of the same scent, but more than this, it can cause a recollection of the whole scenario in which the first experience took place; that is, the scent is a pregnancy as defined by René Thom, as it is able to pack the single elements of the first scenario into a unit.[2] Thirdly, we have a conceptual understanding of *schematic structure*. By schematic we are referring to *spacial relations* independent of any substantial reference, but that only imply geometric and topological properties of space, for example up/down, in/out, etc.

We are also referring to formal relations between actants which are present in a given scenario. This amounts to the concept of *semantic roles*. The actants are filling different roles which are organized in different schematic structures for the different

---

[2] The notion of *pregnancy* is formally equivalent to the notion of *value* in Edelman (1992). Edelman claims that categorization on all levels depends on a dynamic interaction between perceived forms and a value system, i.e., between saliences and pregnancies.

scenarios. Through combinations one can get very elaborate structures, but it seems as if there are only few qualitatively different *primitive* dynamic structures in which the actants can interact. By primitive we mean a dynamic structure which cannot be decomposed further. Such a dynamic structure we call a *dynamic schema*. The previous statement is a result which can be drawn from the catastrophe theoretic reorganization of Fillmore's attempt to exhaust the description of semantic roles, (cf. Petitot 1985). In catastrophe theory, a role is defined as a formal place in a dynamic structure, whereas in Fillmore it is defined semantically, with the result that the number of roles explodes. In the case of animals, even the number of semantically defined roles is probably very limited: for example, prey, predator, rival, con-species, alien.

Of course, we also have concepts for temporal structures, i.e. we have a schematics for *time and aspect*, and finally, we have schemas for the distribution of elements and for numbering and the like; we can collect those under the heading of *multiplicity schemas*.

So far I have mentioned conceptual structures pertaining to gestalts, combinations of collections of gestalts into conceptual units, called a scenario, and finally conceptualizations of schematic structures which make it possible, via memory, to have stabilized representations of the different scenarios. In the following I will only refer to conceptualizations of relevance to linguistic representation. In this perspective, one can say that the gestalts "correspond" to nominals and adjectives, whereas the scenario involves the verb because the packing of the scenario is due to a dynamic interaction of some sort. The schematic structure is then the equivalent of the closed class structure in language which makes a linguistic representation of the conceptualized scenario possible. However, the conceptual structure I have been describing until now gives rise to a linguistic representation whose semantic form belongs to the first level, which I have denoted sem$_1$. This means that the conceptualization takes place in direct reference to the content world of Eve Sweetser.

In certain cases, however, the conceptualization which is expressed in a linguistic phrase requires a *doubling* of the mental representation, which means that the conceptualization refers to a content world reality and at the same time, and possibly in a dynamic conjunction, to a mental representation of a possibility, expressing a modification of the content world semantics. Either a formal possibility in the present, a possible realization in the past, or a pure possibility in the future. Let me illustrate with an example provided by Sweetser: *the letter, if it was ever sent, never arrived.* The embedded clause represents a doubling in the mental space in the sense that it is a meta-comment on the mental representation of the content world reality, that is, a mental representation of a mental representation. The most simple way of defining what we mean by *doubling* is by saying that it consists of a mental representation of a content world plus a second representation of some abstract feature of this content world, where abstract simply means that the first representation is independent of the second, whereas the second is dependent on the first. Let us for example take the metaphor that *A is B*: A is here a content world representation which exists independently of my seeing it as a B; B is then the abstract representation, which is a pure possibility. The dynamic conjunction of the two produces the metaphor. By this very schematic description we can now give a positive definition of the semantic forms of the first level: *they are the conceptual forms which do not require a mental doubling.*

III The Structure of the Schema.

The schematic structure of sem$_1$ works in direct reference to the content world. The content world consists essentially of *space, time, dynamic structures,* and *the distribution of elements in space and time;* that is, the content world can be described by mathematical models. As the form of the schematic structure is motivated from the morphology of the content world, which by itself can be described through mathematics, it would be reasonable to expect that the schematic structure itself is motivated by mathematical structures. Here the ways part, I suppose. In cognitive linguistics one would claim, conversely, that mathematics consists of concepts which are transported from the conceptual structure of language. It would therefore be in vain to expect that mathematics could constitute a formal objective foundation for schematic forms. However, there are strong reasons to believe that mathematics constitutes an ontologic reality of its own. For example, if we take dynamic systems we have no way of explaining the morphology of the system outside the realm of mathematics. Moreover, the morphology can in many cases be reproduced independently of the substrat of the dynamic process,[3] so that one can say that when we refer to certain structural properties in the world then mathematics does not just provide us with an explanation but that these properties *are* mathematical structures.[4] If we

---

[3] Of course, this does not mean that for the form to emerge one can dispense with matter, but just that different substrats belonging to different scientific domains, as for example a chemical and a biological substrat, can cause the same mathematical form to emerge. The stabilization of forms is therefore subjected to mathematical regularities which are independent of the substrat.

[4] There are of course more sophisticated arguments for the ontological independence of mathematics (cf. Petitot 1992b).

accept this very strong ontological commitment, then we are forced to accept the hypothesis that the linguistic forms which pertain to sem_1 have some underlying objective foundation which can be described mathematically. The argument is the following: mathematical structures and mathematically determined morphologies are inherent to the content world (strong ontological commitment), the schematic forms of linguistic structure are motivated by the morphology of the content world (a trivial statement), and from this it follows that the schematic forms are motivated by mathematically determined morphologies.

To illustrate the above, one can for example prove that the structure of the category of force-dynamic verbs, which has been analysed by Talmy, (in Talmy 1985), is not arbitrary, but is a logical consequence of mathematical possibilities, if we understand the interaction of two antagonistic forces as a dynamic system. It is not possible to show this in detail here, but it has been done elsewhere, (cf. Østergaard 1996). One might note that the dynamic schemas for archetypal verb phrases, which were found by René Thom (cf. Thom 1972 and 1980), all belong to the sem_1 category and are therefore also examples of the claim made here.

Let us take an example of spacial schematization. In English, one has at least two different systems (schemas) for referring to the relative position of two objects. We have prepositions of the type "behind" and "in front of" where the relation between the objects is seen from the point of view of the speaker: for example, "the cup is behind the bottle" requires that the speaker is in front of the bottle.[5] On the other hand, we have another system of prepositions, "north of", "south of", etc., which are used in expressions like "the house is north of the church" and "the forest is north of the city". In English, this last system is only used if the object of reference is stationary and relatively large, but there are Indian languages in which the terms "north", "south", etc. serve as the equivalents of the English prepositions "behind", "left", "right", and "in front of" even on a small scale, so that the equivalent of the sentence above would be "the cup is north the bottle" (cf. Talmy 1983). In this case, the relation is schematized independently of the speaker"s position, and instead the situation is seen from a point which lies above the horizontal plane in which the objects are located. We thus have two different schemas for referring to the relative position of two objects. The selection of one of these schemas is the equivalent of selecting a perspective, i.e. a point in space from which the objects are viewed.

---

[5] One can also say "the house is behind the church" without actually standing in front of the church, so it is possible in mental space to translate the point of view. Often this translation is marked by a conditional: "if you stand in front of the church the house is to the left".

It must be stressed that with the terms *perspective* and *selection* we are referring to the selection of a perspective which is *objectively grounded* in the structure of the external space. For example, if we have an object in space, then the possibility of selecting different points of view on the object is determined by the objective properties of space. It is in this sense that we are to understand *perspective*. Later, we will discuss a type of perspective which is *only* determined by the internal structure of the mental space of the speaker. Returning to our two schemas, we can now see that they are solely determined by the structure of space. In the case of "behind"/"in front of", the objects are conceived as lying in a two-dimensional plane. As there is no canonical point of reference, the most natural selection will be the speaker's perspective. If the objects are getting bigger it seems more natural to conceive them as placed in three-dimensional space and then use the third dimension as a canonical axis of reference. *The different schemas are then determined by how the phenomenon is conceived geometrically.* Moreover, the schemas are in this example related in such a way that by moving the reference point P continuously around in space we change from one schema to the other, but this change of schema is of course discontinuous. The "behind"/"left"-schema is always used if P is in the same plane as the objects, but as soon as the point goes into the third dimension, we shift to the "north"/ "south"-schema.

In Talmy (1983), one can find a more elaborate account of how geometry and topology determine the schemas by means of which language refers to space. It should be clear from the above that there is no unique correspondence between geometrical/topological properties of the scenario referred to and the schematic structure in the referring medium, but that the schema *selects* an objectively given geometrical and/or topological *aspect* of the scenario. Different schemas can therefore apply to the same scenario, but they do not have to be co-localized inside the same overall structure as in the previous case, where the overall structure is the three-dimensional space. In Talmy (1983), we find the following example of a physical manifestation which can be schematized in different ways, but without any continuous connection between the underlying objective structures of the schemas. The manifestation is a man going from one side of a wheatfield to the other and the linguistic examples are: "the man went *across* the wheatfield" and "the man went *through* the wheatfield". In the first case, we schematize the field as a horizontal, bound plane, and in the second case, as consisting of stalks of wheat which constitute a medium.

It is also obvious, and expectable, that we have a selection from language to language. However, one can venture the hypothesis that we frequently will find some "universal" schemas which apply to the prototypical cases and selection is then performed on the non-prototypical ones. For example, action-schemas, as in "the child kicked the ball", and motion-schemas, as in "the boy went to the shop", are probably very general schemas which will capture the prototypical cases in most languages.[6] However, an activity like "seeing" is not a prototypical action, so one would expect that "see" could be schematized in either of the two ways mentioned above. Indeed, in English, "the boy saw the ship" is structurally and thereby schematically equivalent to the action expressed in "the boy kicked the ball", whereas in Samoan it is schematized as a motion, something like "saw the boy to the ship", expressing the idea that seeing is a motion from the perceiver to the object perceived. This example is from Langacker (1991: 304), and it once more shows, now on a cultural level, that the speaker selects a perspective on the scenario which he wants to describe, but that the selection is determined by objective features of the external world, which in this case is the existence of action and motion.

Thus, in sum, on the first semantic level, sem$_1$, we find geometric, topological, dynamic, and quantitative *properties* of the external world which determine the conceptual level in the sense that language selects one or more *aspects* of these properties to describe a given scenario. The selected aspects constitute the *schema*. Two different aspects can independently describe the same scenario, which provides us with two different ways of schematizing the same physical manifestation. This gives two different *perspectives* on the same manifestation, but these perspectives are objectively founded in the above-mentioned properties. This realistic grounding of meaning cannot, however, account for all aspects of language. For example, the perspective of the speaker can be due to the internal structure of the mental space and not to the structure of the external space. In this case, we can get an internal mental relation to a mental representation of an external content, so we get the doubling which has been mentioned earlier. This can account for abstract representation in which some schematized material constitutes an internal ideational structure which can relate to a mental representation of external content. One can venture the hypothesis that this is only possible if there is an elaborated symbolic representation of the conceptual structure.

---

[6] This does not mean that the conceptual content of these sentences will be expressed syntactically in the same manner in the different languages. One has to distinguish between schematic form and linguistic expression.

IV   Symbolic Representation

In *Gödel, Escher, Bach*, Hofstadter presents the idea that to understand meaning one needs the notion of mappings between qualitatively different levels. In the following we will view the symbolic level as separate and different from the conceptual and schematic organization. The symbolic level should not be confused with the level of expression, where the speaker enounces an utterance — the so-called enunciation. The structure of mappings between the conceptual and the symbolic levels can be seen as a part of the neural organization of meaning; the mappings will then correspond to synaptic connections between separate structures in the brain, at least according to the biologist Edelman (cf. Edelman 1992). Here we do not have to worry about the details of the neural structure, but this structure gives rise to mappings on a higher order, which we can describe as follows. The concepts are mapped onto the symbolic level, not necessarily one-to-one, but the point is that the symbolic level is itself mapped onto the conceptual structure. A symbol, for example *tree*, is not just the image of the concept /tree/ under the above mapping, but it is itself mapped onto the conceptual structure; for example, it maps onto the concept /noun/. The sentence *"tree* is a noun" is then a meta-linguistic reflection which is only possible because there is a structure of mappings between the conceptual and the symbolic levels which constitutes a *loop*. The loop makes it possible for language to comment on language.

In relation to the schematic level we find the same loop structure. The mapping of the schematic structure we will recognize on the symbolic level as *syntax*. For example, force-dynamic verbs like "make", and "force" are considered "more" schematic than for instance "kick", "move", and "kill". This is reflected on the syntactic level because the force-dynamic verbs often have a subordinate clause in which the verb is nonfinite. One can say "he made the ball roll", but not "he kicked the ball to roll". This exemplifies that schematic differences are mapped into syntactic differences on the symbolic level. However, because of the loop between the schematic structure and the symbolic level, any syntactic construction is again subjected to a schematization. We have schemas for syntactic constructions as well as for conceptual structures; one can, for example, consult Taylor (1989), in particular the chapter entitled "Syntactic Constructions as Prototype Categories".

In the first place, the schematic structure represents *aspects and perspectives on the topological, geometric and dynamic properties of external space and time*. For this to happen it is necessary that a primary mental space be generated from which this perspective can be taken; this mental space corresponds to the sem$_1$-level. It probably emerges during the first years of children's language aquisition, when children learn to express intentions, including concepts, simple actantial schemas, relations between actants, spacial location, etc. If the syntactic form itself is schematized, this requires the emergence of a new mental space, in which it is possible to select an *aspect of the syntactic form*, and from this perspective reorganize it on the level of expression. However, if the schema organizing the primary semantic material refers to mathematical properties of external space, what do the syntactic schemas refer to? What are they aspects of? If we call the first mental space M_1 and the second M_2, then the secondary reality from which the second mental space emerges has formal properties, some of which can be characterized in the following manner.

a) *Inferential structure*. From the structure of M_1 it is possible to infer the existence of elements which do not themselves belong to M_1. This is the construction of a "possible" epistemic world which, however, is regulated by the *material laws* governing the space of reference represented in M_1. It is also, of course, governed by modal forces and modal laws, but those are to some extent co-existent with the doubling of mental space in the sense that it is the modal forces which motivate the application of inferential structure on the content world representations. Ultimately, this is of course due to memory.

b) The construction of *possible worlds which are not epistemically regulated*. These constructions consist essentially of the rearrangements or permutations of elements in M_1, the removal of elements, and the adding of elements. We can then formally describe the mental space M_2 as a mapping between another basic mental space U representing the content world and subsets of that same mental space (that is why it cannot constitute a metaphor). If the mapping is the identity map, it does not cause any change of perspective. If it is not the identity, but one-to-one, it represents a permutation of some elements in the content world. If U is mapped onto a proper subset of itself, the operation corresponds to the removal of elements in the representation; we shall later exemplify this with negation. Finally, if U is mapped one-to-one into a larger space it corresponds to the adding of elements. Of course, it can also map into a larger space in a manner which is not one-to-one but which is a "blending" of the two preceding mappings and therefore causing a more complicated description. These mappings and constructions are essentially *regulated by iconic and scale properties*: for example, if one wants to add something to a kitchen scenario, it should be relevant for the scale and our iconic representations of kitchens. Fairy tales often seem to violate this cognitive principle by introducing elements which are either too small or too big (e.g., giants). Maybe even fairy tales can be characterized by this.

c) *Projections*. In this case a whole scenario is projected onto just a part of the same scenario. The difference from b) is that the projection is not a discrete but a conti-

162

nuous mapping. In semantic terms we would say that the target of the projection constitutes a profile of the whole scenario, in the same manner as the projection on a screen is a profile of a three-dimensional figure.

To a), b), and c) one has to add a principle of blending in the sense of Turner and Fauconnier (cf. Turner and Fauconnier 1995). The formal properties, which constitute the reality of M_2, have to be blended with the elements of M_1 in the actual expression. In the above description of these properties we referred to M_1, but this reference is not inherent in the formal properties themselves; they can be described "algebraically", independently of M_1. In other words, we have an abstract space of *possible transformations* existing independently of the morphology and dynamic structure of the perceived world, and this space has its own internal structure which can be analysed "algebraically". *Blending* is itself an operation in M_2, making it possible to relate epistemic variations, permutations, iconic variations, scale variations and projections to the world represented on the first semantic level. The two mental spaces are related in a dynamic and structurally stable way, so that it becomes possible to "apply" the space of possible transformations to the content world.

That there is an internal structure in a), b), and c) has already been demonstrated for the epistemic case a), for example from a cognitive point of view in Sweetser (1990), and from a semiotic and dynamic point of view in Brandt (1992).

To return to the question of syntax, the different syntactic schemas represent different perspectives the speaker can take on the world, but now we do not mean a perspective objectively founded in the structure of space/time/dynamics, but a perspective determined by the principles outlined in a), b), and c). If such a perspective gets an operative effect in the mental space(s) of the speaker, then it causes a selection of a specific syntactic construction to express the semantic content. The principles mentioned above will therefore be reflected in the syntactic structure of language. The speaker selects a syntactic form according to a), b), and c) — this selection is essentially equivalent with the operation of blending. However, there has to be a *motivation* for the selection. This motivation is probably *modal*. Therefore, as we already mentioned under a) above, there is a dynamic structure underlying the emergence of the linguistic forms that pertain to the mental space M_2. It is because the speaker is placed in a field of conflicting forces that he develops the capacities for making inferences, omissions, projections, abstractions, lies, etc. This has been demonstrated in a considerable number of works by Brandt (cf. Brandt 1992 and 1995). This being said, once the modalization has taken place, the linguistic form is determined by certain operations which can be analysed according to the principles mentioned above.

Let us look at the following two sentences from Langacker (1991): *line A intersects line B* and *line B intersects line A*; they refer to the same phenomenon in the content world, but as Langacker remarks, they do not have exactly the same meaning because there is a difference in the focus of interest expressed in the two. Although the motivation for this difference is modally determined, the possibility of expressing it is determined by the structure of an abstract space of possible permutations, in this case a very simple one where only two elements are permuted. This is the operation mentioned under b) which is mentally represented in M_2 and then implemented on the semantics of the content world M_1.

Another example which falls under b) is *negation*. Firstly, it is not a question of denying the content of perception. Negation is an operation which removes one or more elements in a given *representation* of the content world, so it does not work on the world but on the level sem$_1$. Secondly, negation has to do with epistemic and affective evaluations of the representations of the other, therefore, the modal structure underlying negation is much more complicated than in the first example. Nevertheless, there are some formal possibilities on which the modal dynamics works, so we can determine negation according to the formal description in b) in the following way: suppose S_1 and S_2 have some mental representations U_1 and U_2 of the same scenario in the content world; S_1 *negates* an element a that belongs to U_2 by means of a mapping from U_1 into U_2, excluding the element from the domain of the image. Therefore, the quotient $U_2/$ *(Image of the mapping)* constitutes the negated part. If the image is the empty set, the whole representation is negated. In this way one can consider negations as belonging to an order higher than the direct representations of the content world; they belong to the level of *mappings* between mental spaces.

As an example of *projection*, c) above, we can mention passive constructions. In a passive sentence like "the door was opened" there is a participant, the agent, which is not specified, although it is an integrated part of the scenario; however, this is of course not a question of negation. One has to recognize that the sentence presents the full schematic form of the action taking place in content world, so in fact the sentence represents a projection from the full scenario to a part of it. It is the same as recognizing a three-dimensional figure by looking at a projection on the wall. In the linguistic case, the projection is of course a perspective selected not for external but for internal reasons. The fact that the sentence represents the projection and the projected figure at the same time shows that this is a perfect example of blending, because the figure belongs to the content world representation, whereas the selected perspective belongs to an inner mental-world representation.

Coordinations of sentences, by means of "and", "or", "because", "if...then", "although", etc., all belong to the first group, a), because they represent epistemic evaluations of representations of a content world. They are all operations which cannot be derived from the content world. There are geometric and topological structures in space, but there is no *"if"-structure*. The origin of these operations therefore lies in the doubling of the mental space, in the existence of memory, which makes it possible to relate actual perceptual input with absent structures stabilized in memory and to have mental representations of two conflicting versions of the content world at the same time. In Brandt (1995), the connectors are analysed from this point of view. As soon as we have a doubling of the mental space, certain operations between the spaces become possible which are not inherent in the content world. We get the emergence of a secondary *world of possibilities*, which is essentially what has been denoted M_2.

It goes without saying that metaphors are dependent on the doubling of mental spaces. In this context we can say that irrespective of how one wants to conceive of metaphors, the concept of *mapping* is indispensable. But mapping belongs to the M_2-reality, any construction involving mappings falls under the b)-category above. It is the mapping which makes it possible for the subject to see a structural identity between two different mental representations and thereby construct a metaphor or an abstraction of some sort.[7]

Let us summarize the last part briefly. The doubling of mental space makes certain operations on the representations of the content world possible. These operations are therefore integrated parts of the second mental space. Each operation corresponds in fact to an internal perspective on the content representation. By an operation of *blending* this internal perspective combines with the content space to give rise to a syntactic form on the side of expression.

To substantiate the above, one can pay attention to the fact that in children's acquisition of language, it is only in the late phase that they are able to master negation, passive constructions, embeddings and coordination of sentences (cf. Brown, 1973 and also Petitot 1985: 137). We can see this as an argument for the distinction between at least two levels of mental spaces, and also for our claim that the last one

---

[7] The concept of *mapping* is the blind spot of the theory of metaphor of cognitive linguistics. This is of course a field in considerable development, but at least in its earlier phases there was a tendency to consider the content-world as the source for every metaphor. Therefore, any mental construction was essentially the result of a mapping from the source domain, i.e., the content-world. But the mapping itself, is that an element in the content-world? Apparently not, because in that case the whole theory would implode into just being a theory about the content-world. The mapping is therefore an Archimedean point, from which the linguist constructs his theory of metaphor.

embeds the first one, making possible a schematization of external space/time. The one doing the embedding, M_2, is a representation of the internal representations through which the child can relate to its own relation to the world. M_2 is therefore the source of modal expressions, abstractions, and formal operations such as embeddings and juxtapositions. M_2 comes later than M_1, because it depends on a feedback mechanism from the symbolic representations of M_1 to the schematic level in which the symbolic level is itself schematized, enabling the speaker to select from the syntactic possibilities according to an internal mental state. By the introduction of loop-mappings the space of epistemic and abstract realities is grounded in the existence of a specific symbolic system in which meaning is expressed by means of strings of symbols, whereby "algebraic" operations become possible which make way for the possibility of several options to express a given content. The different "algebraic" variations can then naturally be attached to the different mental states of the speaker which are expressed jointly with external references. This would not be possible if for example language consisted of holo-sounds expressing a schematic content in a holistic way. The "algebraic" decomposition of meaning is necessary for the emergence of higher order consciousness through which meta-linguistic comments can appear.

We can illustrate the previous remarks by the following figure:[8]

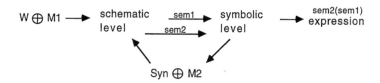

Fig. 1

The weird notation W⊕M1 just signifies that we have some unspecified relation between mental representations and external forms which causes a schematic level to emerge. The schematic forms are represented in symbolic strings with sem₁ as the corresponding semantic form. The development of the mental capacity to take different perspectives on the representations of the content world puts the speaker in a perpetual dynamic situation. Firstly, we have a dynamics between representations of the external content world and the internally motivated perspectives. Se-

---

[8] This figure is inspired by Edelman (1992).

condly, this amounts to a conflict, labelled $Syn \oplus M_2$, between the selected internal perspective and the syntactic constraints language puts on expression. This causes a sensitivity to syntax, i.e., a schematization of syntactic forms which now become attuned to the inner mental representations. The syntactic schemas are then again expressed in symbolic strings, but now the semantics, sem_2, refers to the speaker's construal, independent of the objective properties inherent in the situation. Finally, the expression is a joined structure in which the first semantic level is embedded in the second.

V Example

Of course, just to make a distinction between the two semantic levels, sem_1 and sem_2, is fairly trivial, so one should be more explicit about how the embedding of sem_1 in sem_2 takes place. In cognitive linguistics one does not conceive the relation as an embedding, but rather as a question of mappings between the two levels so that "image-schematic" material is transferred from one level to the other. In more sophisticated versions the relation is seen as a *blending*. This is in accordance with the approach taken here in so far as one sees it as a "blending" between an "image-schematic"/iconic level and the symbolic level, i.e., the perspective in this paper is that these two levels are essentially separated because certain procedures for grammaticalization express a subjective construal in the mental space M_2. The subject can take a perspective on the image-schematic representations and express this perspective by "formal" rearrangements of the elements. The problem is then to examine whether or not we can find any general laws regulating this superposition of formal structure on image-schematic forms.

Another problem is how one can justify the "model" presented in Fig. 1. It is a consequence of the model that any schematic representation of basic grammatical notions cannot be based on objective properties inherent in the content world but has to refer to the speaker's construal from the point of view of M_2-space. This seems indeed to be the case if one follows Langacker's exhaustive analysis of basic grammatical relations such as subject, object, etc. Let us take the case of the *subject* of the sentence, which is analysed in Langacker (1991: 305-313).

According to Langacker, the kind of cognitive salience which characterizes grammatical subjects can best be described by what the tradition calls *topicality*. Topicality is determined by four factors, of which two pertain to the objective properties of the situation and the other two are determined by the speaker's construal. The first factor is the *semantic role*. The prototypical subject with maximal topicality is here the agent.

The second factor is the subject's location in what Langacker calls the *empathy hierarchy*:

speaker > hearer > human > animal > physical object > abstract entity

It seems as if the subject always has to rank higher than the object in this hierarchy and therefore a prototypical subject will be human. However, a participant's location in the hierarchy is an objective determination of the situation. This is not the case for the third factor, which is *definiteness*: a participant is marked as indefinite if the speaker and hearer do not have prior knowledge of its presence, but this is not a property of the external content, only of the mental space, M_2, of the speaker. Here too we have a hierarchy: definite → specific indefinite → indefinite, in which the subject ranks higher than the object. The fourth topicality factor is the *figure/ground* organization, which of course can be motivated by the situation but is in general due to the speakers perspective and therefore is a subjective factor.

Langacker wants to find a schematic form of the notion *subject* by means of these topicality factors, but it is clear that the first three cannot be general determinations of the subject. The subject can take any semantic role, be placed anywhere in the empathy hierarchy, and be indefinite (Langacker's example: *workable strategies are being sought by corporate management*). Langacker tries the weaker claim that for transitive sentences the subject is agent-like. For example, one could examine whether the subject can be described as an *action-chain head*; however, this will not do for examples like "I remember my childhood very well". One could then try the more general description *active participant in an asymmetrical relationship*, but then we get problems with the sentence mentioned above: *line A intersects line B*. With respect to this last sentence, Langacker remarks that we do not quite get the same meaning if we interchange *line A* and *line B*. Therefore, one can say that the motivation for the selection of the subject is that it is the focus of the interest of the speaker, i.e. it is a *figure*; therefore, finally, the schematic form of the notion subject can be described in the following manner:

What all transitive subjects have in common is not a particular semantic role, but rather the status of figure within the clausal profile. Of course, this characterization is not inherently tied to transitivity - it is equally applicable to intransitive subjects.[9]

---

[9] Langacker (1991: 312).

168

This example shows that it is not possible to make a general description of the schematic forms of basic grammatical notions just with reference to the morpho-dynamic properties of the external space, for example semantic roles and/or the type of saliency implied by the participants. It shows that at least the problem of figure/ground alignment has to be involved, but by figure/ground I am not referring to gestaltic properties of external forms, but to the formal possibility of selecting a perspective or a focus of interest on the situation which is not motivated by the morpho-dynamic structure. It is important to stress that although *line A intersects line B* has the same syntactic form as "the cat eats the mouse" and therefore can be said to represent a dynamic schematization of the referent, in the first case, this is due to a selection among two possibilities, whereas in the second case, it is not. It is therefore necessary to understand this double determination of semantic forms. On the one hand, they are determined by the morpho-dynamics of space/time, which constitutes a deep level and is determined by the objective properties of a world of phenomena subjected to mathematical regularities.[10] On this level, the structure of meaning is independent of its symbolic expression: for example, the force-dynamic categories of Talmy have an internal structure independent of the syntactic level of language. On the other hand, there are structures of meaning which cannot be analysed independently of the way they are expressed syntactically. This is the "surface" level of meaning, originating in the possibility of "editing" the representations of the phenomenal world. This space of possibilities is not without structure and it even has a dynamic form, as it is strongly tied up with the affective structure of the subject, but it is also subjected to syntactic constraints. This is a motivation for qualifying it as a surface-level semantic, i.e., there is a strong semantic effect in the syntactic style of the speaker irrespective of the subject matter.[11]

VI Discourse

One of the most interesting questions one can put to cognitive science is the follo-

---

[10] *Objective* and *mathematical* are of course controversial terms in the above phrase. To justify the claim would be an enormous task; we can only refer to the works of Petitot for a clarification, especially Petitot (1985 and 1992a).

[11] This is clear in the psycho-semiotic analysis of psychotic texts, where any direct reference is often absent and therefore the syntactic constructions become carriers of meaning.

wing: Is there a continuous relation between cognitive forms as they appear in language and discursive formations? If this is the case, those cognitive forms which organize discourse must obviously stem from the sem$_1$-level. This seems to be the position taken by Lakoff, for example, to whom mathematics will be the ultimate test for such a claim (cf. Lakoff 1996). Lakoff's observations are not necessarily wrong; on the contrary, the problem is just that the investigations are always punctual. A given concept is separated and then examined from the point of view of the linguist. By this method one overlooks at least four things:

1) All the concepts in, for example, mathematics play a specific role in a global discursive formation, and this role is not necessarily related to or exhausted by how the concept is described semantically. Instead, the role is determined by specific problems and placed in a conceptual network so as to solve these problems.

2) Most concepts are the results of *discoveries*, this is the case, for example, with irrational numbers and non-Euclidean geometry. The discoveries are the results of the attempt made through discourse to solve specific problems, but they are not necessarily the solutions to the problems; often they are unpleasant by-products, as in the two examples above.

3) The emergence of new concepts depends on the *historical state of the discourse*, the specific argumentative forms that the discourse has accepted, its development of techniques for solving problems, and especially on its degree of formalization.

Example 1. In the eighteenth century, mathematicians tried to give a consistent presentation of the theory of real functions. In this attempt they were led to the necessity of considering actually presented infinite sets. For example, given an infinite set of sets, one element is taken from each set. This gives an actual "existing" infinite collection of elements. There is no cognitive justification for this procedure, but it was necessary for technical reasons.[12] However, from this technique, elevated to an axiom in the mathematical tradition, it is possible to prove totally counter-intuitive statements about known mathematical structures. This example therefore defies that the development of a discourse is solely determined by the cognitive level. One can get results which defy cognition.

Example 2. The discovery of non-Euclidean geometry was dependent on an axiomatic and formal representation of the Euclidean one. The key point in this respect was that the axiomatic representation contained a quantification: namely, in

---

[12] The concept of *infinity* presented here is different from the concept invoked when one says that space is infinite or that time is eternal, etc. Although there is a cognitive basis for this infinity of limits, it does not account for the concept of an actual existing infinite set of elements.

the fifth axiom: *Given a line and a point outside the line then it is possible to draw one and only one line through the point which does not intersect the given.* Although the axiom seems cognitively well-grounded, it is still formally possible to change the quantifier from, for example, one to none, or from one to infinitely many, etc. What came out of these formal exercises were new consistent geometries, although the actual aim was to invalidate the changed axiomatic system. Later, these geometries appeared to be significant for the understanding of the content world's morphology, as, for example, in the general theory of relativity. However, here the important thing is that the description of the emergence of non-Euclidean geometry corresponds to the model presented in Fig. 1. As the first element, we simply have space with some primary schematic form, essentially equivalent to the axioms of Euclidean geometry. The corresponding semantic form is identical with what we call Euclidean space; this is the space in which the dynamics of Lakoff's *embodiment* takes place. However, this causes a mathematical discourse to emerge, though this discourse is never stabilized because of the possibility of formal changes in the schematic structure. This possibility, which is not inherent in space itself, is represented by the mental space M_2 in Fig. 1. It causes new schematic forms of space to appear which are then integrated in the mathematical discourse as non-Euclidean geometries. Note that the semantic forms of these non-Euclidean geometries can be precisely located, as for example in the form of a sphere. Let us summarize by repeating Fig. 1 with the appropriate terms added:

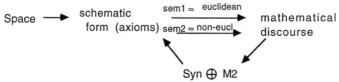

Fig. 2

The conclusion to be drawn from Example 2 is that the dynamics of Fig. 2 is a very general one, valid for cognition as well as for thinking and thereby for the formation of global discourses.

4) One of the main features of higher order discourses is that there is no upper limit to the formation of embedded structure; that it is possible to embed thoughts in thoughts an indefinite number of times. The development of scientific discourses is dependent on this faculty. This is of course contrary to language, in which the punctuation mark ensures that the number of embeddings is small, restricted by the confines of a sentence. Moreover, when scientific discourse is presented in langua-

ge, then embedded units of thought do not correspond to the sentence structure. Therefore, we are dealing with a faculty which transcends the faculty of information transmission by means of language. What remains to be examined is how the structure of scientific discourse *is* organized. One idea, which was presented by the French mathematician Lautman in the thirties, is that discourse is organized by means of logical schemas, i.e., patterns of thinking which exist independently in different discourses. As an example, one can mention the notion of *completion*: if an object is incomplete in certain respects, then by a successive series of steps or embeddings one can construct a complete version; for details we can refer to Østergaard (1995). Of course, the question of the ontological status of the logical schema remains. Probably there is some inherent structure in the subject matter which presents itself globally. Discourse is then a representation of this global presentation by means of local embeddings of thoughts. It is not possible to go into detail on this mechanism here; we just want to point to the fact that embeddings and juxtapositions work differently in higher order discourse than in ordinary discourse.

VII Conclusion

If by icon is meant a sign defined by its relation of resemblance to the "reality" of the exterior world, then we can clearly locate a level of iconicity in our presentation of schematic forms; this is the level which is labelled sem_1. However, this level is superposed by non-icon operations which in fact ground the subject, because it makes it possible for the agent or the speaker to relate freely to the iconicity of the first level. The speaker can situate himself in possible worlds by means of operations which are not themselves iconic. A negation, for example, does not have an iconic base. This gives rise to the schematic forms labelled sem_2.

Similar remarks can be made concerning higher order discourses; cf. 3) above. The difference is that the conceptual structure is very unstable because of a flow of new discoveries into the discursive field, cf. 1) above. Moreover, the formal operations available for constructing new statements about this flow of discoveries clearly surpass what can be found in language; for example, there is no upper limit to the number of embeddings that can be found.[13]

---

[13] Oddly enough, this is Lakoff's main argument against Chomsky's generative linguistics. In the Chomskian tradition, the formal scientific description of language is also an intrinsic property of language; therefore, the non-limitation of embeddings, which is an intrinsic property of scientific discourse, is transposed into language, contradicting the empirical findings.

References

Brandt, Per Aage. 1992. *La charpente modale du sens.* Aarhus: Aarhus University Press.

—. 1995. 'Domains and Meanings.' *Journal of Pragmatics,* 25: 281-305.

Brown, R. 1973. *A First Language.* Harvard University Press

Edelman, Gerald. 1992. *Bright Air, Brilliant Fire.* London: Penguin.

Hofstadter, Douglas. 1980. *Gödel, Escher, Bach.* New York: Vintage Books

Langacker, R.W. 1991. *Foundation of Cognitive Grammar.* Vol II. Stanford: Stanford University Press

Lakoff, George. 1990. *Women, Fire and Dangerous Things.* Chicago: Chicago University Press

Lakoff, George & Nunez, Rafael E. 1996. "Metaphorical structure of mathematics." In *Mathematical Reasonings: Analogies, Metaphors, and Images.* Lyn English (Ed.). Hillsdale, NJ: Erlbaum

Petitot, Jean. 1985. *Morphogenése du sens.* Paris: Presses Universitaires de France.

—. 1992a. *Physique du sens* Paris: Editions du CNRS.

— 1992b. 'Continu et Objectivité. La bimodalite objective du continu et le platonisme transcendantal.' In *Le labyrint du continu.* J.M. Salanski & H. Sinaceur (Eds.). New York: Springer.

Sweetser, Eve. 1990. *From Etymology to Pragmatics.* Cambridge: Cambridge University Press.

Talmy, Leonard. 1983. 'How Language Structures Space.' In *Spatial Orientation: Theory, Research, and Application.* H. Pick & L. Acredolo Eds. Plenum Press.

—. 1985. 'Force Dynamics in Language and Cognition.' In *Parasession on Causality and Agentivity* 293-337. Chicago: Chicago University Press.

Taylor, John R. 1989. *Linguistic Categorization.* Oxford: Clarendon Press.

Thom, René. 1972. *Stabilité structurelle et morphogenése.* New York: Benjamin.

—. 1988. *Esquisse d'une sémiophysique.* Paris: InterEditions.

Turner, Mark. & Fauconnier, Gilles. 1995. 'Conceptual Integration and Formal Expression.' Forthcoming in Mark Johnson (ed.) *Journal of Metaphor and Symbolic Activity,* vol 10, number 3.

Østergaard, Svend. 1995. 'Matematik og Skematik.' *Almen Semiotik,* 9-10: 40-62.

—. 1996. 'The Dynamics of Verbs.' *Semiotica* 118 - 3/4: 307-320.

Diagrammatic Reasoning
and Levels of Schematization

Michael May

I *Seeing as* and *Seeing in*

In the discussions of pictorial representation in the philosophy of art we find different ways of differentiating "seeing as" and "seeing in" a picture (Wollheim 1980). From the logical point of view the *seeing as* can be considered as a an abstract relation of representation (*see* X *as* Y) and from the cognitive point of view as an instance of categorial perception, where some perceived phenomena (X) is identified by assigning a type (Y) to it, i.e. *subsuming* it under a concept (Wollheim 1980). Where the *seeing as* phenomenologically is an experience of an identified particular, the *seeing in* is an experience of a state of affairs seen in the particular. The *seeing in* involves a "twofold attention" (Wollheim 1980), where the viewer identifies a set of figurative objects and simultaneously sees a whole state of affairs in their depiction.

The painting *Dejeuner sur l'herbe* (1961) by Pablo Picasso contains a set of figurative objects that we — in spite of their deformation relative to the human form — interpret as male and female bodies. We also engage in a more "imaginative seeing" (Schier 1986), however, where we interpret the scene on which these figures appear and the possible events that could take place there: we see "a picnic event" in the picture. In this imaginative seeing we freely *disregard* details of the picture and *complement* it with details not actually present in order to see some abstract idea in the picture. Through our knowledge of paintings we might even see the painting as portraying another painting, i.e. the painting with the same name by Eduard Manet (1863). Following Schier (1986) we could assume that we generally have a "three-fold" experience of and attention towards pictures such as paintings: a direct *seeing as*, a more imaginative *seeing in*, as well as an attention towards those *details and features that support the interpretations* at both levels.

Although these distinctions are not without problems (Schier 1986), I will defend a more general version of this "three-fold attention" hypothesis which revolves around the role of *imagination* in the perception of representations in general, i.e. not only "pictures" (graphical images), but also images in other *media* (acoustic images would give rise to similar distinctions between *hearing as, hearing in* and *details/ features of the sound*) as well as other categories of representations, such as diagrams.

In the case of *diagrams*, it becomes more obvious that we need to *know the intended interpretation* to be able to see them *as* diagrams of a specific type and to see *in* them those relevant relations, which they are intended to represent, and that the "three-fold attention" is needed in order to follow a graphically articulated proposition or argument. The imaginative aspect of *seeing in* diagrams — disregarding and complementing parts of the diagrams — is often overlooked in discussions of representation systems, because the two levels of interpretation, from the logical point of view, will be considered as a single "interpretation function" from syntactic elements of the image or diagram to the domain. This simple view of visual reasoning can be illustrated as in Figure 1 below (cf. Wang, Lee & Zeevat 1995).

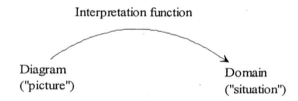

Fig. 1. *The simplified view of visual reasoning in logical semantics*

A case in point could be the "syntax directed approach to picture semantics" proposed by Wang & Zeevat (1996) and Wang, Lee & Zeevat (1995), which is interesting because of its algebraic approach. As a consequence of not considering any intermediate level of representation that could introduce schematic but nevertheless meaningful interpretations of images and diagrams prior to the specific interpretations imposed by the picture description language, they have no guiding lines for interpretation: 'There are no rules to guide users in giving a proper interpretation to pictures,' it is claimed by Wang & Zeevat (1996). In the absence of any semantic categories to guide users, the notion of "pictures" seems to comprise *diagrams* as well as *images*, i.e. all types of graphical objects regardless of their type. There is no consideration of different types (images and diagrams, different types of diagrams, etc.) of graphical representations as something that could impose *semantic structure* on the interpretation. Given that, following this approach, we aim at a formal description of diagrammatic representations, limiting our conception of semantics to syntactic similarities between "pictures" and what they represent, we run the risk of having to encode each new graphical object in its own *graphical signature*, i.e. its own graphical primitives, functions and predicates.

This is also the point of departure in Eric Hammers impressive survey of the formal aspects of different graphical systems or "graphical languages" for the expression of logical reasoning (Hammer 1995), such as Euler circles, Venn diagrams, existential graphs ("Peirce diagrams") and higraphs: 'for each type of diagram one will need to address the question of what an adequate mathematical model will be. It will require case by case attention' (Hammer 1995: 10). However, as a consequence of his detailed examination of the formal properties of those graphical systems, he is able to indicate how each of these types are related to each other. For instance he observes that the system of *higraphs* introduced by David Harel (Harel 1988) is an extension of Euler circles. Euler circles represent subsets of a domain with closed curves, and higraphs basically extend this feature with the ability to represent binary relations between these subsets using arrows. *Any Euler diagram is accordingly also a higraph*. Similarly *any Euler diagram will be equivalent to some Venn diagram*. The converse is not true: not every Venn diagram is equivalent to a Euler diagram. Euler diagrams are less expressive than either Venn diagrams or higraphs, but in so far as we can describe the logical properties of each of these graphical systems (properties such as: Venn diagrams are "closed under conjunction", Euler circles are not), we are able to *order them according to their invariant properties*, i.e. the properties that are invariant *under the operations that are allowed in each system*. Eric Hammer does not follow this all the way through, but it is a consequence of his observations that we should be able to establish a *taxonomy* of these graphical systems by ordering their properties.

The aim of such a taxonomy should of course not only be to describe an arbitrary limited set of graphical systems for the expression of logical reasoning — although each type will require "case by case attention" — but hopefully to arrive at a hypothesis about *the category of logic diagrams,* i.e. the universal properties of *all* logic diagrams and the morphological space of possible forms "covered by" the specific types of logic diagrams such as Euler circles or higraphs. The importance of this observation beyond the domain of logic is that we might extend the approach further and hypothesize about *the category of diagrams* in general, that is hypothesize about the *properties universally shared by all diagrams* (supported and restricted by the given media such as the graphical media) of which logic diagrams would be a *subcategory*. From this point of view we would expect to find properties characterizing other subcategories of diagrams such as *maps* or *graphs*.

Let us assume that we have succeeded in establishing a taxonomy of diagrams along the lines of what is outlined above. What would that imply with respect to the semantics of graphical objects? In the approach to *picture description languages* mentioned earlier we have no taxonomy of diagrams and no categories available for imposing semantic structure on the particular graphical object. Consequently the authors cannot, for instance, distinguish those aspects of the interpretation that depend on the gestalt laws of perception for instance from those aspects of the interpretation that depend on semantic categories. This is exactly a situation where we should distinguish *seeing as* and *seeing in*.

A nice simple example of this problem is given by the authors in relation to a discussion of invisible properties of graphical representations (Wang, Lee & Zeevat 1995). They introduce a notion of the "null" graphical object, meaning a graphical object that cannot be seen, and they represent it by the constant symbol ⊥. A geometrical object such as a circle A may correspond to more than one situation because, for any invisible property involving null objects such as the situation described by the predicate *in*(⊥, A), there are at least two different situations corresponding to the same diagram, one containing *in*(⊥, A) and the other its negation ¬ *in*(⊥, A). The problem with the representation (1) in the figure below, according to the authors, is that the different interpretations (the situations *seen in* the diagram!) are not made visually distinct to the viewer. (1) could for instance represent two circles that happen to overlap. They therefore claim that graphical objects used in visual communication 'should always be seen by the users'; but in what sense of "seen"? They claim that 'it does not make sense from a visual point of view to think that there is a square inside the filled circle' in (1), 'unless it can be seen' as in (2) or it can be 'partially seen' as in (3), where we can recognize a square according to the gestalt laws of visual perception.

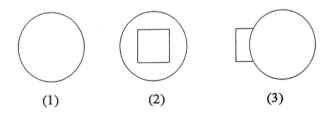

Fig. 2. Illustration of the problem of the "null" object (after Wang, Lee & Zeevat 1995)

The conclusion drawn by the authors is that the *geometrical* characterization of a diagram (or "picture" as they often say) should reflect correctly what one can *see in* the diagram. They want to establish such a simple mapping between the "geometry" and the "situations" it represents because they want "pictures" expressed in a graphical *language* to be viewed as *models* of a graphical *theory* of the language in the mathematical sense, i.e. in analogy to model theory in mathematics; the graphical theory should give the correct *axioms* for this.

There is however a fundamental flaw in this. My "pet example" of this is the case of Venn diagrams. It is a very important feature of our reasoning with simple logic diagrams such as Venn diagram that their geometrical characterization in axioms that (from the formal point of view) constitute the representational space or the scene on which specific situations in the domain can be represented is necessarily violated by the operations involved in actually representing these specific situations! The fundamental mapping of logic diagrams like Venn diagrams is the mapping from *sets* to *regions* in the plane. On the basis of this underlying mapping we interpret regions and relations between regions as sets and relations between sets. The interpretation might be seen as a kind of inverse function of the underlying mapping. This is however misleading because the mapping of sets to regions is precisely "underlying" in the sense that it only sets the "background" or the "scene" for the representation of a specific state of affairs in a particular diagram, the interpretation of which is *not* a simple inverse of any of these two mappings, but a *construction* based on both of them.

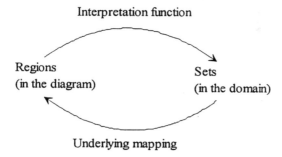

Fig. 3. A (partially misleading) illustration of the interpretation as an inverse function of the underlying mapping (see text).

The underlying mapping that makes the representation possible is in this case dependent upon a topological invariant originally stated by Camille Jordan and which is known as the *Jordan curve theorem* (Gardner 1982). According to this theorem any simple closed curve in the plane will partition the points in the plane into two regions, an "inside" and an "outside" region; this is intuitively evident, but has nevertheless not been easy to prove. The partition of the plane is used to represent set membership. Let us look at the simple case where we just have two sets A and B. In order for the representation to work, we will have to draw the curves such that they intersect. The underlying map will in this case give us three different regions — or four if we also introduce the "universe of discourse" U represented by a square enclosing the curves.

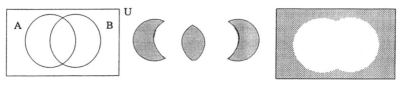

Figure 4. The four non-overlapping areas in the Venn diagram of two sets is shown as separate disjoint parts.

However the whole point of Venn diagrams — as opposed to Euler circles — is that it should be possible to express all possible situations. John Venn had argued that in constructing a diagrammatic system for expressing logical propositions *the diagrammatic and the symbolic scheme should be in complete accordance and harmony with each other*, the basic flaw of Leonhard Eulers circles being that this was not secured. Venn accordingly had to make sure, that all the different dyadic relations of propositional logic could be represented in a different spatial configuration of two simple closed curves (and similarly for the representation of triadic relations with three curves, etc.). Since there are $2^4 = 16$ different dyadic relations of two logical propositions when considering two truth values, we need to differentiate 16 different spatial configurations. This means that we need to have access to 16 regions, but according to the Jordan curve theorem we have graphically only produced 4 of these (cf. Figure 4) — the "minimal regions" having no other regions as a proper part (Hammer 1995). But this means that we somehow have to *construct* the other regions from these four. From the *logical point of view* all combinations arise from Boolean combinations (intersection, union and negation) of the original sets A, B and U. But according to the geometry of the mapping that constructs the minimal regions, the regions corresponding to the original sets are no longer available because of the intersection. The region A for instance is now intersected and therefore separated in two regions according to the Jordan curve theorem:

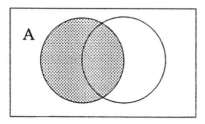

Fig. 5. The region corresponding to the set A is seen as a unified region although it is intersected in the diagram as a geometric object.

From the *cognitive point of view,* this does not pose any problem, but the point is that seeing the region corresponding to A as a unified region (corresponding to the shading of A in Fig. 5) is a cognitive construction: we can easily see two or more regions as one region, and on top of this *seeing as* we can *see* the set A represented *in* the diagram. These cognitive constructs violate the geometric description of how the underlying mapping works, i.e. the representation of sets into regions based on the principle of the Jordan curve theorem. The reason why this is not a problem in reasoning with the diagrams is our ability to dynamically abstract from properties and relations in the geometric figure that are not relevant at a given moment in the reasoning process.

This is also stressed as an aspect of the *intended interpretation* in the approach of Wang, Lee & Zeevat:

> [...] one often sees that the information carried by a diagram is subject to a certain kind of *abstraction.* In other words, one often emphasize some of the properties of the graphical objects, but at the same time intentionally ignores (or abstracts away from) the other properties. (Wang, Lee & Zeevat 1995: 359)

In the case of Venn diagrams this abstraction does not only include the abstraction from metrical properties like the size of the closed curves, but also the momentary disregarding of intersections that is actually relevant for (other parts of) the reasoning process. What is relevant or not relevant is accordingly not simply a static abstraction from something that is not 'relevant for the subject matter' (Wang, Lee & Zeevat 1995), but a *dynamic abstraction from relevant information.*

In a previous study (May 1995) I have used the case study of Venn diagrams to show how the role of diagrams in logical reasoning is also misconstrued in cognitive semantics by George Lakoff. In his eagerness to present an alternative to "object-ivist semantics" (Lakoff 1987), he gives an overly simplified account of diagram-matic reasoning as a kind of direct perception of image schematic structures that do not involve any symbolic inference but only cognitive operations like superimposition and focusing (Lakoff 1988a). The example he uses depicts two Euler circles A and B and a point x inside A. The set or class A is depicted as a subset or subclass of B, and following the (symbolic!) rules for the construction of Euler circles (that are different from the corresponding Venn diagrams) the circle A is accordingly represented inside B without any intersection, as shown in Figure 6.

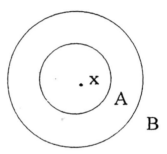

Fig. 6. Lakoff's example of visual reasoning based on the container as an image schema. The figure corresponds to Euler circles and the implied reasoning to the property of transitivity.

Lakoff seems to be unaware of the problems inherent in Euler circles. For example we cannot represent whether 'some B are not A' (so we might have B = A), although this seems to be a conclusion following from the diagram. In a Venn diagram shading would be used to represent empty regions and the point x would indicate that A is not empty.

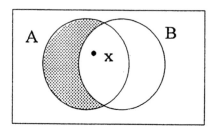

Fig. 7. The Venn diagram corresponding to the information given in the Euler diagram in Figure 6. By the symbolic convention of shading it is shown that 'No A is not B' (i.e. 'All A is B'), and that 'There exists some A', which is labeled "x". It is not know whether 'Some B is not A' (and this can be seen in the Venn diagram but not in the corresponding Euler circles).

Lakoff implicitly identifies the Euler circles with the abstract image schemas of cognitive semantics, since he refers directly to the geometric figures of Fig. 6 as container-schemas (Lakoff 1988a). Accordingly, Lakoff does not differentiate between the gestalt properties of vision operating on the geometric figures (including high-level cognitive operations such as superimposition and focusing) and abstract semantic relations *seen in* the diagram (such as transitivity). His example in relation to our figure 6 above is that it is seen instantly, *without making any deductive inference*, that 'x is in B', because the container-schema has "built-in logics" that arise from their topological properties independent of the symbolic structures which we would otherwise need to express transitivity and other properties, such as axioms of the form:

$\forall$ x, A: container(A) $\Rightarrow$ in(x, A) $\lor$ $\neg$ in(x, A)

$\forall$ x, A, B: container(A) $\land$ container(B) $\land$ in(A, B) $\land$ in(x, A) $\Rightarrow$ in(x, B)

In his own words Lakoff states that:

One of the most interesting properties of image-schemas is that they have *built-in logic's*. For example, bounded region schemas, also called container-schemas, have essentially a Boolean logic. Consider two container schemas A and B, such that A is in B, and object x is in A. We 'see' instantly, without doing any logical deduction, that x is in B. All we need to do is shift our focus to the relationship between x and B. [...] In general, image schemas have logic's built into their topological structures, and spatial inferences arise via the application of attentional mechanisms. (Lakoff 1988b: 302).

Transitivity does not however follow by itself simply from the topology of what is seen by looking at the geometric figures, because seeing is a semiotic process that involves interpretation at several levels. Rather than confusing the level of the geometric figures seen with the level of abstract schematic structures such as the container schema, we ought to understand how the interpretation is constructed in cognition by imposing structure on what is seen and understood. We could speak of these levels as *levels of schematization.* We impose a container schema on the geometric figures of Fig. 6, but even under this interpretation it does not follow directly ('without doing any logical deduction') that x is in B. In fact we could understand the figure as representing the situation that 'x is in A, but not in B', since we could interpret the same abstract schematics as representing *modal barriers* ('x cannot move into B') rather than *logical boundaries.*

The conclusion — *and it is a logical conclusion and not an instant perceptual fact* — that 'x is in B' is dependent on the *implied abstract properties of the diagram*, such as the properties of transitivity, which again mean that it is dependent upon the classification of the geometric object *as representing a diagram of a particular type* (Euler circles, Venn diagrams, etc.). The properties are "implied" in the sense that they can only follow from the *knowledge* of Euler circles (or Venn diagrams) and of symbolic logic in general, and therefore from the whole mathematical construction of such a mapping between logic and geometry, and not directly from (an unmediated) perception.

Already in 1882, Augustus de Morgan criticized in a letter to John Herschel the attempts to reduce logical consequence in mathematical reasoning to syntactic consequence in a purely formal, uninterpreted, system of symbols. What was lacking from the formalist reduction was, according to de Morgan, the acknowledgment, that *mathematical reasoning cannot be detached from the representation of knowledge* (Richards 1980: 359). It would seem that in his polemical attempt to deconstruct the "symbolic" and "objectivist" paradigm in logical semantics and in cognitive science, Lakoff has introduced the inverse "iconistic" reduction of mathematical reasoning, but with the same consequence of overlooking the representation of knowledge. The logic of transitivity (and the excluded middle and other logical properties) is not "built into" the *cognitive topology* of container schemas in any simple way, since any concrete logic diagram based on containment can have several interpretations dependent upon the intended interpretation of the diagram and the implied knowledge of the conceptual structure relevant for the intended interpretation.

Lakoff's account of logic diagrams does not only tend to underestimate the symbolic determination of their interpretation, but as we have seen he also seems to identify the conceptual structure of image schemata with the geometric or "pictorial" structure of a concrete image. This is seen most clearly in his appeal to connectionism (Lakoff 1988b). Seeing, in Lakoffs analysis, seems to be equivalent to immediate "insight", and there is therefore no *contemplative function of the schema* in its mentally constructed and genuinely *iconic* sense, where it can be distinguished from the concrete *diagram* as a real geometric object or "picture".

Going back to the abstraction of diagrammatic reasoning discussed earlier, the adding and subtracting of parts of the diagram is a necessary aspect of reasoning in order for us to be able to bridge the gap between *the geometry of what is "seen"* and *the semantics and "cognitive topology" of what is thought*, and in this sense *seen in* the diagram. We see less (i.e. disregarded boundaries) and more (i.e. an image schema) in the geometric object in the act of "seeing in" a diagram.

How could such a "seeing in" be realized by a cognitive agent? In the case of Venn diagrams, the idea of an immediate insight would suggest that we could somehow manage to see all the different spatial configurations at one glance, as if we saw through a series of transparent layers of configurations that were all projected on the plane and "superimposed" there, with all the manifest boundaries. According to this hypothesis *we would see all the models that interpret a concrete diagram "at once" by seeing them directly in the resulting projection.* This solution does however not seem very plausible from a cognitive point of view.

One other solution that seems more plausible would imply *"mental manipulation" of mental equivalents of the diagram* (or parts of the diagram) over some time in order to construct different spatial configurations. Somehow the cognitive agent would observe and discover properties and relations in these constructions, and draw conclusions from this mental process of construction, manipulation and observation. This is exactly the suggestion of Charles S. Peirce, who introduced the concept of *diagrammatic reasoning.*

II Diagrammatic Reasoning

Charles Sanders Peirce introduced the concept of *diagrammatic reasoning* long before it was reformulated and rediscovered by the Artificial Intelligence community (Glasgow, Narayanan & Chandrasekaran 1995). For Peirce it was related to an iterative process of *construction, manipulation and observation* of parts and relations in external diagrams or mental equivalents of such diagrams by a cognitive agent. The purpose of constructing diagrams is that they serve as a kind of mental model or analogy of the object of reasoning, where the model or analogy makes it easier to manipulate parts of the model in order to observe and evaluate different consequences. It is a kind of mental experimentation such as we know it from thought experiments or from simulations of complex models on computers, ex that the Peircian concept is much broader.

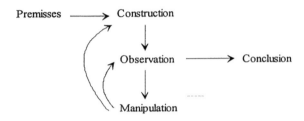

Fig. 8. The iterative process of diagrammatic reasoning

The concept was introduced in relation to the philosophy of mathematics. In "On the algebra of logic" (1885), Peirce argued for a conception of mathematics, that would place it among the observational and experimental sciences, since

> [...] even simple syllogism, involves an element of observation; namely deduction consists in constructing an icon or diagram, the relations of whose parts shall present a complete analogy with those of the parts of the object of reasoning; of experimenting upon this image in the imagination, and of observing the result, so as to discover unnoticed and hidden relations among the parts. (Peirce 1885)

Interpreting diagrams often involves some kind of reconstruction of them as external "snapshots" of a continuos transformation or process. The continuity is not just a property of the domain of the diagram, i.e. what it is "about", but there is an *implied continuity* in reasoning with a series of diagrams that is an important part of the force of the arguments involved. A series of diagrams would be like a "moving picture of thought".

The concept of the iconic involved in Peirce's theory of diagrammatic reasoning is very abstract. *Iconicity* can be like *images*, like *diagrams* or like *metaphors*, according to Peirce, and the iconic is not a separate type of sign, but only one particular aspect of the sign-relation, namely the relation between the carrier of a sign (representamen) and its object, this relation being characterized either as iconic, indexical or symbolic. Where images actually preserve some physical-geometrical *properties* of the objects depicted in a pictorial image (or the sound objects portrayed in a sound image, etc.), the iconicity of the diagram is far more abstract. It does not necessarily "look like" (or "sound like", etc.) the objects it represents, since it only preserves the *relational* structure between significant parts. The manipulation of algebraic forms is for Peirce an important manifestation of iconicity, since we here impose structure preserving mappings on the different forms, as in the case of propositional logic and its representation in logic diagrams. A generally stated rule for the manipulation of formal symbols, such as

$$(x + y)\, z = x\, z + y\, z$$

could be replaced by an abstractly stated rule, like 'multiplication is distributive over addition', 'but no application could be made of such an abstract statement without translating it into a sensible image.' In other words, the algebraic formula not only states the rule, it also shows how to use it in manipulating objects (signs) *qua* the iconicity of its form. Understanding the algebraic rule given above will imply that the cognitive agent can somehow translate this "declarative" proposition into a "procedural" manipulation of more tangible parts and relations among them in a specific instance of applying the rule, as shown in the diagram below, where the symbols have been replaced with numbers to illustrate the meaning of distributivity.

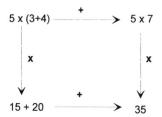

Fig. 9. An example of the abstractly stated rule of distributivity of multiplication over addition translated into a procedurally tangible diagram of the parts and relations involved.

The function of iconicity is to convey information by *preserving some relational form between objects and their interpretation*. The construction of diagram-icons is therefore to Peirce not a question of illustrating a point or an otherwise symbolic argument, it is a necessary condition for reasoning.

All necessary reasoning is diagrammatic; and the assurance furnished by all other reasoning must be based on necessary reasoning. In this sense, all reasoning depends directly or indirectly upon diagrams. [...] The diagram represents a definite form of relation. [...] The pure diagram is designed to represent and to render intelligible, the form of relation merely. Consequently diagrams are restricted to the representation of a certain class of relations; namely those that are intelligible. [...] A diagram is an icon of a set of rationally related objects. By rationally related, I mean that there is between them, not mere one of those relations which we know by experience, but know not how to comprehend, but one of those relations which anybody who reasons at all must have an inward acquaintance with. (Peirce 1906: 314, 317).

We have seen that it is simplistic to assume that we "directly see" properties and relations in a logic diagram. We sometimes have to add or disregard properties and relations that are not relevant at a particular moment of reasoning. Now, according to Peirce diagrams 'make their conclusion *evident*' to an observing and thinking mind, and he describes the process of dynamic abstraction as follows.

It is [...] a very extraordinary feature of diagrams that they *show*, — as literally *show* as a percept shows the perceptual judgment to be true, — that a consequence does follow, and more marvelous yet, that it *would* follow under all varieties of circumstances accompanying the premises. It is not, however, the statical Diagram-icon that directly shows this; but *the Diagram-icon having been constructed with an Intention, involving a Symbol of which it is the Interpretant* [...]in the light of this intention determines an initial symbolic interpretant. Meanwhile the diagram remains in the field of perception or imagination; and so the iconic diagram and its initial symbolic interpretant taken together constitute what we shall not too much wrench Kant's term in calling a *Schema*, which is on the one side an object capable of being observed while on the other side it is general. (Peirce 1906: 318)

One contemplates the Diagram, and one at once prescinds [abstracts] from the accidental characters that have no significance. They disappear altogether from one's understanding of the Diagram; and although they be of a sort which no visible thing be without ..., yet their [disappearance] is only an understood disappearance and does not prevent the features of the Diagram, now become a Schema, from being subjected to the scrutiny of observation. (Peirce 1906: 317)

The theory of *diagrammatic reasoning* as introduced by Peirce seems in some ways to be more advanced than the modern theory of "image schemata" as presented by Lakoff, especially with regard to the interplay of iconic and symbolic forms. As I have indicated before, the interpretation of diagrams will generally have to rely on a conceptual structure and therefore on pre-established intuition and pre-established knowledge (about the symbolic conventions and about the structure of the domain in general, etc.). This is true of any diagram, as it has been noted by Efraim Fischbein in his study of *Intuition in Science and Mathematics* (1987). According to Fischbein the intuitive appeal of a diagram or a diagrammatic model has two important aspects.

Firstly, it offers a synoptic, global representation of a structure or a process and this contributes to the globality and the immediacy of understanding. Secondly, a diagram is an ideal tool for bridging between a conceptual interpretation and the practical expression of a certain reality. A diagram is a synthesis between these two apparently opposed types of representations — the symbolic and the iconic. [...] Diagrams are not, generally, the direct image of a certain reality. [...] It is the figural expression of an already elaborated conceptual structure, like any other symbolic system. (Fischbein 1987: 154, 157).

Returning to the idea of two different levels of schematization in reasoning with diagrams, we could try to take another look at the difference between *seeing as* and *seeing in*. We could argue that the *seeing as* is the relation implied in logical semantics as an "interpretation function" on the geometrical object (cf. Figure 10). This *seeing as* is however a sign relation that can only be established by an interpretation (which is itself a sign) of the geometric object as a particular type of *diagram* (a logic diagram for instance, and more specifically Euler circles or Venn diagrams or Higraphs). This means that the geometric object and the diagram are not on the same level: *the diagram interprets the geometric object*. This way we can also differentiate the operations that belong to the geometric object and those that belong to the diagram. In the case of Venn diagrams for instance, we can perform a series of geometric operations on the objects that does not make any difference on the level of the diagram. We can change the geometric object by reseizing the circles or by deforming the circles to elliptic curves or we could even draw boxes instead of circles as long as they intersect in the required way. It would not affect our categorial perception of the domain according to the category of logic diagrams, according to which we interpret the geometric objects.

On the other hand we can perform other types of operations, which would also (at least sometimes) have geometric equivalents, namely those operations which would change the logical status of the diagram. This would be operations like shading a region to indicate that a subset represented in the diagram is empty (cf. Figure 7 above) or introducing a new object such as a third curve to represent possible relations to a third set C. Intoducing a third set or predicate C would of course demand a new geometrical object (a third intersecting simple closed curve), but it would also correspond to a logical operation.

The *seeing in* would then be the relation between the *diagram*, including the logical operations allowed according to its type, and the *model* thought of in the interpretation. This model is not simply identical to the domain object of the first level, since we here allow purely "mental" events that do not necessarily have an interpretation in the domain. The model is the constructed "thought object" from which we get the "meaning" we see in the diagram. In this imaginative seeing we can add or subtract parts of the diagram under consideration as long as it is meaningful, i.e. as long as it makes sense in the model. We have seen however that such an imaginative seeing as well as the (re)construction, manipulation and observation of diagrams in thought or on paper (or simulated in computers) only takes places under the regulatory interpretation of a wider conceptual structure such as the image schema and the symbolic knowledge of the domain. In the case of Venn diagrams their logical interpretation was mediated by container schemas and the symbolic knowledge of mathematical structures (the property of transitivity for instance). On this level we can again differentiate between different types of operations: the logical operations belonging to the diagram and the cognitive operations belonging to the conceptual structure. Cognitive operations could be generalized operations of visualization such as focusing on a semantically relevant aspect or dynamically abstracting from some part of the diagram that is irrelevant for a particular conclusion. These distinctions can be summarized in the figure below.

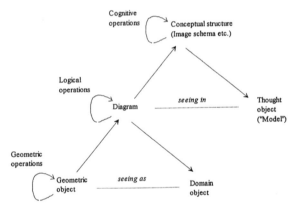

Fig. 10. Levels of schematization involved in diagrammatic reasoning and an attempt to "locate" the difference between "seeing as" and "seeing in". The diagram is the logical construction that mediates between the geometric object of perception and the conceptual structures.

III Logical Semantics or Cognitive Semantics?

In the discussion above I implied a conception of semantics, in which semantic structure could be imposed upon a geometric figure: for instance, in a constructive process of interpretation, rather than a conception of semantics, where the interpretation is simply a function from a geometric figure to the domain it represents. There are several such conceptions that allow us to introduce "intermediate level" representations with varying degrees of *internal structure* roughly corresponding to different conceptions of *"invariants* across situations" (Cooper 1988), such as *image schemas* (Lakoff 1987; Lakoff 1988a; Johnson 1987), *cognitive grammar* (Langacker 1987), *conceptual semantics* (Jackendoff 1983; Jackendoff 1987), *conceptual spaces* (Gärdenfors 1990a, Gärdenfors 1990b), *mental spaces* (Fauconnier 1985; Fauconnier 1988; Fauconnier & Turner1996) and *situations* (Barwise & Perry 1983; Cooper 1988; Barwise 1989, Seligman 1990). With the exception of situation semantics or situation theory all of these approaches contribute to the field of *cognitive semantics*, and they all stress the mediating role of *spatial representations* in the construction and understanding of meaning across different cognitive domains, such as visual perception and natural language, cf. Jackendoffs "intermediate-level theory" (Jackendoff 1983, 1987).

The notions of space and spatial representations are implied in different ways. Gilles Fauconnier sums up his position as follows (Fauconnier 1988). Language does not link up directly with a real or metaphysical world, and expression in natural language does not in itself carry meaning in the sense of a propositional content. Rather, these expressions should be viewed as "instructions" to carry out constructions at the intermediary cognitive level. These constructions are discourse-driven but under-determined by the linguistic expressions, i.e. the construction of meaning is also dependent on the pre-established knowledge of different semantic domains and types of situations (cf. situation semantics), pre-established schematic constructions (image schematic constructions) and the perception of the discourse situation, etc. The notion of "mental spaces" does not refer to a mental experience of space but to the *interconnection* of semantic domains in these cognitive constructions. It is accordingly a highly abstract *topological* concept of space that is implied, but it is nevertheless 'quite powerful in accounting for semantic and grammatical *regularities*'.

In the work of Peter Gärdenfors, "conceptual spaces" are seen as a framework for cognitive semantics. The semantics of a language is primarily a relation between the language and the cognitive structure that interprets it, rather than a direct relation between expressions in a language and the referential domain ("the world") as it is assumed in "truth-functional" semantics. 'Meaning comes before truth', i.e. we have to answer questions about meaning before we can raise any questions about truth. Conceptual spaces consist of a number of *quality dimensions*, such as the three ordinary spatial dimensions or dimensions such as color, pitch or temperature. Dimension is here understood literally, because each of the quality dimensions is endowed with certain topological or metric structures. Color is for instance a quality dimension with 3 dimensions corresponding to the circular structure of *hue* ("the color circle") and the linear dimensions of *saturation* and *brightness*. Together they form a color space ("the color cone") where each perceivable color will correspond to a convex region in this conceptual space. Predicates in a language that denote primary properties can generally be assigned regions in a conceptual space and the regions corresponding to natural predicates like color will be coherent and convex. *Mappings* between conceptual spaces is introduced in order to account for constructions like metaphors, since (some) metaphors can be seen to express a *similarity* in topological or metrical structure between different quality dimensions. In the frameworks of Fauconnier's "mental spaces" metaphorical constructions are described more generally as a "blending", where two input spaces are *projected* onto a "blend" space.

With Gilles Fauconnier's "mental spaces" and Peter Gärdenfors' "conceptual spaces" as examples we have focused on the highly abstract topological notion of *space* introduced in different versions of cognitive semantics. Although this could seem only to serve the formalization of semantics, there is however also a claim about the cognitive importance of spatial representations as the representational format for the conceptual structures, which is seen by Jackendoff (1983, 1987) as a level of cognitive representation 'at which linguistic, sensory and motor information are compatible'. Without such a mediating format, we would not be able to "translate" easily between linguistic meaning and visual scenes as indeed we are. Upon hearing a linguistic description of a situation, we can imaginatively construct a mental image of the scenic structure of the situation and its relevant objects and events, although we have not seen it ourselves. We can imagine the situation *as if* we could see (and hear) it directly in the description (cf. *seeing in*). Similarly we can easily construct a linguistic description from a complex situation we have actually experienced by focusing on its relevant parts and analyzing their grammatical relations — the categorized parts of the situation being schematized as subjects, adverbs and verbs, etc. — *as if* we could directly see a kind of abstract grammar in the situation.

This brings us back to the central problem of *schematization* and the role of *invariant structures* in reasoning. We saw that we should be able to order different types of diagrams *according to their invariant properties*, i.e. the properties that are *invariant under the operations that are allowed in each graphical system*. We also saw that graphical systems such as Venn diagrams are dependent upon an underlying mapping that makes the representation possible, and in the case of Venn diagrams this was (among other things) based upon a *topological invariant* formalized in the Jordan curve theorem.

Finally we have seen that the different alternative conceptions of semantics all introduce "intermediate level" representations with varying degrees of *internal structure* corresponding to different conceptions of what is "*invariant across situations*" (Cooper 1988; Talmy 1978). Rather than setting up a conflict between logical semantics and cognitive semantics, we could perhaps imply a kind of constructive common ground in these abstract notions of invariant structures across situations in so far as it is acknowledged that these invariants could correspond to a separate level of representation (a "cognitive topology").

References

Barwise, Jon & Perry, John. 1983. *Situations and Attitudes*. Cambridge, MA: MIT Press.

Barwise, Jon. 1989. *The Situation in Logic*. CSLI Lecture Notes, N. 17. Stanford.

Cooper, Robin. 1988. 'Facts in Situation Theory: Representation, Psychology, or Reality?' In *Mental Representations*. Ruth M. Kempson (Ed). Cambridge: Cambridge University Press.

Fischbein, Efraim. 1987. *Intuition in Science and Mathematics. An Educational Approach*. Dordrecht: Reidel.

Fauconnier, Gilles. 1985. *Mental Spaces. Aspects of Meaning Construction in Natural Language*. Cambridge, MA: MIT Press.

Fauconnier, Gilles. 1988. 'Quantification, Roles, and Domains.' In *Meaning and Mental Representations*. Umberto Eco, Marco Santambrogio & Patrizia Violi (Eds.). Bloomington: Indiana University Press.

Fauconnier, Gilles & Turner, Mark. 1996. 'Blending as a Central Process of Grammar.' In *Discourse and Language*. Adele E. Goldberg (Ed.). Stanford: Stanford University Press.

Gardner, Martin. 1982. *Logic Machines and Diagrams* (2nd. Ed.). Chicago: University of Chicago Press.

Glasgow, Janice N., Hari Narayanan & B. Chandrasekaran (Eds.). 1995. *Diagrammatic Reasoning. Cognitive and Computational Perspectives*. Menlo Park CA: AAAI Press & MIT Press.

Gärdenfors, Peter. 1990a. 'Frameworks for Properties: Possible Worlds vs. Conceptual Spaces'; Manuscript 1990.

—. 1990b. 'Mental Representation, Conceptual Spaces and Metaphors', *Synthese* 1990.

Hammer, Eric. 1995. *Logic and Visual Information. Studies in Logic, Language and Information*. Stanford: CSLI Publications Ltd.

Harel, David. 1988. 'On Visual Formalisms', *Communications of the ACM*, 31.

Jackendoff, Ray. 1983. *Semantics and Cognition*. Cambridge, MA: MIT Press

—. 1987. *Consciousness and the Computational Mind*. Cambridge, MA: MIT Press.

Johnson, Mark. 1987. *The Body in the Mind. The Bodily Basis of Meaning, Imagination and Reason*.

Chicago: University of Chicago Press.

Lakoff, George. 1987. *Women, Fire, and Dangerous Things. What Categories Reveal About the Mind.* Chicago: University of Chicago Press.

—. 1988a. 'Cognitive Semantics.' In *Meaning and Mental Representations.* Umberto Eco, Marco Santambrogio & Patrizia Violi (Eds). Bloomington: Indiana University Press.

—. 1988b. 'A Suggestion For a Linguistics with Connectionist Foundations.' In *Proceedings of the 1988 Connectionist Models Summer School.* David Touretzky, Geoffrey Hinton & Terrence Sejnowski (Eds): San Mateo, CA: Morgan Kaufmann.

—. 1990. 'The Invariance Hypothesis: is Abstract Reason Based on Image Schemas?', *Cognitive Linguistics* 1990, Vol. 1, Nr. 1: 39-74.

May, Michael. 1995. 'Diagrammatisches Denken: Zur Deutung logischer Diagramme als Volsstellungs-schemata bei Lakoff und Peirce', *Zeitschrift für Semiotik*, Band 17, Heft 3-4.

Peirce, Charles S.. 1933-1961 [1885]. 'On the Algebra of Logic. A Contribution to the Philosophy of Notation', in: *Collected Papers of Charles Sanders Peirce*, Vol. III, (C.P. 3.359-3.403). Cambridge, MA: Harvard University Press.

—. 1933-1961 [1902]. 'The Simplest Mathematics.' In *Collected Papers of Charles Sanders Peirce*, Vol. IV (C.P. 4.227-4.323). Cambridge, MA: Harvard University Press.

—. 1976 [1906]. 'Prolegomena to an Apology for Pragmatism.' In *The New Elements of Mathematics* Vol. IV. Carolyn Eisele (Ed). The Hague: Mouton.

Richards, Joan L. 1980. 'The Art and Science of British Algebra: A Study in the Perception of Mathematical Truth', *Historia Mathematica* 1980, Vol. 7: 343-365.

Schier, Flint. 1986. *Deeper into Pictures. An Essay on Pictorial Representation.* Cambridge: Cambridge University Press.

Seligman, Jerry. 1990. 'Perspectives in Situation Theory.' In *Situation Theory and its Applications*, Vol. 1. Robin Cooper, Kuniaki Mukai & John Perry (Eds.). CSLI Lecture Notes N. 22. Stanford.

Talmy, Leonard. 1988 [1978]. 'The Relation of Grammar to Cognition.' In *Topics in Cognitive Grammar*. Brygida Rudzka-Osty (Ed.). Amsterdam: John Benjamins. Original version published in the *Proceeding of the TINLAP-2* (Theoretical Issues in Natural Language Processing), ed. David Waltz (University of Illinois 1978).

Wang, Dejuan, John Lee & Henk Zeevat. 1995. 'Reasoning with Diagrammatic Representations.' In *Diagrammatic Reasoning*. B. Chandrasekaran, J. Glasgow & N. H. Narayanan (Eds.). Menlo Park, CA: AAAI Press/MIT Press.

Wang, Dejuan & Henk Zeevat. 1996. 'A Syntax Directed Approach to Picture Semantics', *AVI'96 Workshop on Theory of Visual Languages*, May 1996.

Wollheim, Richard. 1980. *Art and its Objects.* (2nd Ed.). Cambridge: Cambridge University Press.

Don't Make a Scene!
On Iconicity, Quantifiers and Fuzzy Frames

Berit Brogaard

The present text intends to outline the prospects of a cognitive semiotics based upon an extension of the traditional philosophical distinction between intension (sense) and extension (reference) to three cognitive categories quite analogous to the three Peircian sign categories: *icon, index*, and *symbol. Pure sense qualities* may under these circumstances be conceived as kinds of icons, a set of *quantifiers* as indices on the iconical scene, and symbols as *framed* and activated qualities. In a figurative sense, the quantifiers can be regarded as stage directions in the mental theater; however, the *quantifiers* and the *frames* might be due to a theory about *fuzzy sets* related to basic principles of iconicity. Fuzzy theory, just like prototype theory, is based upon the hierarchical organization of quantifiers and upon concepts in general. The two theories, however, are very dissimilar in the sense that they invoke *unbounded* and *bounded types*, respectively. The *quantifiers* responsible of framing, then, may be a set of *fuzzy concepts*, and although *personal frames* are probably constituted as *fuzzy sets*, the non-individual frames seem to be a mere set of *bounded types*.

I Aims

This paper is concerned with some basic consequences of the cognitive constraint: the fundamentals of a *cognitive semiotics* concerning the question of how we can think something with respect to what we see. Traditionally, questions concerning framing, quantification and (inter)subjectivity, did not concern any semiotic inquiry. *Cognitive Science*, however, has been one of the important factors in the emergence of the class of "economic" models of cognition in which cognitive claims are viewed as context-dependent, risky, or uncertain commitments.

A general conception of the contemporary *phenomenological* doctrine in the field of *cognitive science* might be that the methodology of both forms bridges within three main approaches to human cognition, the three approaches being *logical, psychological*, and "purely" *phenomenological*.

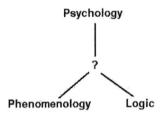

Psychology

?

Phenomenology   Logic

Fig. 1.

The proposents of the psychological-logical branch may include for example Ronald W. Langacker, Ray Jackendoff, Jerry A. Fodor and Eve Sweetser; the phenomenological-logical branch, Per Aage Brandt, Len Talmy, Barry Smith, Jean Petitot, Mark Turner, and Gilles Fauconnier; and the phenomenological-psychological branch, Charles J. Fillmore, Philip N. Johnson-Laird, George Lakoff, Mark Johnson, and Eleanor Rosch.

In general, a "pure" logical approach may concern the effort of clarifying the essence and true relations of scientific phenomena; on the other hand, a "pure" psychological approch may seek insight into the meaningful structures which connect psychic phenomena, not causally, but intentionally, and a "pure" phenomenological approach may concern the genesis of meaning in the space between "real" objects and the sphere of desires, personal and cultural values, etc.

The problem in the phenomenological-psychological and the psychological-logical approaches to human cognition is, as I see it, that they are limited to investigating the objective manifestations of human cognition and existence in general within circumscribed categories. However, only a science which is unaware of its own procedure and which forgets its methodological limits can, in my opinion, claim to give a complete account of its object.

The phenomenological-logical approach, then, is an effort to clarify the sciences, starting with the science of logic, by examining and describing the essence of experiences (an effort to get to the things themselves) and then to ask where experience and knowledge come from in a causal sense. The latter question, central to contemporary pheomenology, thus becomes an effort turned towards the experiences which underlie the sciences: those of psycho-physical beings.

A cognate approach, close in attitude to the phenomenological-logical approach but turned towards state-space representations and concerned with iconicity and framing properties, might be that of a *cognitive semiotics*. The "natural" objects of such a *cognitive semiotics* might be the pictural reasoning of human beings (apperception and memorization), and the pictural features of state-space representations in langu-

196

age (science, poetry, and common sense); and to give a complete account of its objects, the methodology might link itself to mathematical and neurobiological models, e.g., fuzzy logic and the like.

The central point which I shall stress in this context before turning towards the minor aims of my article, is that there may be some relation between such a *fuzzy set theory* and the nature and structure of the world. The organization of the world as it is represented in the mind, whether it reflects the organization *in* the world or in the brain, could be termed the projected world or the *natural world*, which is a world of possibilities, corresponding to a possible totality of facts. The phenomenal reality need not be discontinuous in itself, but its chaotic nature *vis-à-vis* human understanding forces us to conceive of it as discontinuous.

What is more interesting in this context, however, is that the mental processes that create the organization of the sense stimuli are both *automatic* and *unconscious*. Therefore, one of the topics I want to explore, related to the *fuzziness* of the natural world, is the nature of basic level thinking mapped onto the three Peircian sign-relations: *icon, index,* and *symbol.* An icon, generally speaking, is a sign that has a resemblance or similarity to its object; an index is a sign that indicates its objects in some manner or other, and a symbol is a conventional sign, which has no connection, whether of similarity or indication, with its object other than its serving as the name of that object (but note that persons denoted by a proper name have no "*common characters*" attributed to them save the fact that they all answer to the proper name; so, proper names may not be symbols).

A fruit of the general distinction between iconicity, indexicality and symbolicity instead of the prior distinction between internal minds and external objects, is that the relation between the comprehension of a thing that a person may be having in perceiving that thing and how it looks or otherwise appears to her, can be spatially distributed over a scale of properties with a relatively fixed but dynamical relationship amongst its parts.

Moreover, if we make the assumption that these oscillative states can have reference to the world external to the system, the possibilities mentioned before may be actualized via a set of *quantifiers* pointing out the iconical relations amongst the mentally recalled properties of an external object.

So, although a discussion of the influence of iconicity upon the (re)introduced concepts of *quantification* and *fuzzy sets* is essential to the overall aim of this article, the aim is more ambitious to outline how perception is related to memorization and thinking in general. In the first part of this paper, I intend to present in some detail the Peircian arguments for an iconical reasoning. In the last part, I will discuss the problem of framing and the problem of quantifying a continuous world.

II   Everyday Thinking

Everyday thinking is generally characterized by an intimate interaction between perceiving, investigation, remembering, deducing, and action, with constant monitoring and guidance from reversibility. According to Peirce, 'all thinking is dialogic in form. Your self one instant appeals to your deeper self for his assent' (6.338). The mutual reference in this dialogue is the ground of the sign, i.e., a vague idea (in the next section, I am going to discuss this crucial topic in more details).

What is central to this paper is the mental signs which Peirce has chosen to call *non-symbolic thought-signs*. As I see it, non-symbolic thought-signs are related to the fact that we rarely make deep or difficult deductions, or remember surprising or profound concepts. According to Peirce, the

> non-symbolic thought-signs are of two classes: first, pictures or diagrams or other images (I call them Icons) such as have to be used to explain the signification of words; and secondly, signs more or less analogous to symptoms (I call them Indices) of which the collateral observations, by which we know what a man is talking about is examples (6.338).

'The icons', says Peirce, 'chiefly illustrate the significations of predicate-thoughts, the Indices the denotations of subjects-thoughts' (6.338). It seems to me, however, that there are at least two possible ways of viewing the denotations of subject-thoughts: The relation of the signification of subject-thoughts to the thinking subject indicate that *indices* represent *intersubjectivity*. But there is also an iconical element related to *intersubjectivity*. If other subjects are similar to the thinking subject itself to a certain degree, it is reasonable that the feelings and thoughts of the thinking subjects, may also be true to other subjects. The relations amongst the similar, relevant and common qualities of the thought of the subject itself and the assumed thought of the other subject constitute an iconical sign. That means that intersubjectivity is, of course, not mere existence in a group having a common concern, rather it is a kind of fertile indistinction of persons, a universal quality of the will to mutual participation. The intersubjectivity may in respect to each subject be called infra-objective, for it is not the awareness of any particular object or of some abstract object in general — perhaps of some common character related to the subjectivity itself.

The present paper seeks to describe pre-reflective or intuitive reasoning. Intuitive reasoning, as suggested above, may be related to intersubjectivity via some common character. Together with the disturbance which is "broadcast" from a "transmitting" real or imaginary object, the common character constitutes the immediate, nonrepresentative awareness which is prior to all pictorial reasoning or *non-symbolic thought-signs* in general. These signs are quite commonly imagined to be like logical reasoning in structure but unconscious. I think, however, that even any deep level structure may be quite distict from that of classical logic and most reflective reasoning — even though some features such as quantification at a pre-memorized level may be logic in nature.

In classical logic the validity of deductive reasoning has no exceptions and any evaluation of circumstantial evidence is not possible. In contrast, the validity in everyday (intuitive) reasoning become less plausible with the length of the deductive chain, and evaluations of circumstantial evidence is possible here, even though they might be biased because of the heuristic and/or characteristic of memory. Also, in traditional reasoning only standard *quantifiers* are allowed, in everyday reasoning, however, all quantifiers are useful. The last proposition applies only to pictorial and/or conscious reasoning, the lower levels "reasoning" probably uses rather more restricted quantifiers.

Peirce has named three subdivisions of *reasoning* to cover the three references of the sign (cf. 'A sign is something which stands to *somebody* for *something* in some *respect*' (2.228) [I underline]): The sign "to somebody" is covered by Speculative Rhetoric,[1] the sign "for something" by Critical Logic, and the sign "in some respect" by Speculative Grammer.

III The Problem of Iconicity

Speculative Grammar, as mentioned above, is the most fundamental of Peirce's three main divisions of reasoning (or logic in general). Speculative Grammar treats particularly the meaning of signs,[2] that is, 'the reference of [...][signs] in general to their ground' (4.116). Peirce claims that a sign is anything which 'determines something else (its interpretant) to refer to an object to which itself refers (its *object*)' (2.303) (Note, however, that the object determines both the sign and the interpretant (cf. Dinesen 1996)).

Thus, the sign stands for an object to an interpretant in some respect, that is, the sign represents the common character of the dynamical object and this respect is

---

[1] Note that speculative rhetoric in principle is located between logical necessity and "pure" chance.

[2] Although there is a clear distinction in Peirce's early philosophical work, I will not in this paper make any distinction between representamen and sign (cf. Dinesen 1996: 291).

called the *ground*[3] (Ibid: 289) (According to Dinesen (1996) the dynamical object means an event taking place in time):

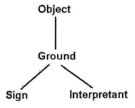

Fig. 2.

Langacker uses the term *ground* for 'the speech event, its participants, and its immediate circumstances (such as the time and place of speaking)' (1990: 318). If we recall that 'all thinking is dialogic in form. Your self one instant appeals to your deeper self for his assent' (6.338), we can characterize the cognitive *ground* of the sign as the thought event, its cognitive levels, and the immediate circumstances. Langacker continues: 'The class of "deictic" expressions can now be defined as those which necessarily do invoke the ground and thus include it in their scope' (1990: 318). The grounded entity considered as a sort of schematically characterized object or event raises the question whether the icon (distinct from any deictic notion) has got any ground at all.

I think the answer may be no, despite the fact that the icon is associated with its object via the ground — since the icon has apparently no dynamical object and is probably in itself not a sign (this is not to say, however, that the sign may not be iconical in nature or perhaps *in natura*). Peirce claims that 'the icon has no dynamical connection with the object it represents; it simply happens that its qualities resemble those of the object' (2.299). Thus, the red quality of an icon may resemble a Danish mail box, an apple, a quantum of blood, etc., and the elongated form of a church tower (conceived as an icon) may resemble a phallus, a weapon, the castle in a game of chess, etc. 'Unless there really is such an object, the icon does not act as a sign, but this has nothing to do with its character as a sign' (2.247). Yet, with respect to perception, sometimes there might be such an object, and therefore the icon may sometimes act as a sign in perception. It must be pointed out, however, that the icon in itself or the sense quality in itself is a mere possibility that cannot exist separately — i.e., only by actualization or generalization of this possibility is it

---

[3] Note that the "ground" in 1867-68 means the "common character" of the sign, in 1897 the "ground" is now the "idea" in a "Platonic sense" (cf. Dinesen 1996: 289).

possible for the quality to emerge; and that is as a sign. Suppose, by way of illustration, we attempt to understand what is meant by the quality *red*. We think normally of *red* in the sense that it might be external to us for an object *in some respect*; the concept of *red*, then, is not "communicable" without its object, since at least the quality must take up some space, and then the quantum of space may function as an object for the quality as a *sign*.

Once again, iconicity does not function distinctly from a given object; some character of the icon is transformed to a character bounded in a real or imaginary object, and then the character can be transformed to another character of the object via fluid bounderies. This transformation of the icon as a "first" to an "icon" as a "second" or "third" may be based upon some resemblances or analogies. Analogies and resemblances, then, are crucial to the principle of iconicity, but it is important to be aware of their limitations. No two sets of phenomena are exactly alike, and the use of the term "analogy" instead of "iconicity" may severely limit the modes of reasoning by causing us to lose sight of *differences*. Peirce says about this problem: 'For instance, yesterday I saw a blue colour; and here *is* a blue colour. (...) I find myself disposed to say the two [ideas] are closely allied; *in that disposition their similarity consists*. For they are two different ideas' (7.392).

Because iconicity is more multi-faceted than a rigid conception of similarity would allow, and because the icon itself is a mere possibility that cannot exist separately, it is more appropriate not to include the concept of iconicity without having an eye to the indexical and symbolic features (invoked via the ground of the sign). Take, for example, a Native American called Lion Claw after a scratch from a fight with a lion. The sign produced of the scratch of the lion claw is an index only to the extent that a person deduces that the Native American once had a fight with a lion (or another animal); however, if the scar looks like something else according to a common character between the seem and the mental feeling, the sign will be an icon (e.g. if the scar resembles the slim figure of the Indian squaw). And if the scar is an emblematic entity indicating the pronoun and status of Native American, the sign that emerges is a symbol. The icon and the index embody sign-relations of likeness and of existential connection, respectively. The symbol is conventional in nature, but since a *common character* of the sign-relation connects the symbol to its dynamical object, the symbol is not arbitrary in the intuitive sense of the word. Now, it seems to me (as suggested above) that the icon is not only *dependent* on the *ground* of the sign, but also that it emerges from the *ground* as either realized, virtualized or actualized.   The examples which I have mentioned do not in themselves point to any new aspects of the problem of iconicity, however, in the scope of apperception and memorization, we will see for instance that the temptation to ignore negative similarities in our pleasure at seeing positive ones is crucial for the performance of mental images. When we strive to recognize a face, a perfume, or a tune, there is a concious apprehension of an effort of synthesis — of the present awareness putting out quantifiers to the past and, when the recollection is succesful, drawing complexes of past memorizations into the present as a part of the present judgment or memorization. Sometimes either spontaneously or in response to an effort of comprehension, the importation of complexes from the past can then be said to formulate the present perceptual judgment or memorization. This is to say that before the implication of an entity from past memorization the "creation" exists in present perception only as a possibility. The ability to ignore negative similarities enables us to mean what we are saying in sentences like 'She is the spitting image of her mother'. We are then looking at her as a iconical sign without being aware of the dominance of resemblance.

IV   The Problem of Apperception and Memorization

Basically, the pair perception-apperception is a process of *recognition* in the form of an internal pattern of neuronal firing sequences, one that reflects the memory of previous events, and which has to be integrated with sequences of stimulus to produce recognition. In spite of this, perception-apperception presupposes knowledge,[4] i.e. the recognition of the general characters of the dynamical object, which again is the projection of the previously memorized entities upon the sensory stimuli. Furthermore, seeing something as different from its background implies knowing to some degree what it is for two things or two sense qualities to being different. Hence, the mental figurativity may be created by pointing out the *resemblances* and *differences* between the observed or recalled object and a previously memorized object. The perception-related processes, then, are based upon *iconicity*, but the iconical procedure does *not* in itself create any dynamical relation between the object and the icons. It is rather the process of *switching* among the similarities and the differences in the observed object and the previously memorized object that connects the qualities (icons) with their object. In the next section, I shall consider in more detail the relations amongst sense qualities (icons), the process of *switching* between sense qualities (icons), and the process of pointing out resemblances and differences (framing), but first a few more points concerning apperception and

---

[4] Knowledge becomes knowledge *of* a thing, where the "of" is emphasized to suggest the *de*tachment.

memorization need to be noted here.

The set of sense qualities or *icons* may fail to have appropriate spatial or temporal dimensions. They may fail to have the appropriate energy or to have an appropriate wavelength or an appropriate mass. Also, the pattern stored in an early-state array may be adequately dissimilar to another pattern or the recollection of the pattern may be confused. Here, the process of memorization plays a central role. If an icon fails to exhibit appropriate the characters for a mental image it may be considered by the memory as a member of a set of trash.

Indeed, the role of memorization can go even deeper. The evidence for incomplete representations is apparently strong, since subjects frequently implicate fewer sets of icons than they should. For example, it is often impossible to remember the delicate details of a face, or to remember colours, amounts, etc. This allows (with or without implicating personal liberty) a space of freedom or a margin to fill with icons related to some foreign but loosely bounded micro-frames; and to go even futher, the metaphorical creation is basically obtained from several ostensions or from picking up icons from separate frames. It seems to be difficult, then, to distinguish the processes of apperception and memorization from metaphorical creation or comprehension.[5] The metaphor, however, may only be genuine if it is effectively definable by referring to one framework but fully definable only by referring to two or more frames. In contrast, the metaphors in science, especially in natural science seem to be un-framed (or only embodied in micro-frames), but indeed quantified; the extreme ease and unforced naturalness of metaphors of science in their general acceptance and comprehensibility obscure the fact that they are metaphors at all. Like in physics: "motion", "travel", "force", "power", "pulsion", "energy", "wave", "ray", "vibration", "resonance", "matter", "fluid", "element", "ether", "light" (applied to invisible processes), or in molecular biology: "expression" (of a gene), "transfer" (tRNA), "template", "transcription", "transformation", "translocation", "encode", "code", "DNA fingerprint", "signaling", "nonsense mutations". All these metaphors may be effectively definable only by referring to one framework, that is, to the specific scientific one. They are in a sense invisible or dead, so perhaps their original frame has been lost, or perhaps the character of the frames is more comprehensive than normally assumed, some frames being more bounded than others. The comprehension and prior formation of the physical metaphors may be due to a transfer from the ordinary use of these terms to a re-

---

[5] In fact, as supposed by Per Aage Brandt, it seems likely that quasi-inferential perceptual mechanisms that generate perceptual beliefs work like the mechanisms in a complex system of embedded metaphors.

ference to our own sensations of causality, and the biological metaphors from our sensations stemming from linguistic and social experience. The question, however, arises whether biological metaphors are metaphors at all or rather metonymic extensions; that is to say, the linguistic and social macro-frames are shrunk into useful sets of micro-social frames. For this reason, the following suggestion of a certain *fuzziness* in apperception and frames looks more promising as a solution to the problem concerning apperception and memorization (including comprehension-related memorization).

V The Fuzzy Environment

The simplest conception of *fuzzy sets* is a 'generalization of the ordinary concept of sets to the case where the memberships of elements are not clearcut, or in other words, the "boundary" of the sets under consideration is not sharply defined' (Chang 1975). Memorized images are indeed fuzzy in the intuitive sense of the word, as analogous to "ambiguous". In fuzzy logic, however, fuzziness is a strictly defined mathematical concept,[6] i.e the continuous variability of the characteristic function over the real interval $[0,1]$ (nothing; everything[7]).[8] Hence, memorized images may not necessarily be images of fuzzy sets but rather bounded types; a category considered as fuzzy and as typical seems to me to be two different things: bounded *types* implies more comprehensive patterns or deeper membership than the typical unbounded element does. For instance, a "typical Dane" is tall, has blond hair, blue eyes, and Scandinavian attitudes. What makes someone a Dane (bounded typicality), however, is her parents' nationality, her place of birth, citizenship, and

---

[6] What basically distinguishes mathematics from cognitive science is that the latter operates on concepts which are exposed to produce contradictions.

[7] In modified fuzzy sets negations are also included.

[8] I suggest an outline of a fuzzy representation (in the context of appercetion) as follows: A fuzzy representation may belong to the *natural world* and constitute the continuous variability over the real interval $[0,1]$ (nothing; everything). The first two elements of the representation (I, F), then, denote the classes of all real or imaginary icons and of all possible *micro-* and *macro-frames* in the mind, respectively. The third element of the fuzzy representation denotes the degree (p) to which the *frame* holds "true" for each of the icons. The *quantifier* (Q), then, denotes the fuzzy representation which stretches the degree of membership for any member of a fuzzy set. The fuzzy set again denotes the core of a m-fuzzy set (M) consisting of its elements (x) with full membership: $Q : \{x = (I,F, p) \mid x \in M \ d = 1\}$.

residence. Thus, it may be true to characterize someone as a typical Dane even though she is not Danish at all. A prototypical or bounded member of a category is related to a greater extent to its appearance than is the fuzzy member of the same category. Recall that, according to Peirce, the *ground* of a representamen is a sort of idea relating the sign to the dynamical object (2.228), and furthermore that 'the icon has no dynamical connection with the object it represents; it simply happens that its qualities resemble those of the object' (2.299). Thus, the bounded type seems more to be related to (but not analogous to) the *ground* of the sign, and the unbounded fuzzy entity to the *icon* which in itself has no dynamical object. If the processes of memorization do perform more bounded types than do the processes of perception-apperception, it may *eo ipso* invoke the unique identification of more comprehensive patterns (*ex ungue leonem*).

According to Mervis and Rosch the fuzzy set function can be characterized as category-representativeness (or typicality) as used in prototype theory (Mervis & Rosch 1981). Even though a *fuzzy set* just like the *type* addresses the similarities and dissimilarities among the members of a category, the two approaches are diametrically opposed. The prototype theory is based upon the Aristotelian logic which assumes *a priori* relations. *Vice versa*, the Fuzzy sets are based upon the fact that no universal relation is assumed a priori; an entity, then, may never be defined as either "A" or "not-A". Take for example the apples in Paul Cèzanne's 'Nature Morte avec Cruche et du Fruit' of Paul Cèzanne from 1890-91. The plastic apples may each belong not only to both "apple" and "not-apple", but also to both "typical apple" and "not apple" and even to "typical fruit" and "not fruit". Thus the borders of fuzzy sets are far less unique than traditional Aristotelian logic. Statements like an apple which is not an apple' are not logically empty nor necessarily contradictory.

The discussion so far, intent on the rationales by which categorization is performed, has overlooked several aspects of the fuzzy set itself. The very idea of the fuzzy set, as mentioned above, is mathematical in its constitution; nevertheless, it seems to me that *fuzzy sets* can be used in two ways for cognition: as a characterictic of certain mental states formed in human minds and as an instrument for the formation of these states. The former is a practical matter in the framework of phenomenology rather than a detached one of objective description. The other may supply the *objective* (true[9]) dimension or *frame* in which the object-bounded qualities can appear. This distinction is neither entirely abandoned nor rigorously adhered to in the sections below, but the origin of the fuzzy set theory must be borne in mind.

---

[9] The term "true" is here used for instance in a mathematical sense.

Like a member of a fuzzy set, apperception is essentially a being in-between. As such it stands continuously between alternatives. The demand of qualities on one hand, and that of object relations and frames on the other; and instead of having to confront only one path, there are often given two or more roads to follow. Such a road or *fuzzy quasi-uniformity* is formed among the sense qualities of a range of objects and the energy bringing the sense qualities together in a new range of objects. The actual dynamical structures of an object are based upon a dynamics of the gaze, i.e. the internal or external visual scanning of the internal or external objects. Take for example the perception-apperception of a church tower: now (and in this context at a unconscious level) the object looks like a part of the church and now like a phallus. These unconscious and fast shifts amongst the qualities of the object are necessary for an appropriate representation of the object. However, very different materials may be used to establish the appercept and all must conform to one or another of a very limited set of specifications. Thus, to talk about shifts among the qualities of an object is only an appropriate metaphor for the actual *quasi-uniformity* formed in apperception. Under normal circumstances the church tower is rather, for example, 80% a part of a church and 20% a phallus and includes of course materials from elsewhere (in this example the phallus, etc.).

The apperceptual level, however, cannot by itself or by its fuzzy logic retain the relatively fixed relationship amongst its parts; unless the apperceptual entities are bounded in a *frame*. Once again, all pairs of perception-apperception, at least concerning human beings, require a fairly extensive set of supporting conditions to facilitate the quasi-uniformity of dynamical figurativity. The common frames, then, come very close to the *bounded type* and the *ground* of the sign except they are not identical. This interface among quantification, framing, and grounding will be examined in the next section, with reference to fuzzy sets and iconicity.

VI Quantifiers and Framing

When a person observes a fact, she "sees" it through concepts which are usually derived from a theory that might be a common-sense theory. Both this theory and the concepts constitute a range of *frames*. I want to distinguish the *micro-frame* from the *macro-frame*, and if nothing else is written, I will consider the *frame* as a *common frame*.[10] In contrast to the *common frame* the *common ground* of the sign is related to

---

[10] See Barry Smith (1994) for the distinction between what he calls fiat object and bona fide objects.

mutual knowledge about the universe. The frame does not relate to any ultimative mutual knowledge. In that sense, the frame is more like a personal entity, even though it is often shared by an ethnic group of people or any other collective. The widest frame of the universe, then, might be the *common ground*.

The micro-frames can be characterized as basic level concepts, related to the properties and boundaries of a restricted range of elements (perhaps only fire, water, air, and earth). The micro-frames of the *physical metaphors*, then, might be characterized according to natural elements: "energy", "ray", "light", "power" belonging to the macro-frame "fire"; "wave", "travel", "force", "motion", "power", "pulsion", "vibrations" and "fluid" to the macro-frame "water"; "resonance" and "ether" to the macro-frame "air"; and "element" and "matter" to the macro-frame "earth".

According to everyday propositions, a good example is Lakoff's outline of the framing-properties included in the frame "Tuesday": 'Tuesday can be defined only relative to the movement of the sun, the standard means of characterizing the end of the day and the beginning of the next, and a larger seven-day calendric cycle — the week'. That is to say that "Tuesday" in one sense is a microframe, constituting, for instance, the thought or proposition: "Tuesday, I will do ... "; however, in another sense it is a macro-frame composed of the micro-frames "movement of the sun", "the beginning and end of the day", "week", etc.

It seems to me that a set of instruments is required to point out these micro-frames and macro-frames in any continuum of dynamical sense qualities. I will term such an instrument a *quantifier*. Quantifiers are used to indicate quantities along certain dimensions, whether of amount or frequency. Dimensions such as universal/particular, large/small, and negative/positive can be used to categorize quantifiers. If they are considered as kinds of stage directions, perhaps analogous to the zoom of a camera or the like, they then might be visualised as fuzzy sets of variable sizes which are in a *fixed order* relative to each other but which can be moved up and down a continuous scale.

Several interesting features are bound up with the fluid structure of the quantifiers. A certain real or imaginary object can never be possessed as a whole; each perspective is capable of indefinit futher development. We can think of the fuzzy instrument (quantifier) as a dynamical *chorema* with scattered boundaries and the ability to shrink and widen like the sphere of an atom. The quantifier, then, is not a sign that stands for something which can itself be an object of awareness. The quantifier is unique in that even though it points beyond itself to non-determined dimensions, that *towards* which it points is available only in and through the *ground* of the sign.

According to Langacker the class of "deictic" notations[11] can, as mentioned, be defined as 'those which necessarily do invoke the ground and thus include it in their scope' (1990: 318). The quantifier conceived as a "deictic" notation then separates a set of *icons* (qualities) from another set of icons with respect to their immediate or dynamical object.[12] The fact that the dynamical interpretant corresponds to the characters of the dynamical object and the final interpretant to a certain final truth results in the invocation of a dynamical or a final interpretant. If for example a scientist aspires to a certain final truth, her instinctive quantification of a scientific frame may invoke a final interpretant.

Quantifiers, then, might be termed *ideas*,[13] but if quantifiers are transcendental principles, and at the same time are regulators of our thinking, it seems to me that classical freedom and necessity collide.[14] Generally, humans may have more control over the spatio-temporal perspective of their sensory systems than they have over their mass, size, reaction time, wavelength sensitivity or bio-chemical constitution; and it *is* in fact likely that quantifiers play a role in delicate neurophysical and chemical processes. They may then specify that stastically neurons converge in a *common* or shared average firing pattern which is characteristic for a particular environmental signal, thereby creating a certain frame. Hence, quantifiers must be a set of abstract agencies in the form of *indices* rather than ideas, and conceived as macroscopic determinacies, but constituted as microscopic indeterminacies. Awareness of the quantifiers is then awareness of having a choice, experienced as a moment of reflection, a glimmer of rudimentary satisfaction or a iconically organized consciousness. However, if the quantifiers apply to some intentionality, the question then arises of what makes the quantification intentional at all.

The modal competence involved in the intentionality implies, as I see it, a *virtual "narrative" programme* and also the *competence* necessary to realize that programme (*ex nihilo nihil fit*). *In absentia*, the virtual "narrative" programme may be the modal change of a given state caused by the influence of an object upon the subject. The subject itself and the object are then presupposed in the "paradigmatic" structure of the

---

[11] Quantification is the process of pointing out some qualities and negations, and hence, quantification, as I see it, share some structures with the class of deictic notations.

[12] Seen from the perspective that the quantifiers do invoke the ground of the sign.

[13] According to Peirce, the 'sign stands for something, its *object*. It stands for that object, not in all respects, but in reference to a sort of idea, which I have sometimes called the *ground* of the representamen' (2.228).

[14] If both are taken as ultimate metaphysical principles.

quantifier, and the *quantified frame*, therefore, stretches a state-space presentation, which emphasizes the *modal* structure of any apperceptual entity.

VII Existential Choices and Fuzzy Frames

Clearly then, *quantifiers* have a range of meanings and under certain circumstances the meaning of quantifiers may vary depending upon the context in which they occur, but in most cases they seem to be connected only to the subject or the group. When the quantifiers settle down two things may happen: The frame may be unbounded and dynamical or it may be sharply defined, the latter being related more often to the group than to the subject. The *frame*, however, has to have the possibility of getting a fuzzy nature for the member of the group to get the possibility of an existential choice. What this implies, of course, is that existential choices are dependent on the existence of fuzzy frames (unbounded), which again are based upon the fuzzy nature of the *quantifier*.

If for instance someone says 'don't make a scene!', he actually means 'don't make a new frame,' but because he considers the common frame to be unframed or because he is not aware of the common frame, he says 'don't make a scene!' and means exactly the opposite. Thus, *he* is standing outside of a common bounded frame, that is, he opens up the possibility of the common frame aquiring a fuzzy nature; in this way he is perhaps creating an existential choice which may influence the common frame. Peirce indicates a similar problem, using Napoleon as an example: Napoleon 'walked, ate, slept, worked in his study, rode his horse, talked to fellows, just as every other man does. But he combined those elements into shapes that have not been matched in modern times' (4.611).

Thus, all existential choices are made in response to a potential discovery, i.e., either the actualization or realization of a prior possibility. The choice of particular extensions does not have any correlates in objective reality; the choice then is a mere belief, and the aim of living might be for the subject to describe the actual history of the subject itself. The *actual* history is just that one possibility that happened to be realized. In contrast to this, the poet wants to describe the *real* history of himself, that is, he wants to create an autonomous and bounded frame with only *iconical* relations to any common frame.

Thus, it seems to me that a semiotic existential choice may be the act of transforming the possibility of a set of icons either to a set of actualized indices or to a set of realized symbols. By ontology and cosmology there is a certain amount of freedom allowed both in actuality and in reality. The ontological *credo* of the frame is implicated in the *actualized* history of the subject, and the cosmological *credo* of the frame is implicated in the *realized* history of the subject (both, however, influenced by the chance *in* and habit taking *of* the world).

Peirce claims that freedom or 'originality is not an attribute of the *matter* of life, present in the whole only so far as it is present in the smallest parts, but is an affair of *form*, of the way in which parts none of which process it are joined together' (4.611). If we consider the quantifiers (or perhaps the quantified sets of icons) as fuzzy sets of *variable size* which are in a *fixed order* relative to each other but which can be moved up and down a continuous scale, it seems to me that originality or spontaneity is an affair of the quantification in general, i.e. an affair of quantifying and framing in the fuzzy sense of the words.

VIII   Summary and Conclusion

Quantifiers and fuzzy sets have been (re)introduced in this text to show that, for instance, while there are some powerful reasons for prototype theory, the prototype principles do not exist without the principle of iconicity. A quantifier points out a fuzzy set of icons or sense qualities which overtly belongs to the dynamical object, and the icons themselves limit the fuzzy set further, thus, for example, the recognition that icon A seems more likely than icon B (or an aspect of icon A seems more likely than an aspect of icon B) limits the membership in a certain fuzzy set. Note that the lower and upper quantifier could still be entirely unconstrained. Take for instance the two F's in the figure below (the present example is invented for this sake and must be considered with reservations). The scattered F represents a fuzzy graph and the black F an ordinary graph (cf. Kaufmann 1975: 44). It is possible to attribute a value p (x,y) to each point (x,y) on each of the two graphs.

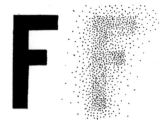

Fig. 3.

Here, the two values (x,y) for membership in the fuzzy set "F" are combined to the degree of membership via the m-Fuzzy set that only valuate fully membership (i.e. "F" or "not F"). The important factors in recognizing the pictures are the position and the intensity of each point; furthermore, since the total magnitude of the "F" in this case does not influence recognition, the relative positions, closeness, and density of the points may also be implicated. The *common frame*, which is the set of ordinary "F's", is activated via the quantifier that settles down on the set of imaginary or real icons (with varying form and intensity). Again, the *degree* to which the frame holds "true" for each of the points depends on the position and intensity of the points. If a point in the border of the full figure does not hold "true" with the frame it may be due to the lack of imaginary and real points and to the position of the core points. Thus, the temptation to ignore negative similarities in our pleasure at seeing positive ones is essential for the processes of recognition.

In their quality of being something between a bounded and an unbounded type, the characters in this example and in general are quite curious. Nevertheless, it has, I think, been conclusively established that unbounded and bounded types are two different things. The conditioned character of the fuzziness of A on an unbounded type T (given A, on the supposition that T) is more like the prior assumption that A is given, on the supposition that an aspect of A is iconically equivalent to an aspect of T. Hence, it seems to me that recognition is not necessarily affected by what we might choose to say is conventional or what we might think of as bounded typicality. No doubt, such an assumption seriously complicates our comprehension of cognition, for, in the long run, cognition may not be satisfactorily ruled out on an *a priori* ground.

In conclusion, I will summarize the (re)introduced concepts in this simple hierarchic model:

Sense qualities or icons
-------Quantifiers---------
Fuzzy frames or indices

Bounded frames

Let me summarize: the quantification of the continuum of sensory or recalled icons is based upon the indexical structure of a set of quantifiers. The quantifiers settle down as fuzzy frames. For me, then, *sharp* personal frames are notably absent, but personal fuzzy frames are indeed present. If the fuzzy frames also include the bounds of logic, those bounds are not logically empty. The bounded frames or vehicles together with the content of the frames may be analogous to symbols. This finally leaves the conceiving subject with a substantial framework within which to address the dynamics of a (semiotic) world.

References

Brandt, Per Aage. 1995. *Morphologies of Meaning*. Århus: University of Aarhus Press.

Dinesen, Anne Marie. 1996. *Time, Evolution and Modality*. Center for Semiotic Research, University of Aarhus, Aarhus.

Kaumann, A. 1975. *Introduction to the Theory of Fuzzy Subsets*. New York, San Francisco, and London: Academic Press,

Lakoff, George. 1987. *Women, Fire, and Dangerous Things*. Chicago and London: The University of Chicago Press.

Langacker, Ronald W. 1990. *Concept, Image, and Symbol: The Cognitive Basis of Grammar*. Berlin and New York: Mouton de Gruyter.

Mervis, C.B. & Rosch, E. 1981. 'Categorization of Natural Objects.' *Annual Review of Psychology*, 32: 89-115.

Peirce, Charles Sanders. 1960. *Collected Papers* vol. 1-8 (CP). Charles Hartshorne and Paul Weiss (Eds.) Cambridge: The Belknap Press of Havard University Press.

Sheldon, C. L. 1975. 'On Risk and Decision Making in a Fuzzy Environment.' In *Fuzzy Sets and Their Applications to Cognitive and Decision Processes*. Lotfi Zadeh, King-Sun Fu, Kokichi Tanada & Masamichi Shimura (Eds.). New York, San Francisco, and London: Academic Press.

Smith, Barry. 1994. 'Fiat Objects.' In *Parts and Wholes: Conceptual Part-Whole Relations and Formal Mereology*. N. Guarion, L. Viev & S. Pribbenow (Eds.). Amsterdam: European Coordinating Commitee for Artificial Intelluigence.

Iconicity in Music

Torben Fledelius Knap

I

Like other culturally created intentional messages, the phenomenon of music has been the object of scientific investigation. Semiotics has here proven itself to be one of the most fruitful methods of investigation of such phenomena, and music is an especially interesting object of scrutiny for semiotic analysis. The aim of this article is to demonstrate, with the help of the analysis of two musical compositions, some general features in the formation of meaning, features that seem to evade analyses of other carriers of meaning (i.e., media) but which seem obvious in the case of music.

Music is not a firm and reliable medium in a standard information theoretical way — one might not even classify music as a form of communication — but somehow it nevertheless has the standard character of communication: it tells something which some composer or musician intentionally made it tell. By starting out from music, one can show how the formation of meaning *per se* has a direct foundation in the real world. Formations of meaning are not arbitrarily related to the phenomena they capture. The way semiotic studies music describe the production of meaning is of special interest, since it demonstrate that the meaning produced actually exists prior to the medium.

It seems to be a fact that meaning carried by a medium has a general and transmedial way of functioning at its basic level. This is due to the fact that meaning grounds itself in the real world externally to the medium that carries it. Meaning exists before the medium. The medium thus creates nothing but the ability for humans to transport a message through an pragmatic intersubjective space. A human thought or idea can be mediated throughout all conceivable media as a message, and it will still be reconstructed in the field of the addressee as (more or less) the same original idea intended by the sender as a transcendent thought in the first place. A semantic construction hence turns out to be autonomous whatever the medium that may carry or mediate this construction.

A signification (and the meaning of the signification) is more basic than the medium by which it is carried. A formation of a meaning emerges in the field of the

213

human subject due to the human subject's direct interaction with the real phenomenal world, and it is not as a consequence of the devices of the medium of communication. The meaning of a phenomenon constitutes itself in the human mind as a result of an automatic and involuntary cognitively based mentalizing process which in its essence is not foounded on any medium. This is what the study of music can tell us something about.

Linking the analysis of music as a mode of expression to the analysis of modes of expression as such will reveal that any individual mode of expression basically follows the same rules as does music. Even "language-like" media, which are characterized by their high degree of symbolicity, can only tell us something about the phenomenal world to the extent that they are not detached from the world about which they are meant to tell something. Any language type, or medium, only gives meaning to somebody because a human being intentionally uses it to convey something related to a situation in the real, unmediated world.

II

In 1936 the Russian composer Prokofiev was asked to write a piece of music which would both motivate children to listen to classical music and increase their understanding of this particular musical genre. The famous fable *Peter and the Wolf*, surely one of the most excellent examples of "program" music ever, was the result of this request. The orchestra's various instruments play the roles of different animals that in this way are animated through music. A narrator names these instruments and tells the listener about the animals that are represented by each instrument. The flute is a bird, the oboe is a duck, the clarinet a cat, a group of strident sounding brass instruments the wolf, and so on. Peter is represented by the entire string session, the grandfather is a bassoon, and the hunters that hunt the wolf are represented by various kinds of drums.

After the narrator has introduced all the agents of the fable, and every agent in the guise of an instrument has revealed itself through a small "riff" of its own sound, the play (i.e., the fable) begins. It starts out with the animals (i.e., instruments) starting to interact along the lines of the pattern of the fable. In this fashion, a scenario starts unfolding in the field of the imagination of the listener. In the beginning of the fable, the narrator steps in to tell, in words, what the animals are supposed to be doing. However, as the fable carries on, the narrator becomes a background figure not present during long intervals, as the receiver is now intuitively able to follow the plot of the story by inferring from the sounds of the instruments in dialogue with each other as "space builders" alone.[1]

The fact that children understand the plot in *Peter and the Wolf* so easily, even when the voice-over is removed, is probably not becuase they have internalized the linguistic logic of the narrator but rather that there exists an iconic similarity between the sounds of the instruments and the sounds of the corresponding animals. The question then is what is similarity between the culturally produced sounds of instruments and the sound of the "corresponding" animals in the natural world. We can point to some general features that humans employ when they make inferences from the sound of an instrument to the image of a living animal. The animal appears through the intonation of a sound as a picture in the listener's imaginary mental space.[2] To this end we will now turn our attention towards another piece of "program" music: Saint-Saëns' *The Carnival of the Animals*. This piece consists of a series of short "portraits" of various animals presented one by one without any explanatory voice-over.

In addition to an introduction and the ending, Saint-Saëns' *Carnival* consists of thirteen one-minute descriptive "portraits" of the following "animals":

1. The March of the Lions
2. Hens and Roosters
3. Fast Animals
4. Turtles
5. The Elephant
6. Marsupial
7. Aquarium
8. Long-eared Agents
9. The Cuckoo in the Deep of the Forest
10. The Aviary
11. Pianists
12. Fossils
13. The Swan

It turns out that people independently of each other, and in different contexts, make correct inferences from the musical sound to the representation of specific

---

[1] The term "space builder" is used by Gilles Fauconnier as a devise in his theory of mental spaces and linguistic structure (Fauconnier 1994), but will in this article denote a material entity able to trigger mental imagery in the field of the receiver of a text, or a message.

[2] A mental space is built as a mental imagination on the grounds of space builders.

animals. A pilot project carried out by the author of this article has shown that, in tests, three groups of students, independently of each another, displayed a high degree of correctness in correlating the musical fragments of the *Carnival* with the proper animal when confronted with the predicates of the 13 pieces of music (denoting the animals) written in a random sequence on a blackboard — and given no other guidelines. By listening to the pieces of music one at a time in a random order the students succeeded in putting together the written title on the blackboard and its proper piece of music in approximately 80 percent of the instances.

This is indeed remarkable. When absolutely no instructions for qualified guesses are given in the Saint-Saëns' piece — that is, as distinct from Prokofiev's *Peter and the Wolf* — just where does this great certainty come from? As mentioned above, a symbolic, explanatory voice-over narrator accompanies in the latter piece almost the entire musical composition. On the grounds of an elaborate explanation of each single guess by the students (i.e., an explanation of what the student established as the parameter(s) for his guess), the following picture of how the test teams generally reached their results appears.

Three generalizable parameters occurred the most frequently. The students noticed:

1. the quality of the sound;
2. the metric and rhythmic dynamics (including intensity), and
3. arbitrary conventional features.

As concerns the quality of the sound, the ones situated at a high level were regarded as belonging to small, light or flying animals, while the tones at the deep end of the scale were considered as belonging to large or heavy animals. The metric aspect of the music caused the informants to infer fast-moving animals from high-speed metrics; whereas low-speed metrics was converted to a mental picture of slow-moving animals. At the arbitrary symbolic level, the informants found a variety of "cliches" that do not in any way justify making direct inferences from the sounds of the music to a mental picture without the necessary action of squeezing in between the two an extra explanatory layer saying "that is the way this animal is traditionally depicted in music."

This pilot project further showed that none of the qualified guesses were based only on one of the three parameters mentioned above. In every inference made, the students employed more than one parameter at the same time, and those sequences of music that could be inferred from the most parameters simultaneously caused the fastest and most unambiguous answers. The pieces that caused spontaneous answers were those which combined deep tones with slow metrics and those which combined high tones with fast metrics. Almost all the test subjects could infer an elephant on the basis of a piece of music that employed deep tones in slow metrical pulsations and was characterized by a high intensity (volume). A piece displaying itself as tones at a high tonal level in high speed metrics (to a certain point with irregularities in the metrical intervals) and with a lower intensity (volume) most often evoked mental images of hens and roosters.

The march of the lions was most frequently inferred from a relation between the marching rhythm in the music and not as much from aspects in the music that could be assigned to the lion as an animal. The march of the lions is to be distinguished from the other portraits by being played in a very rigid rhythm in such a manner that the intervals between the beats in this piece — unlike all the others — are of the same duration and have the same intonation.

The "Pianists", quite surprisingly placed between the animals in Saint-Saëns, is unfolded as a mental picture of piano-playing humans, since the piano simply calls attention to itself as an instrument that is being played. This is done by the restless playing of those scales from which music originally appears as music. Reference is made here to that particular movement which listeners may assign to an image of a pianist who plays "etudes". Etudes are not music but only scales, which expresses those rules on which the logic of the piano is founded. "The Swan", on the other hand, was more or less arbitrarily inferred from the notion that a very beautiful piece of music has to denote such a beautiful animal as the swan, i.e, in our culture swans are commonly taken to be especially beautiful creatures.

We have focussed on "The Elephant", "Hens and Roosters", "The March of the Lion", "Pianists", and "The Swan" since these particular pieces seem to be the most prototypical and substantial in their appearance: The listener — according to the intention of program music — easily creates a picture in his imagination during the act of listening.

The pithy way in which these pieces function as mental "space builders" furnish us with the possibility to put forth a generalized thesis of how music builds images of a mental kind. Finally, this may lead to a hypothesis about whether the generalized patterns, which are characteristic of the formation of meaning in program music, are also characteristic of the formation of meaning in general. We now turn to the account of this hypothesis.

III

As listening human beings we probably make use of three distinct registers when we are to infer the concrete story through our reception of program music:

1. A qualitative iconic aspect. We form the quality of a tone on the basis of an inherent cognitive competence by which the human being as a species is equipped (Bastian 1988). Frequencies of vibration in the range of 20-20,000 Hz are conceived of as sound by human beings. But two different tones with two different frequencies (inside the area mentioned before) standing in a 2:1 correspondence are heard by human beings as two separate tones, creating the musical octave. If for example the concert pitch A (440 Hz) is played along with its frequency doubling (880 Hz), humans hear the octave that creates the frame of music in the key of A. If a vibration is located between these two frequencies, it is heard by humans as a tone which is part of the music played in this octave.

A tone emerging in this way is an icon. As an icon, this tone has qualities in itself which function to generate meaning: Thus deep tones indicate the quality of "heavyness" and high tones that of "lightness". But it becomes evident to infer mental pictures from music as "space builders" at precisely the moment we also hear the quality of the tone from a dynamic perspective and make use of another basic innate cognitive competences.

Even though heavy animals can appear in the imaginary field of the listener in form of qualitative iconicity alone (deep tone, deep voice, etc.), it turns out to be the dynamic dimension of music superimposed onto the quality of the sound that causes the animals' patterns of movement to be imagined, thereby also bringing about a clearer mental picture of them.

2. A kinaesthetic (dynamic) iconic aspect. As human beings we are equipped with a cognitive competence that enables us to discern sounds that appear after each other. Even desire seems to be involved in actualizing this competence. For example, in an enthusiastically applauding audience, if a single individual wants to strengthen the entire enthusiasm of the group he begins to applaud simultaneously (i.e., he claps with the same intervals between the single clapping movements), and furthermore , each individual of the audience will increase the motoric force of their movements to increase the dynamical, metric emphasis.

Human beings not only possess this purely metric competence. They also possess a metrical-rhythmic (musical dynamic) competence. The latter is activated when the metric beat is divided into steps in such a way that some beats are more intense than others in the metric progression. When humans organizes the metrics into beats in this way, a rhythm emerges for the human being as an iterative entity. This iterative entity refers to the feeling that a dynamic-motor intentional force must be initiated every time a new step is about to begin. The iconic quality of the tone seems to be based on notions of heaviness and lightness. Metrics in music, in contrast, seems to build pictures of something moving by motor force in the mental field of the inferring listener. One may say that Man imagines movement in this dynamic register on the basis of kinaesthetic iconicity.

3. A symbolic aspect. Some symbolic arbitrariness is also present, although program music is generally based on a "space building" strategy in its use of quality icons and kinaesthetic icons. We often encounter conventional codified messages which replace natural iconicity. The piano-playing pianists in Saint-Saëns cannot be inferred solely from the fact that this piece is played by a piano. If that were the case, how then would this particular sequence distinguish itself from the other twelve pieces of music in *The Carnival of the Animals*? The way in which the piano is played is the aspect that causes the sound of the piano to call attention to itself as the sound of a piano: The pianist plays in scales. The scales within the universal octave are strongly determined by culture. The scales played in the "Pianists" piece therefore function on equal terms with, for instance, conversational symbolic language.

"The Swan" must be inferred from the symbolic register as well. If no mention was made of a piece that was supposed to resemble a swan, it is unlikely that the music would be employed as a "space builder" in a "swan scenario". The piece would have been experienced as "beautiful". Still, several other pieces are beautiful as well whether or not they have to do with swans. Swans are, of course, not beautiful *per se* simply because swans are seen as especially beautiful animals in our culture.Thus, when we as listeners infer the swan from a piece of music, this involves a codified activity that performs the task of correlating beauty with music. The general inferences that are mentioned so far in terms of the creation of mental spaces can be schematized as follows:

THE MENTAL WORLD

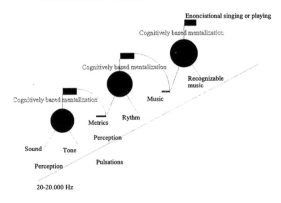

THE MATERIAL WORLD

Fig. 1.

This figure shows that the listener necessarily must relate three distinct, cognitively created *gestalts* in order to understand music. Children understand *Peter and the Wolf* without great difficulty. This is due to the fact that (1) the quality of a sound is thought to belong to the music as a tone; (2) the quality of a tone is heard as something which is related to temporality and to the metrics of the music; (3) the dynamics of the tones creates in the imaginary field of the listener an image of a certain quality that moves in space; and (4) the human subject will be able to enunciate the music by mimicking it as a repetition of what has now for the subject been "framed" as a piece of recognizable music. This *Gestaltung* in the imaginary field of the receiver is inherent to a *marking* of this precise piece of music. This marking will make the subject able to point specifically to that piece again later on simply by humming it, or by playing it on an instrument.. This leads to the following conclusion: In the first place, the subject does not bring about arbitrary signifiers for the purpose of remembering the music or recalling it from memory. So, although the music is "marked" by the subject as a specific piece to be recollected and pointed to by an intentional act, no arbitrary symbol is needed to do so. The recollection of a specific piece of music is based on the pure iconicity of the music itself: In this sense, one remembers a piece of music only by means of music itself.

This is crucial to a general theory of how meaning is produced, transported, and received in general. My claim is that every system of language and every mediating practice that we usually regard as working in complete arbitrariness (such as symbolic, written and spoken language, pictorial language, etc.), is only *compressing* the meaning it wants to confer through the pragmatic intersubjective space. This mean that any signifier *de facto* functions as an index to the iconicity of the whole mental scenario of the receiver.

IV

I have now discussed some aspects of *Peter and the Wolf* and of *The Carnival of the Animals* with the purpose of showing that mental scenarios are built on the basis of sounds, metrics, and rythms. In other words: Figures in the mental images have an iconic resemblance to the sounds, metrics and rythms that are meant to provoke the mental imagery of the person listening.

The basic pattern for "programme" music is to provoke the listener to superimpose the quality of the sounds with the metrics and rythms in order to get to the "point".

We can conclude that music is a non-arbitrary, non-symbolic medium, which nevertheless is a medium suitable for telling stories. My claim is that "normal" symbolic stories told by means of arbitrary signifiers too are capable of producing meaning (i.e., mental images in the field of the adressee) only insofar as the symbolic signifiers are grounded in a non-arbitrary experience. Every signifier used for the purpose of producing meaning must have the ability of creating mental images in the very moment of their enunciation. If the signifier does not happen to do so, then it will be set aside by the adressee as a *noise* that disturbs the mental space building of proper scenarios.

Meaning as such stems in the first place from our experience of the "real", physical world (cf. Lakoff 1987, Lakoff &Johnson 1996). Meaning that reaches a level of arbitrariness in normal communication is effectuated by the fact that every experience can be compressed mentally in such a way that only a single index of the experienced scenario is nessesary in order to frame the experience in memory. On the other hand, what is needed to unfold the experienced scenario again is the very same index.

A diversity of different indexes framing different scenarios (by reference to iconic representations of the scenarios) can be framed together as a cluster of indexes by an index of a higher level of abstraction. In this perspective, the "arbitrary sign" is nothing but an index of a certain iconic value that holds together index clusters. The sign is in this sense only "arbitrary" if is is taken for an index of iconic value at a very high level of abstraction. Although conventionally constructed, the sign will only produce meaning if it points to mental scenarios. The latter structured as a system of indexical reference.

In the act of communication, two persons may reach a point where one of the two does not understand the meaning of the words that the other person is using. What we normally do in such a situation is to move the discourse down one level in the system of index levels. What is normally referred to as meta-language is a particular habit of a person which, in order to make himself properly understood, approaches the real-life mental situation of which he is actually speaking. This situation can be approached by moving downwards in the edifice of index clusters to a non-abstract level at which he is sure to re-connect to the other person in the conversation. Exemplifications are often used as a device for blowing up scenarios in which the other person in the conversation is able to "picture" himself.

The arbitrary system of language is useful only to the extent that one is able to connect signifiers to meaningful mental scenarios. When the mentalizing process is disrupted, the communication becomes blurred and in the end impossible to sustain. "Can't you *see* what I mean" is a frequently used complaint for an agent in a conversation that is not being properly understood by the other person.

The iconic aspects of experiences are the foundation of all symbolicity, and it is for that reason that meaning does not come around as the pure effect of the use of arbitrary signifiers in a linguistic system. This is what the phenomenology of music tells us about.

Although both *Peter and the Wolf* by Prokofiev and *The Carnival of the Animals* of Saint-Saëns can be bought in bookstores, written out as scores in a linguistic notation system, the notes written in black ink between lines on a white sheet of paper does not yield much meaning to the person bying them, unless he is able to hear the tones that the notation system refers to.

References

Brandt, Per Aage. 1994. *Dynamiques du sens*. Århus: Aarhus University Press.

Bastian, Peter. 1988. *Ind i musikken*. København: Gyldendal.

Fauconnier, Gilles. 1994. *Mental Spaces: Aspects of meaning Construction in Natural Language*. Cambridge: Cambridge University Press.

Jackendoff, Ray. 1992. *Languages of the Mind*. Cambridge, MA and London, England: MIT Press.

Lakoff, George. 1987. *Women, Fire and Dangerous Things*. Chicago: University of Chicago Press.

Lakoff, George & Johnson, Mark. 1996. *Metaphors we live by*. Chicago: University of Chicago Press..

Contributors

Per Aage Brandt
Dr.phil., Professor, Center for Semiotics, Aarhus University. The author of some 200 scientific papers on, among other things, the semantics of literature and language, the semio-aesthetics of works of art and music, and cognitive science. Among his recent books are *La Charpente modale du sens* (John Benjamins, 1992), *Dynamiques du sens* (Aarhus University Press, 1994), and *Morphologies of Meaning* (Aarhus University Press, 1995). With Wolfgang Wildgen he directs the *European Semiotics* line of books at Peter Lang. Email: pabrandt@inet.uni2.dk

Berit Brogaard
MA, PhD, Department of Philosophy, SUNY at Buffalo (USA). The author of works on ontology, bio-semiotics, Peirce, Lesniewski, and other related matters published in Danish and international journals. Along with Martin Skov, she is currently writing a book on the ontology of things. Email: bbp@acsu.buffalo.edu.

Erling Davidsen
PhD, Assistant Professor, Department of Comparative Literature and Semiotics, Southern University of Denmark at Odense. Latest publication: 'Imagination og derealisering i Coleridges The Rime of the Ancient Mariner.' ("Imagination and de-realization in Coleridge's The Rime of the Ancient Mariner.", to appear in *Ny Poetik*, 2000).

Helle Munkholm Davidsen
MA, PhD Scholar at the Department of Comparative Literature and Semiotics, Southern University of Denmark at Odense. Latest publication: 'Against theory' (to appear in *Semiotica* 128 1/2, 2000). Email: helle.m@litcul.ou.dk.

Troels Degn Johansson
MA, PhD Scholar at the Danish Forest and Landscape Research Institute. The author of works on psychoanalysis, film studies, and aesthetics in general, published in various journals and books. During 1996-1998 the coordinator of the NSU circle *Modernity and Visual Aesthetics*. Currently chairman of the Nordic Summer University. Email: tdj@fsl.dk.

Torben Fledelius Knap
MA, PhD Scholar at the Department of Nordic Philology, University of Copenhagen. The author of works on psychoanalysis, media theory, and cognit-ive science. Email: fleknap@hum.ku.dk.

Michael May
PhD, a Research Fellow at the Danish Maritime Institute. Papers on cognitive science and the semiotics of hyper-media. The author of *Diagrammatisk tænkning.* ("Diagrammatic Thinking", Roskilde University, 1993). Email: mim@danmar.dk.

Hanne Roer
PhD, an Assistant Professor at the Department of Greek and Latin at the University of Aarhus. The author of works on Medieval philosophy and literature, especially Dante. Email: oldhr@hum.au.dk.

Martin Skov
Since 1990 a student at the Department of Nordic Philology, University of Copenhagen. The author of works on semiotics, cognitive science, linguistics, and aesthetics. Co-editor of *Almen Semiotik*, a journal of semiotics, and the books *Perspektiver i nyere dansk litteratur* (Forlaget Spring, 1997), *The Roman Jakobson Centennial 1996* (= *Acta Linguistica* vol. 29, 1998), and the forthcoming anthology, *Dynamisk semiotik* (Gyldendal, Spring 2000). Along with Berit Brogaard he is currently writing a book on the ontology of things. Email: mskov@stud.hum.ku.dk.

Göran Sonesson
Dr. phil, Director of the Seminar of Cultural Semiotics at Lund University, Sweden. The author of numerous papers on visual semiotics and the semiotics of culture besides the classic book *Pictorial Concepts* (Lund University Press, 1989). He is the President of the Nordic Association for Semiotic Studies (NASS), Vice-president of the Swedish Society for Semiotic Studies (sffs), Swedish representative to the executive commission of IASS, and a member of the Editorial Committee of *Visio, The Journal of the International Association for Visual Semiotics.*
Email: goran.sonesson@artnew.lu.se.

Frederik Stjernfelt
PhD, Associate Professor, Department of Comparative Literature, University of Copenhagen. Editor of the Danish periodical *KRITIK* and a critic with the weekly newspaper *Weekendavisen*. His most recent books are *Formens betydning. Katastrofeteori og semiotik* ("The Meaning of Form. Catastrophe Theory and Semiotics" (Akademisk Forlag, 1992) and *Rationalitetens himmel* ("The Heaven of Rationality", Gyldendal, 1997). Email: stjern@hum.ku.dk.

Svend Østergaard
PhD, Associate Professor, Center for Semiotics, University of Århus. Numerous papers on (the philosophy of) mathematics, cognitive linguistics, and Borges and Proust in Danish and international journals. Selected publications: *The Mathematics of Meaning* (Aarhus University Press, 1996) and *Kognition og katastrofer* ("Cognition and Catastrophes", Basilisk, 1998). Email: semsvend@hum.au.dk.